Information Technology and Global Governance

Series Editor
Derrick L. Cogburn, American University, Bethesda, USA

Information Technology and Global Governance focuses on the complex interrelationships between the social, political, and economic processes of global governance that occur at national, regional, and international levels. These processes are influenced by the rapid and ongoing developments in information and communication technologies. At the same time, they affect numerous areas, create new opportunities and mechanisms for participation in global governance processes, and influence how governance is studied. Books in this series examine these relationships and influences.

Fiona M. Alexander · Laura DeNardis · Nanette S. Levinson · Francesca Musiani

# Geopolitics at the Internet's Core

palgrave
macmillan

Fiona M. Alexander
School of International Service
American University
Washington, DC, USA

Nanette S. Levinson
School of International Service
American University
Washington, DC, USA

Laura DeNardis
Communication, Culture,
and Technology Program
Georgetown University
Washington, DC, USA

Francesca Musiani
National Centre for Scientific
Research (CNRS)
Paris, France

ISSN 2946-3297 ISSN 2946-3300 (electronic)
Information Technology and Global Governance
ISBN 978-3-031-89477-0 ISBN 978-3-031-89478-7 (eBook)
https://doi.org/10.1007/978-3-031-89478-7



Cover credit: dem10 | Getty Images

This Palgrave Macmillan imprint is published by the registered company Springer Nature Switzerland AG
The registered company address is: Gewerbestrasse 11, 6330 Cham, Switzerland

# Preface

Did America Surrender the Internet to China, Iran, and Russia?

Personal Account of Fiona M. Alexander, former Associate Administrator of the NTIA

"You are risking personal criminal liability of up to two years of prison," said U.S. Senator Ted Cruz to the career public servants who worked in the Commerce Department's National Telecommunication and Information Administration (NTIA). He was threatening me, my staff, and colleagues, telling us to consider our careers and the prospect of jail time, just for doing our job. My first reaction was to try to keep a straight face during a serious hearing with consequences for the future of the Internet and the digital economy, while my boss at the time, NTIA Administrator Larry Strickling, physically outraged by the Senator's threat launched into a passionate defense of the team.

What exactly was our crime? We were carrying out a two-decade long policy, spanning three U.S. presidential administrations (both Democrat and Republican), bipartisan Congressional resolutions of support, and countless oversight hearings, to privatize and internationalize the management of the Internet's Domain Name System (DNS). Typically likened to the plumbing of the Internet, the DNS, something to which the average user never gives a second thought, relies on the routine updating of three databases. Collectively called the Internet Assigned Numbers

Authority or the IANA functions, the activities include: (1) coordinating the assignment of technical Internet Protocol parameters; (2) updating the Internet's root zone file, the authoritative mapping of domain names to Internet addresses; and (3) allocating Internet numbering resources. The U.S. government's stewardship, the legacy of DARPA and NSF funding, had slowly been phased out in favor of a system of direct private contracts and the multistakeholder model for policymaking.

So, what was the reason that Senator Cruz, and others, argued that Washington, D.C. bureaucrats like me should remain in charge of a largely invisible part of the Internet? First, there was the mischaracterization of the effort as an illegal giveaway of U.S. government property. With the Internet built on a completely voluntary system of standards, largely privatized, no single government or entity owns the Internet. There was simply nothing to relinquish. Second, and most troubling was the suggestion that by shifting the responsibility for the stewardship of a technical system to the companies and stakeholders that actually own and operate the networks and removing the bureaucracy of Washington, we were surrendering the Internet to Russia, China, and Iran. The fear was that this would kill free speech online in America. Also, not true, because as a condition we had imposed a requirement that the NTIA role not be replaced by a government or intergovernmental solution, and perhaps more relevant to this charge, free speech online is protected because of the open decentralized nature of the Internet not the action of a single government.

On September 30, 2016, I found myself sitting in a courtroom in Texas, as Judge George C. Hanks, Jr, presided over a lawsuit brought by the attorneys general of Arizona, Oklahoma, Nevada, and Texas attempting to stop the privatization. As I listened to the arguments being presented, nervously wondering if I would have to testify, I reflected on my time as an American University student and NTIA intern, when all of this had started. Pausing on the milestone moments in my nearly 20-year life at NTIA that followed—my first ITU Plenipotentiary Conference and ICANN meetings, the World Summit on the Information Society and the Internet Governance Forums, my first time at the Internet Engineering Task Force, the Affirmation of Commitments—I couldn't help but mull over the fact that all of the work, by so many people, all over the world now came down to the decision of one single man in a Galveston, Texas, courtroom of half of dozen or so people.

As Judge Hanks ruled to deny the plaintiffs' application for declaratory and injunctive relief, I let out a big sigh. As soon as the gavel hit, I pulled out my phone and emailed back to NTIA two words: "We won." The we, the global Internet community, and the win, that our vision for an open, decentralized, participatory system, reflecting the ideals of the Internet founders, had been validated for the technical coordination of the Internet, including the Internet Protocol.

On the drive back to the airport, my phone pinged non-stop: White House colleagues past and present, Internet governance friends from around the world, the chair of the IETF, the CEO of ICANN. I was unexpectedly conferenced into a public interest tech advocacy group's board meeting. Everyone wanted to confirm the outcome. Everyone wanted to celebrate our collective success codifying a global and open Internet.

As my plane careened down the runway at Reagan National Airport in Washington, D.C. that night, I reached for my phone. It was 11:59 p.m. The witching hour of midnight was upon us. After years of contentious debates and geopolitical conflict, millions of dollars spent on lobbying and an epoch that was single handedly responsible for drawing the world's attention to this thing called "Internet governance," the multistakeholder approach, and a little known agency within the Commerce Department, how would we announce this achievement? A splashy press release, a conference, a White House pronouncement? At 12:01 am, two simple sentences on the NTIA website appeared:

> *"The federal court in Galveston, Texas denied the plaintiffs' application for declaratory and injunctive relief. As of October 1, 2016, the IANA functions contract has expired."*

Arguably the world's largest Internet policy debate, to date, had concluded.

A great irony, and a condition that speaks to the fragility of the Internet and its governance, was that a single U.S. Federal Judge would make a decision that was technologically complex and involving twenty years of work by thousands of people around the world, within a day of being presented a case.

And yet the Internet still lives. And the Internet Protocol remains at the center of almost every geopolitical conflict in the digital world.

Washington, DC, USA Fiona M. Alexander

*Acknowledgments* Our first thanks go to the distinguished Internet technologists and scholars surveyed or otherwise providing input for this book including: Carolina Aguerre, Bernard Benhamou, Stéphane Bortzmeyer, Sandra Braman, Vinton Cerf, David Clark, Steve Crocker, Keith Davidson, William Drake, Anriette Esterhuysen, Patrik Fältström, David Gross, Maria Hall, Richard Hill, Geoff Huston, Wolfgang Kleinwächter, Karen Rose, Jean-Jacques Sahel, Robert Shaw, Andrew Sullivan, and Emily Taylor. We are also grateful for the anonymous peer reviewers whose suggestions strengthened this book.

The authors also wish to acknowledge the important support of their home institutions: Georgetown University, the Georgetown Program in Communication, Culture, and Technology, and the Georgetown Center for Digital Ethics (DeNardis); the French National Centre for Scientific Research (*Centre national de la recherche scientifique*, CNRS) and the *Centre Internet et Société* of CNRS (Musiani); and The School of International Service, Internet Governance Lab, American University (Alexander and Levinson).

A special thanks to Series Editor Professor Derrick Cogburn, a pioneering contributor to the development of our field, and to the highly talented entire team at Palgrave Macmillan led by Stewart Beale, Senior Editor, and Chitra Gopalraj, Production Editor.

Finally, our deepest appreciation goes to each of our families for inspiring support and sustenance in bringing to fruition what has been a multi-year, extraordinary and intensive cross-disciplinary and cross-continental collaboration.

*Competing Interests* The authors have no competing interests to declare that are relevant to the content of this manuscript.

# Contents

# About the Authors

**Ms. Fiona M. Alexander** is a former government executive with extensive digital policy experience. She served at the National Telecommunications and Information Administration (NTIA) where she was the principal official responsible for the analysis, development, and execution of international Internet, cyber, and communications policy within the Executive Branch of the United States government. She is Distinguished Policy Strategist in Residence in the School of International Service, Distinguished Fellow at the Internet Governance Lab, and a Strategic Advisor to the Khan Cyber and Economic Security Institute, all at American University. Fiona is a Non-Resident Senior Fellow at the Center for European Policy Analysis (CEPA) and co-founder of Salt Point Strategies, a consulting group that provides public affairs advice, strategy, and advocacy to clients navigating the emerging high-tech economy. She has a Bachelor's Degree in International Studies from Old Dominion University and a Master's Degree in International Relations from American University.

**Dr. Laura DeNardis**, a global expert in cybersecurity and Internet governance, is Professor and Endowed Chair in Technology, Ethics, and Society at Georgetown University in Washington, DC. Her book *The Internet in Everything: Freedom and Security in a World with No Off Switch* (Yale University Press) was recognized as a Financial Times Top Technology Book of 2020. Among her seven books, *The Global War* *for Internet Governance* (Yale University Press) is considered a definitive source for understanding cyber governance debates and solutions. Professor DeNardis is an affiliated Fellow of the Yale Information Society Project, where she previously served as Executive Director, and is a life Member of the Council on Foreign Relations. She holds an AB in Engineering Science from Dartmouth, a Master of Engineering from Cornell, a PhD in Science and Technology Studies from Virginia Tech, and was awarded a postdoctoral fellowship from Yale Law School.

**Dr. Nanette S. Levinson** serves as a Director of the Internet Governance Lab and Professor at the School of International Service, American University. She is a past Chair of: International Communication Section, International Studies Association; Information Technology and Politics Section, American Political Science Association; and the Global Internet Governance Academic Network (GIGANET). Currently she co-chairs a HICSS mini-track she founded on Digital & Social Media: Culture, Identity & Inclusion. Recipient of awards including those for distinguished scholarship, outstanding teaching and program development, her research focuses on Internet/cyber governance, knowledge transfer, and innovation. Co-editor of *Researching Internet Governance Methods,Frameworks,Futures*, MIT Press (2020), her recent publications include "Idea Entrepreneurs: The United Nations Open-Ended Working Group & Cybersecurity," *Telecommunications Policy*, 2021 and "Crafting Science Diplomacy In Comparative Perspective: The Case of U.S. Internet Governance" in *Internet Diplomacy: Shaping the Global Politics of Cyberspace*, Marzouki and Calderado, eds., Rowman & Littlefield, 2022. She received her bachelor's, masters and doctoral degrees from Harvard University.

**Dr. Francesca Musiani** is research professor at the National Center for Scientific Research (CNRS) of France, co-founder and director of the Center for Internet and Society of CNRS. She is also an associate researcher at the Center for the sociology of innovation (i3/MINES ParisTech) and a Global Fellow at the Internet Governance Lab, American University in Washington, DC. Francesca's research work focuses on Internet governance "by architecture" and "by infrastructure," in an interdisciplinary perspective merging information and communication sciences, science and technology studies (STS) and international law. In

2023, she was presented one of the annual Awards of the French Foundation for the Social Sciences, the special mention of the Stefano Rodotà Award for Data Protection by the Council of Europe, and the Woman Cyber Researcher Award by the French Circle of Women in Cybersecurity.

# Abbreviations

| | |
|---|---|
| ACLU | American Civil Liberties Union |
| AFRINIC | African Network Information Centre |
| AG | Attorney General |
| AI | Artificial Intelligence |
| ALAC | At-Large Advisory Committee |
| ANSI | American National Standards Institute |
| APNIC | Asia-Pacific Network Information Centre |
| APT | Advanced Persistent Threat |
| ARIN | American Registry for Internet Numbers |
| ARP | Address Resolution Protocol |
| ARPA | Advanced Research Projects Agency |
| ARPANET | Advanced Research Projects Agency Network |
| AS | Autonomous System |
| ASCII | American Standard Code for Information Interchange |
| ASN | Autonomous System Number |
| ASO | Address Supporting Organization |
| ATRT | Accountability and Transparency Review Team |
| AWS | Amazon Web Services |
| BBN | Bolt Beranek and Newman |
| BGP | Border Gateway Protocol |
| BGPSEC | Border Gateway Protocol Security |
| BP | Bundle Protocol |
| CA | Certificate Authority |
| CATNIP | Common Architecture for the Internet |
| CCETT | Centre commun d'études de télédiffusion et de télécommunications (France) |

| | |
|---|---|
| CCM | Capacity Maturity Model |
| ccTLD | Country Code Top-Level Domain |
| CCSDS | Consultative Committee for Space Data Systems |
| CCWG | Cross Community Working Group |
| CDA | Communications Decency Act |
| CEO | Chief Executive Officer |
| CEPA | Center for European Policy Analysis |
| CERT | Computer Emergency Readiness Team |
| CERTS | Computer Emergency Response/Readiness Teams |
| CFAA | Computer Fraud and Abuse Act |
| CIDR | Classless Inter-Domain Routing |
| CIR | Critical Internet Resources |
| CISA | Cybersecurity and Infrastructure Security Agency |
| CLNP | Connectionless Network Protocol |
| CNN | Cable News Network |
| CNRS | French National Centre for Scientific Research |
| CNSA | China National Space Administration |
| COSO | Committee of Sponsoring Organizations |
| CPU | Central Processing Unit |
| CRTC | Canadian Radio-television and Telecommunications Commission |
| CSA | Canadian Space Agency |
| CSIRTS | Cyber Security Incident Response Teams |
| DARPA | Defense Advanced Research Projects Agency |
| DDoS | Distributed Denial of Service |
| DE-CIX | Deutsche Commercial Internet Exchange |
| DEC | Digital Equipment Corporation |
| DFN | German Research Network |
| DISA | Defense Information Systems Agency |
| DISA NIC | Defense Information Systems Agency Network Center |
| DMCA | Digital Millennium Copyright Act |
| DNS | Domain Name System |
| DNSSEC | Domain Name System Security Extensions |
| DoD | Department of Defense |
| DoH | DNS over HTTPS |
| DoQ | DNS over QUIC |
| DoT | DNS over TLS |
| DPI | Deep Packet Inspection |
| DPRIVE | DNS PRIVate Exchange |
| DSA | Digital Services Act |
| DTC | Digital Transformation Centres |
| DTN | Delay-Tolerant Networking |
| EC | European Commission |
| EFF | Electronic Frontier Foundation |

| | |
|---|---|
| ENISA | European Union Agency for Cybersecurity |
| ESA | European Space Agency |
| ETNO | European Telecommunications Network Operators' Association |
| EU | European Union |
| EUNET | European Network |
| FBI | Federal Bureau of Investigation |
| FCC | Federal Communications Commission |
| FDA | Food and Drug Administration |
| GAC | Governmental Advisory Committee |
| GAFAM | Google, Apple, Facebook, Amazon, Microsoft |
| GAO | Government Accountability Office |
| GCA | Global Cyber Alliance |
| GDPR | General Data Protection Regulation |
| GE | General Electric |
| GFCE | Global Forum on Cyber Expertise |
| GGE | Group of Governmental Experts |
| GIGANET | Global Internet Governance Academic Network |
| GPS | Global Positioning System |
| GSC | Global Supply Chain |
| gTLD | Generic Top-Level Domain |
| HHS | U.S. Department of Health and Human Services |
| HICSS | Hawaii International Conference on System Sciences |
| HIPAA | Health Insurance Portability and Accountability Act |
| HP | Hewlett-Packard |
| HTML | HyperText Markup Language |
| HTTP | HyperText Transfer Protocol |
| HTTPS | HyperText Transfer Protocol Secure |
| IAB | Internet Architecture Board |
| IAHC | International Ad Hoc Committee |
| IANA | Internet Assigned Numbers Authority |
| IBM | International Business Machines |
| ICANN | Internet Corporation for Assigned Names and Numbers |
| ICG | Internet Coordination Group |
| ICMP | Internet Control Message Protocol |
| ICT | Information and Communication Technology |
| IDN | Internationalized Domain Name |
| IDNA | Internationalized Domain Name Application |
| IEEE | Institute of Electrical and Electronics Engineers |
| IEEPA | International Emergency Economic Powers Act |
| IESG | Internet Engineering Steering Group |
| IETF | Internet Engineering Task Force |
| IFO | IANA Functions Operator |
| IGF | Internet Governance Forum |

| | |
|---|---|
| IMP | Interface Message Processor |
| IMRS | Internet Multicast Routing System |
| INTA | International Trademark Association |
| IP | Internet Protocol |
| IPAE | IP Address Encapsulation |
| IPng | Internet Protocol next generation |
| IPNSIG | Interplanetary Networking Special Interest Group |
| IPR | Intellectual Property Rights |
| IPsec | Internet Protocol Security |
| IPv4 | Internet Protocol Version 4 |
| IPv6 | Internet Protocol Version 6 |
| IRGC | International Risk Governance Council |
| IRIA | Institut de recherche en informatique et automatique (France; renamed Inria in 1980) |
| IRTF | Internet Research Task Force |
| IS-IS | Intermediate System to Intermediate System |
| ISO | International Organization for Standardization |
| ISOC | Internet Society |
| ISP | Internet Service Provider |
| ISRG | Internet Security Research Group |
| ITRs | International Telecommunication Regulations |
| ITU | International Telecommunication Union |
| ITU-D | ITU Telecommunication Development Sector |
| ITU-T | ITU Telecommunication Standardization Sector |
| IXP | Internet Exchange Point |
| JANET | Joint Academic Network |
| JAXA | Japan Aerospace Exploration Agency |
| JPA | Joint Project Agreement |
| JPEG | Joint Photographic Experts Group |
| JPL | Jet Propulsion Laboratory |
| LACNIC | Latin America and Caribbean Network Information Centre |
| LICRA | International League Against Racism and Antisemitism |
| LINX | London Internet Exchange |
| LIR | Local Internet Registry |
| LMS | Learning Management System |
| MAC | Media Access Control |
| MANRS | Mutually Agreed Norms for Routing Security |
| MIME | Multipurpose Internet Mail Extensions |
| MIT | Massachusetts Institute of Technology |
| MOIS | Ministry of Intelligence and Security |
| MOU | Memorandum of Understanding |
| NASA | National Aeronautics and Space Administration |
| NAT | Network Address Translation |

| | |
|---|---|
| NBC | National Broadcasting Company |
| NCC | Network Coordination Centre |
| NIC | Network Information Center |
| NIR | National Internet Registry |
| NIST | National Institute of Standards and Technology |
| NOI | Notice of Inquiry |
| NRO | Number Resource Organization |
| NSA | National Security Agency |
| NSF | National Science Foundation |
| NTIA | National Telecommunications and Information Administration |
| OECD | Organization for Economic Co-operation and Development |
| OEWG | Open-Ended Working Group |
| OFAC | Office of Foreign Assets Control |
| OSI | Open Systems Interconnection |
| OSI-TCP | Open Systems Interconnection- Transmission Control Protocol |
| OSPF | Open Shortest Path First |
| P2P | Point-to-Point |
| PCCW | Pacific Century CyberWorks |
| PIPA | Protect IP Act |
| PTI | Public Technical Identifiers |
| QIRG | Quantum Internet Research Group |
| QUIC | Quick UDP Internet Connections |
| RALO | Regional At-Large Organization |
| RAND | Reasonable and Non-Discriminatory |
| RFC | Request for Comments |
| RFID | Radio Frequency Identification |
| RFP | Request for Proposals |
| RINA | Recursive InterNetwork Architecture |
| RIPE | Réseaux IP Européens |
| RIPE-NCC | RIPE Network Coordination Centre |
| RIR | Regional Internet Registry |
| RPKI | Resource Public Key Infrastructure |
| RPS | Requests per Second |
| RT | Real-Time |
| RTP | Real-time Transport Protocol |
| SANA | Space Assigned Numbers Authority |
| SIP | Session Initiation Protocol |
| SIPP | Simple Internet Protocol Plus |
| SNA | Systems Network Architecture |
| SOPA | Stop Online Piracy Act |
| SRI NIC | Stanford Research Institute's Network Information Center |
| SSAC | Security and Stability Advisory Committee |
| SSL | Secure Sockets Layer |

| | |
|---|---|
| STS | Science and Technology Studies |
| SYN-ACK | Synchronize-Acknowledge |
| TCP | Transmission Control Protocol |
| TLS | Transport Layer Security |
| UDP | User Datagram Protocol |
| UDPR | Uniform Domain Name Dispute Resolution Policy |
| UK | United Kingdom |
| UN | United Nations |
| UNESCO | United Nations Educational, Scientific and Cultural Organization |
| URL | Uniform Resource Locator |
| US | United States |
| US-CERT | United States Computer Emergency Readiness Team |
| USG | United States Government |
| VPN | Virtual Private Network |
| VoIP | Voice over Internet Protocol |
| W3C | World Wide Web Consortium |
| WCIT | World Conference on International Telecommunications |
| WGIG | Working Group on Internet Governance |
| Wi-Fi | Wirelesss Fidelity |
| WHO | World Health Organization |
| WIPO | World Intellectual Property Organization |
| WSIS | World Summit on the Information Society |
| WTO | World Trade Organization |
| XML | Extensible Markup Language |

# List of Figures

CHAPTER 1

# Internet Protocol Politics

## Introduction

During Russia's 2022 invasion of Ukraine, amid global economic sanctions and tech company boycotts of Russia, the Ukrainian Minister of Digital Transformation asked two institutions—ICANN and RIPE-NCC—to essentially disconnect Russia from the Internet.[1] Do organizations most people have never heard of hold the power to unplug an entire country from the Internet? In part, yes.

Disrupting Russia's Internet connectivity would involve pulling its country-specific "top-level domain" from the "root zone file" at the center of the Internet's naming system and to withdraw its use of assigned Internet Protocol (IP) addresses, the unique virtual addresses necessary to send or receive information online. The institutions declined to do so for a complicated set of reasons, including concern about collateral damage to the universal Internet.[2]

Who exactly are these institutions and what do they do? Routine Internet use requires unique names and numbers. ICANN, the Internet Corporation for Assigned Names and Numbers, is the not-for-profit organization coordinating Internet names and numbers globally and the institutional system that administers the Internet's underlying address book, the Domain Name System, that translates names people use into binary numbers computers understand. RIPE-NCC, or Réseaux IP Européens



F. M. Alexander et al., *Geopolitics at the Internet's Core*, Information Technology and Global Governance,
https://doi.org/10.1007/978-3-031-89478-7_1

Network Coordination Centre, is the regional Internet registry (RIR) responsible for Internet address allocation in Europe, the Middle East, and parts of Central Asia.

Ukraine's wartime request to disconnect Russia from the Internet was not the first time the critical virtual resources of IP addresses and domain names, or the standards that structure them, have landed in the middle of geopolitical conflict.

A few years earlier, global concern about the design and control of the Internet Protocol arose in the context of what was described as "China's controversial mission to reinvent the Internet."[3] Alarm about an authoritarian takeover of the Internet followed a vague proposal by technology giant Huawei and the Chinese Ministry of Industry and Information Technology for a new Internet Protocol to replace the longstanding core architecture of the Internet.[4] The Chinese submitted the strategy proposal, more accurately a white paper, to the International Telecommunication Union (ITU), a part of the United Nations, as part of a larger study group examining future network technologies.

The Chinese white paper contained nothing concrete, but it did make the bold—and debatable—assertion that the current incarnation of IP was incapable of supporting the applications of the future. One of these applications was holographic communications, akin to the holograms portrayed in old Star Trek reruns. The Huawei paper claimed that the Internet Protocol would not support this and that "we need to think about a New Internet Protocol or quite simply the New IP."[5]

Concerns about the Chinese New IP were varied.[6] Some involved political and human rights considerations about China potentially extending its authoritarian system of digital control and censorship deeper into the Internet's infrastructure. The Chinese government had already established a sophisticated system of filtering content and controlling digital platforms in order to crack down on dissident speech, the media, and generally control the flow of online content. They accomplished some of this through IP filtering. The concern was that even greater control could be designed into the protocol itself through this long-term design initiative.

Other concerns involved issues of ongoing innovation and interoperability. Would a "fork" in the Internet road—with two competing versions of the core protocol of the already arguably fragmented Internet—lead to two different Internets? The "New Internet Protocol" white paper itself cited innovation as the impetus for a redesign, but having two competing core protocols would raise the specter of greater fragmentation, already a global concern about taking the Internet from a universal system to one that is further splintered and, to a certain extent, overlain with national boundaries. The rapid innovation of applications and devices on the Internet has depended upon interoperability and a consistent global address space. In other words, those investing in new products and systems do so only with the assurance that their innovations can run over the Internet and be interoperable with other systems.

Because the early Internet technology innovators were largely American firms, part of the Chinese interest in a new protocol involved global competition policy. A new platform could provide Chinese companies with a first-mover advantage that would provide them with a comparative advantage in the global economy.

The greatest concern about the prospect of a "New Internet Protocol" seemed to center on control itself. Who should control the protocols and technical architecture of the Internet? What actors and institutions have this authority and design control? The Internet Protocol arose from the Internet Engineering Task Force (IETF), the standards-setting body responsible for the core Internet Protocols that enable companies to make products that are mutually interoperable.

One of the most controversial aspects of the Chinese white paper was the idea that the design of a modified or redesigned Internet Protocol would shift from the IETF to the ITU, a specialized agency of the United Nations and itself a prominent technical standards-setting institution. Moving responsibility from the Internet's venerable technical community to the United Nations would be a significant institutional power shift.

RIPE-NCC leaders issued a strong statement against a protocol redesign.[7] Part of their concern was about design control. Should a protocol be dictated in a top-down manner, or in a bottom-up, transparent, multistakeholder arena? RIPE-NCC suggested, "The open, inclusive, multistakeholder approach throughout its development—both in the technical forums that created its standards, as well as in the governance of its resources—has made the Internet what it is today."[8]

This exact concern about institutional control over the Internet Protocol's design has a very long history. Years before Facebook or Twitter existed, the 1990s selection of the newest Internet Protocol—IPv6—involved an institutional tension between designs originating with the International Organization for Standardization (ISO) efforts and the IETF community. During this skirmish, addressed later in this book,

Internet engineer David Clark famously said about Internet standardization norms, "We reject: kings, presidents, and voting. We believe in: rough consensus and running code." The phrase "rough consensus and running code" has since become the unofficial motto of the IETF.

Concern about either a Chinese takeover of the Internet Protocol or about questions of control over and distribution of IP addresses is hardly new. Global controversies over control of the Internet address space have indeed long been a core Internet governance conflict. The move to transition years of U.S. Department of Commerce stewardship of these critical resources to what has come to be called the "global multistakeholder Internet community" through ICANN probably best exemplifies the politicization of this core Internet architecture.[9] Before this long-planned transfer, American politician Newt Gingrich suggested that "Every American should worry about Obama giving up control of the Internet to an undefined group. This is very, very dangerous."[10] U.S. Senator Ted Cruz similarly framed this stewardship transition as President Obama surrendering the Internet to authoritarian regimes. A piece in the Wall Street Journal referred to the announced move simply as "America's Internet surrender."[11]

China redesigning the Internet? Ukraine asking that Russia be disconnected? The United States surrendering the Internet? Battles between standards organizations? All of these very brief examples of questions and controversies over the Internet Protocol, whether founded or not, real or imagined, hint at the core importance and geopolitical interest in the evolution of this protocol and how IP is an ongoing flashpoint mediating broader geopolitical conflicts in various cultural and historic contexts.

In uncovering entanglements between IP and a host of public policy issues from content control to security and privacy, *Geopolitics at the Internet's Core* is an important longitudinal case study amplifying and building on the conceptual framework from *The Turn to Infrastructure in Internet Governance* (Palgrave 2016), itself drawing substantially from infrastructure studies traditions in the field of Science and Technology Studies (STS) and to the authors' decades of Internet governance scholarship drawing on these STS traditions, as well as international relations scholarship. The core idea of this STS perspective centers on the social, organizational, and political dimensions of technical infrastructure, both material and human. This conceptual framework draws from a long line of scholarship from STS scholars ranging from Susan Leigh Star and Geoff Bowker to Janet Abbate and Laura DeNardis.[12] It is not just that values are designed into technical systems, such as Lessig's Code is Law contribution, but that systems, once developed, become a proxy for political power.[13]

The *Turn to Infrastructure in Internet Governance* book contributed to Internet governance scholarship and practice by capturing how powerful actors—especially governments—turn to infrastructural control points to carry out functions beyond the original purpose of the technology. Search engines become intellectual property rights enforcement mechanisms. The Domain Name System becomes a tool of censorship. Cloud computing infrastructures become arbiters of speech. Financial and transactional digital intermediaries become tools for deplatforming companies and people. This politicization of infrastructure is powerful because it is effective, carried out by the private sector, and concealed in complex technology often hidden from direct view. This phenomenon often carries with it "collateral damage to the stability and security of the Internet and the protection of online civil liberties."[14]

*Geopolitics at the Internet's Core* examines how and why the Internet Protocol has become entangled with almost every digital policy concern in modern society—from access and privacy to economic competition and content control—and how it serves as a flashpoint for broader governance struggles. This book seeks to make three original contributions. First, and while the phenomenon of infrastructure-embedded geopolitics is established conceptually, this book uses controversies around the Internet Protocol ecosystem to develop a more elaborate and systematized analytical frame that can methodologically be applied to other complex infrastructure controversies, whether quantum communication, artificial intelligence, the Internet of Things, or cryptocurrency. The book is also innovative in that it brings together scholars and practitioners to present original information from both practice and research, a methodological charge in the authors' edited volume *Researching Internet Governance: Methods, Frameworks, Futures* (MIT Press 2020). Most importantly, the book establishes how the Internet Protocol ecosystem at the core of the Internet continues to be a flashpoint for geopolitical conflict and how the resiliency and security of this system is vitally necessary for society, the economy, and human security.

### *Opening the Internet Protocol Ecosystem*

What exactly is the "Internet Protocol" and why does it occupy the center of so many power struggles? The Internet itself has become hard to define. Even the language used to describe the Internet is mercurial. Should it continue to be capitalized (Internet) or should the first letter be demoted to a lower-case letter (internet) as so many started to do? Why is the term "cyberspace" used when discussing national security but "Internet" used when discussing communications or the digital economy, even if the same exact infrastructure is referenced? Despite these linguistic machinations, if the Internet has a technical and historic definition, *it may be the* Internet Protocol.

Among other things, the Internet Protocol is part of the world of technical standards. The Internet works and has a common infrastructure because of technical standards that provide interoperability between products and services, regardless of who manufactures them. These often open standards—open in design participation, open to freely access, and open for anyone to implement in products without significant intellectual property rights restrictions—replaced a highly fragmented information ecosystem predating the commercial Internet in which a proprietary system built by one company (e.g., Apple, IBM, Digital Equipment Corporation, Hewlett-Packard) could not easily exchange information with proprietary systems built by another company. They used proprietary protocols. Open standards changed this.

Since that era of inherent fragmentation, an agreed-upon, universal language has specified everything from how to encode and compress images, audio, and video in standard formats, how to exchange information between web browsers and servers, how to use common cryptography to secure information exchange and provide authentication, how to perform error detection and correction, and every other function required to potentially provide secure communication and transactions between any two points on earth. Many of these technical standards are everyday terms like Wi-Fi, JPEG, HTTPS, VoIP, TLS, DNSsec, and Bluetooth. The Internet depends on standards.

This common language of Internet standards does not mean that there is no "fragmentation" at all, or that there are no proprietary specifications, or that there is a fully universal Internet. More than two billion people do not yet have Internet access. Those that do often face barriers such as political censorship and filtering, or technical and economic barriers.

Many of the "standards" within digital devices are part of proprietary architectures that are closed or patent-embedded. But the availability of common standards has made growth and access possible and represented a significant revolution relative to the closed and incompatible systems that preceded the global Internet.

The common nomenclature for this set of standards is sometimes "TCP/IP." The protocol suite known as "TCP/IP" encompasses the Internet Protocol but actually has many historical meanings. One meaning is conceptual; one serves a taxonomical usage function; and one is a strict technical definition. The later, strict definition of TCP/IP is that it is two protocols: the Transmission Control Protocol (TCP), responsible for establishing a reliable connection between source and destination, and the Internet Protocol. In common usage, however, TCP/IP has become a term that more generally refers to a large family of protocols necessary for the Internet to work, including protocols for file sharing, mail, and other functions. Even more abstractly, the TCP/IP suite is a conceptual model for understanding how protocols work by characterizing their functionality in four "layers," the Link layer, the Internet layer, the Transport layer, and the Application layer. IP operates at the so-called Internet layer.

The Internet, as designed, also requires a universal pool of globally unique names and numbers. This requirement can easily be understood through the prism of physical-world communications. Sending a letter through the postal system requires using a physical address, usually a street number, street address, city, state, zip code, and country. For the mail system to work, each address has to be globally unique. Analogously, digital devices reach each other using a globally unique number known as an IP address, either assigned temporarily for a session or more permanently. Instead of being a physical address (e.g., a laptop owned by John Doe), each address is logical, meaning software-defined and not tied to a particular physical location. The totality of available IP addresses is usually called the "Internet address space."

The Internet Protocol establishes the addressing format necessary for routing information from point A to point B. And, by extension, its design establishes the global addressing space for communication over the public Internet. Describing this role is aided by describing the packet-switching network approach that underlies the Internet. In packet switching, information to be transmitted over a network is broken up into small units called "packets." Each packet contains some of the actual information (called payload) and a header containing the source and destination Internet addresses along with other administrative overhead. Each packet is forwarded to its destination via routers that make decisions in real time about how to reach this destination. Packets may travel along different pathways and are then re-sequenced (i.e., placed in proper order) at the destination.

The original Internet Protocol dates back to the early 1980s and is documented in the Internet "RFCs."[15] The RFCs, or Request for Comments, are an electronic archive that, since 1969, has documented Internet standards and other informational and procedural documents. Lest one think engineers are without humor, RFCs published on April 1 are April Fool's jokes, such as one describing "The Quantum Bug," making fun of concerns about quantum networking by referencing "faster-than-light communication, where packets arrive before they are sent."[16] A hilarious April Fool's RFC released in 1997 fictitiously reminisces about "Internet Protocol version 9," and how Internet providers issued "1 billion addresses to each house" with "a million addresses to be allocated for each discrete unit (e.g. room/floor etc.)" including to "light switches."[17] A quarter century later, light switches and light bulbs actually are connected to the Internet, but not yet "lawnmowers in space" as the RFC also lampoons.

The real Internet Protocol-related specifications are, of course, serious ones that standardize a number of necessary communication features including the format of the packet header, the size of each IP address, and how information is fragmented for transmission over a packet-switching network.

The Internet Protocol is a technical standard, a blueprint that establishes how information should be formatted, addressed, and routed in order for information to move from point A to point B. As IP has evolved, there are two versions in use, the original Internet Protocol version 4 (IPv4) and Internet Protocol version 6 (IPv6). The distinction and implications are discussed in greater detail in later chapters. But IPv4 is the long-dominant Internet address standard that assigns a unique, fixed-length 32-bit number to each address, such as:

00010011001010001000000100100001

This long binary number is usually written in shorthand "dotted decimal" notation such as, in the case of the number above, 19.40.129.33. For those interested, this notation is explained in the Technical Appendix.

The number above is one address out of the entire pool of IPv4 addresses. How many total are there in the IPv4 address space? Each of the 32 places in an IP address can take on one of two values, either a one or a zero. These ones and zeros are called "bits," short for binary digits. The total number of globally unique IP addresses can be calculated as $2^{32}$, or roughly 4.3 billion addresses. At the time this standard was developed (prior to the commercialization and internationalization of the Internet and prior to the Web), 4.3 billion unique addresses seemed an enormously optimistic number anticipating enormous growth.

Around 1990, Internet engineers anticipated that these billions of unique addresses would not suffice to meet global demand and they developed a new standard, IPv6, to massively expand the Internet address space. Each address under this standard would still have a fixed length of bits. But instead of 32 bits, each address would contain 128 bits, such as:

01110100100111011000011010101110111101000110 01
001100100100100111010010011101100001101010
11101111010001100100110010010010101110000

Shorthand notation based on the hexadecimal numbering system is necessary to make this one IPv6 address more human readable. The technical appendix explains this shorthand notation, but the hexadecimal notation for the address above is: 749D.86AE.F464.C927.49D8.92B8.

The entire pool of IPv6 addresses is so large; it has sometimes been described as equaling the number of grains of sand on earth. Unlike this unknowable number of grains of sand, calculating the exact number of available addresses under IPv6 is simple, though colossal, $2^{128}$, or 340 undecillion addresses, meaning 340 followed by 36 zeros.

The "Internet Protocol" sounds technically like one standard but is also surrounded by dozens of overlapping standards that are part of the "Internet Protocol ecosystem." The Internet Protocol itself establishes how addressing and fragmentation of packets occurs. This was first specified in 1980 as the "DOD Standard Internet Protocol" and updated and replaced by many subsequent RFCs (e.g., RFCs 791, 1349, 2474, 6864).[18] Reading any of these RFCs helps to demystify what "Internet Protocol" means.

Related protocols that are part of the broader "Internet Protocol ecosystem" include: IPv6 specifications; IPsec, a network-layer encryption protocol; IP standards customized for the Internet of Things (IoT); protocols that enable Voice over the Internet Protocol (VoIP), including Session Initiation Protocol (SIP); and Border Gateway Protocol Security (BGPsec), Resource Public Key Infrastructure (RPKI), and others.

The Internet Protocol ecosystem also arguably includes the surrounding systems that process, route, and advertise IP addresses and that translate IP addresses into domain names. As such, the broader IP ecosystem includes routing infrastructures, interconnection, and the Border Gateway Protocol (BGP) standard that advertises what IP addresses are reachable through each network (autonomous system). The broad IP ecosystem also includes the Domain Name System (DNS) that translates between the domain names that people use, such as georgetown.edu or wikipedia.org, and the IP addresses that routers use to reach a destination. The DNS is a vast, distributed, massive technological system that itself depends upon standards and involves a hierarchical database, software, servers, and a system of institutions to operate and coordinate all of this.

Putting this all together, this book addresses the Internet Protocol ecosystem as a combination of virtual resources, abstract specifications, tangible infrastructure, functionally specific systems, and the institutions and rules that design, operate, and coordinate these systems. This ecosystem approach is typical of theoretical frameworks from STS, and from the systems approach explored in history of technology and other fields. Historian of technology, Thomas Hughes, in work that predated the commercialization and globalization of the Internet, suggests that:

> "Among the components in technological systems are physical artifacts, such as turbogenerators, transformers, and transmission lines in electric light and power systems. Technological Systems also include organizations, such as manufacturing firms, utility companies, and investment banks... Legislative artifacts, such as regulatory laws, can also be part of technological systems."[19]

The ecosystem framing, while possibly dating back to the 1930s,[20] has had useful relevancy for Internet governance analysis[21] and is highly applicable to an examination of the Internet Protocol. The ecosystem and systems approach recognize the interrelationships among entities and the characteristics, organizations, and institutions within their contexts.[22]

The Internet Protocol ecosystem arguably encompasses a complex, overlapping set of infrastructural and institutional components. These include material and virtual elements, technical institutions, procedures, and laws as well as the policy, social, cultural, and political contexts that shape and in turn are shaped by these infrastructural elements. Taken together, these components illustrate the power of an ecosystem perspective. It is vital not just to examine infrastructural components or underlying technologies of Internet governance—the "thousands of protocols, platforms, algorithms, systems of routing and interconnection, the DNS, encryption standards, the Internet of Things, public key cryptography and other authentication mechanisms"[23] but also to highlight the often invisible interrelationships with the actors, institutions, and private and public power that constitute the ecosystem and its governance. This book defines the Internet Protocol ecosystem as a complex, overlapping set of components including:

- **Internet Addresses**. The IP address space (both IPv4 and IPv6) that encompasses the globally unique addresses identifying the virtual locations of resources online.
- **Specifications**. The collection of specifications that defines various engineering characteristics of the Internet Protocol from frame formats to address size to encryption.
- **Supporting Systems**. The distributed systems that enable IP to function, including routing infrastructures, network interconnection, and the Domain Name System that translates between names and numbers.
- **Institutions**. The technical institutions, procedures, norms, and laws that shape the design and administration of these systems.

Understanding the contemporary collection of actors and institutions keeping the Internet Protocol ecosystem operational can be more complicated than understanding the technology itself. No one actor is responsible for the technologies and systems around IP. There is also not only one governance function, but many, necessary for the basic functioning of the IP ecosystem: setting technical standards for the Internet

Protocol ecosystem; coordinating the distribution of IP addresses; operating and securing the Domain Name System and routing systems; agreeing to conjoin networks and exchange traffic between networks; and establishing both private and public policies that regulate the conditions of information flows and rights on the network.

The question of who "governs" the Internet is a complicated and important question. If IP is the technical center of the Internet, and an ecosystem of technologies with important public policy dimensions, then the question of who designs and administers this ecosystem of technologies is critical, particularly when these functions entangle with various dimensions of public policy.

## The Technical and the Geopolitical

How does one jump to "America's Internet surrender" from the ecosystem of packet headers, address length, encryption, translation between names and numbers, routing, and packet sequencing, and acronym-laden institutions that may seem dry relative to the controversies that have swirled around it? Even technical standards, one of the most invisible and abstract of all the components of Internet architecture and governance, have technology and society entanglements.[24] The interests of standards designers, as well as ambient geopolitical and economic contexts, shape technical design. Once developed, standards reciprocally shape society and have social and economic implications. Like all technologies, they are historically and culturally shaped.

Specific examples help highlight how, like all technologies, technical standards are historically and culturally shaped. The World Wide Web Consortium's (W3C) accessibility standards seek to make information accessible for those with hearing, sight, or other impairments. Standardized algorithms for facial recognition embed cultural biases if they are trained primarily on primarily lighter skin images.[25] Regulatory constraints on encryption standards (e.g., key length) demonstrate how cryptography inherently mediates tensions between individual privacy and economic stability versus law enforcement and intelligence agency access to information.[26] The intellectual property rights embedded in protocols (standards-based patents) have effects on economic competition, the freedom to innovate, and the creation of an information ecosystem of either multiple competing and interoperable products or closed, proprietary systems and monopolies. Standards are not merely technical in nature. The Internet Protocol, too, has connected with the public interest in many ways, as this book addresses.

Several inherent design and implementation features of the Internet Protocol have shaped its surrounding geopolitics.[27] The term geopolitics in this context is not at all relegated to nation-states. The traditional use of the word geopolitics comes from "geography" and "politics," thereby focusing primarily on the nation-state. Especially in the context of Internet governance, geopolitics expansively includes other institutional actors, technologies, and private power, along with the critical role of nation-states and intergovernmental organizations.

The following technological affordances of the Internet Protocol have contributed to the geopolitical attention it has attracted:

**Technical Criticality**: The Internet Protocol is arguably the fundamental and central technology that makes the Internet the Internet. While exceptions exist, most transactions online from accessing a website to sending an email to playing a multiplayer video game use the Internet Protocol. It is the core addressing system of the Internet that standardizes how to append a unique number to an online resource, dictate how each "packet" of information is formatted, and allow routers to exchange information over different networks (i.e., interoperability).

While the Internet is made up of many different innovations and standards developed by many people, companies, and institutions, IP is the common denominator that, over time, has largely made the Internet the Internet and enabled interoperability among networks. This, in part, explains why TCP/IP developers Vinton Cerf and Robert Kahn are often referred to as the Fathers of the Internet. At one point, Internet engineers used the definition of whether a device could be "pinged"—reached via IP—as a delimiter of whether someone was actually "on the Internet."

Given the central role of this protocol in the digital economy, public sphere, and every facet of the real world as the Internet becomes embedded in everyday objects, it is unsurprising that economic and geopolitical forces seek to control or replace this technology.

**Finite Pool of Resources**: The finite pool of Internet addresses available globally is another factor that attracts geopolitical conflicts over IP. This characteristic stems from the initial design decision to use a fixed-length number of bits (0s and 1s) for each address. The long-dominant IPv4 standard, as mentioned, provided a pool of approximately 4.3 billion addresses. IPv6 has dramatically expanded this number but, for a complicated set of reasons discussed later in this book, has not completely replaced the demand for IPv4 addresses. While the word "scarcity" might overemphasize the context, the constrained architecture around IP addresses has for decades remained a global concern.

Architecting a finite pool of fixed-length virtual identifiers, rather than a dynamic design that continuously expands the number of available addresses, embroils the Internet into questions about authority for allocating these resources necessary for using the Internet, and the distributional fairness questions about how they are allocated. Who is responsible for allocating and assigning addresses? How should they be distributed around the world? And how should first-mover advantage, such as American universities and corporations historically having large stores of IP addresses, be addressed over time, if at all?

**Personal Identification**: Another set of technical characteristics creates policy concerns (and opportunities) involving personal identification and privacy. Each use of an IP address must be globally unique, either assigned permanently or temporarily for a session. These identifiers are not linked to a physical object such as a piece of hardware (this was another design alternative) but are virtual, also called logical or software-defined identifiers. As such, they do not necessarily identify a person or device. But, these virtual identifiers, when combined with other information provided by network operators, for example, can be used to identify people as they exchange information online.

Social security numbers in the United States and national identification numbers in other countries were not necessarily designed to be unique identifiers for other purposes over decades, but that is exactly how they evolved. Analogously, IP addresses were designed to be virtual, not physical, identifiers yet are now embroiled in many policy questions about privacy, such as law enforcement requests to identify criminals, authoritarian efforts to identify political dissidents, or marketing and online revenue generation through collecting massive amounts of personal information. Because of this identity usage, the Internet Protocol is a highly politicized technology at the core of many questions about personal privacy ranging from business models and political oppression to mass data surveillance.[28]

**Not Historically Market-Based**: Given the value of IP addresses, and given that the Internet Protocol creates a finite pool of addresses, in contemporary political and economic systems, one might expect the distribution of these addresses to be mediated by market-based supply and demand. Another feature of IP is that addresses were not traditionally bought and sold in open markets (although markets developed over time). The Internet standards-setting community, influential technologists, and the institutions involved in allocating and assigning addresses originally embraced a philosophy that Internet addresses are a shared public resource. They should be "allocated" and "assigned" rather than sold in a traditional way that transfers private ownership of a product or service. While there were exceptions to this, this distributional approach privileged those first involved in the Internet, and ascribed more power to those responsible for allocating these resources. Because markets are not the delimiter of resource allocation, other types of conflicts over political and economic influence have materialized.

**A Choke Point for Control**: Because IP addresses inherently locate information and resources online, they are a locus of filtering and blocking content and services online. Whether firewalls using IP blocking to protect against network intrusion or co-optation by authoritarian governments to censor information, IP addresses have always been a source of content filtering, censorship, content moderation, or whatever is the latest societal term for filtering content.

IP addresses are an integral part of the Domain Name System. While designed for specific technical functions such as resolving domain name queries into IP addresses, the DNS has become a content redirection mechanism for everything from political censorship to sites that violate intellectual property rights around pirated media or the illegal sale of trademarked goods. The practice of carrying out this mediation is often privatized, in that domain name registrars and registries—commensurate with social media companies, web hosting companies, and other kinds of information intermediaries—are increasingly approached to be a source of interventions to address "objectionable content." This approach is such an effective—albeit disproportionate and potentially conducive to collateral damage—content-blocking mechanism because it does not require taking down targeted sites but rather just redirection, such as to a law enforcement message.

## Tales of the Internet Protocol

The Internet Protocol exists within a larger context of "multistakeholder Internet governance" that has dominated the twenty-first century. Chapter Two, *A Radical Governance Innovation*, uses the Internet Protocol as a lens into this governance structure and attendant geopolitical tensions. Sometimes messy and always contestable, this broad framework of oversight, coordination, and public policy has been distributed across the private sector, governments, civil society, and cross-border technical coordinating institutions such as technical standards bodies and ICANN. Championed historically by democratic governments, this model is also associated historically with the idealized vision of "a free and open Internet."[29] It also clashes with other geopolitical forces, such as cybersovereignty governance approaches, tensions between borders and bits, and the ways in which infrastructure is co-opted for political and economic purposes.

To examine how technical and sociopolitical decisions are intricately entangled, Chapter Three, *Technical Design as Governance*, presents three historical Internet Protocol case studies in which societal contexts shape technical design and design reciprocally co-constructs societal conditions. One is the early 1990s selection of TCP/IP versus the competing Open Systems Interconnection (OSI) protocol suite as the set of standards that would form the basis of modern communication. Another is the design and selection of the next-generation Internet Protocol—IPv6—to meet the demands of a commercializing and globalizing Internet. Yet another example involves the privacy implications of the design choices around the IP ecosystem.

Chapter Four, *The Internet Address Space as a Geopolitical Space*, turns attention to IP addresses themselves. The chapter explains the technical architecture and governance of the IP address space and explores a number of geopolitical flashpoints around IP addresses around AfriNIC, political sanctions against Iran, and Russia's war on Ukraine.

While these cases serve to highlight the geopolitical stakes of the IP address space, Chapter Five—*A Twenty-Year Control Struggle from U.S. Stewardship to Private Governance*—explores in depth the most high-profile example of IP address geopolitics: the transition of stewardship over the so-called Internet Assigned Numbers Authority (IANA) functions from the United States to a global multistakeholder institution, ICANN. While Internet governance itself is diffuse and distributed, there are also points of concentration and requirements for centralized coordination, such as assuring the global uniqueness of each assigned IP address. Taken together, these governance controversies help explain the geopolitical stakes of the IP address space and suggest that institutional and geopolitical controversies over allocation and control of these virtual resources will likely continue.

Increasing political interest in moderating content online—everything from purely illegal content to disinformation—has become one of the most contested public policy questions ever to confront the Internet, especially because illegal content varies across regions and what counts as objectionable content is always in flux. Content moderation is carried out primarily by the private sector. Much of this involves social media platforms such as Facebook, TikTok, and X. But deeper layers of infrastructure, whether the DNS, cloud computing providers, and web hosting services are even more powerful mediating forces, with the capacity to cut off large parts of the Internet. The Internet Protocol ecosystem has also become one of the most powerful control points for content censorship and blocking, as well as broader Internet shutdowns. Regardless of the rationale—national security, censorship, intellectual property rights enforcement, defamatory content, hate speech, and beyond—the task of blocking content or disrupting access has moved "down the stack" of technology into infrastructure intermediation. Chapter Six, *The Internet Protocol and Content Battles*, addresses the ways in which IP has been routinely co-opted as a proxy for blocking and restricting content. Examples include IP filtering and blocking for political censorship, intellectual property rights enforcement, and content-blocking efforts to mediate societal concerns related to human safety. These examples help pull back the curtain on the architectural points of control for content mediation and the institutions that mediate and execute this content filtering.

Because of the Internet Protocol's centrality to how the Internet works, as well as its intersection with critical public policy concerns as diverse as privacy and content blocking, it has long been a target of cybersecurity attacks. Chapter Seven, *Internet Protocol Security Entanglements with Geopolitics*, examines the necessary architectures of trust around IP and the associated actors involved. The chapter delves into four key areas of IP-related trust architectures: Certificate Authorities, Border Gateway Protocol, the DNS, and IP addresses themselves. As the Internet continues to move into the real world of medical objects, autonomous vehicles and cyber-physical industrial systems, the importance of securing this infrastructure cannot be overestimated.

The benefits and challenges of digital systems are not evenly distributed, despite the potential availability of the IP ecosystem anywhere in the world. Neither is inclusion in the design and governance of this infrastructure. Chapter Eight, *The Role of the IP Ecosystem in Inclusion*, seeks to expand discussions of digital inclusion beyond typical questions of broadband access and other user-facing metrics to infrastructural inclusion. Who has access to critical Internet resources? Who can use and contribute to technical standards? How can IP-supporting infrastructure from the DNS to Internet Exchange Points increase digital inclusion? Understanding these layered points of capacity-building and capacity absorption has to be part of meaningful economic, political, and cultural inclusion around the Internet.

The Internet Protocol has endured throughout massive technological change and usage cases. For example, the Internet's architecture is already infused with artificial intelligence at every layer from cybersecurity architectures to traffic management. New applications constantly emerge as the Internet moves further into physical objects and up into the solar system. What has not changed is that the history of IP has been characterized by a normal cycle of continual attempts to "redesign the Internet" and a normal cycle of a technology as a proxy for geopolitics. Chapter 9, *Geopolitical and Technical Futures of the Internet Protocol*, draws from the case studies of this book to present a taxonomy of eight levers of power within the IP ecosystem and the prospects of the technology considering the cycle of attempts to redesign and redistribute control over this ecosystem.

The Internet Protocol has been born out of conflict since its inception. One remarkable feature of its evolution is that, as each issue becomes resolved, geopolitical tensions seem to only escalate. The Internet Protocol—rightly or not—has occupied a unique place at the center of many public policy issues in the digital era. If history is any indication, controversies around core Internet architecture are a feature of our sociotechnical world. Internet governance issues are not fixed any more than technical architecture is fixed. Yet, IP architecture and governance systems have remained at the Internet's core. And it has endured as a major mediating site for geopolitical battles over the digital world. How these conflicts unfold will have enormous consequences for human rights, national security, economic stability, and the very heart of the Internet.

## Notes

1. Letter from Ukrainian Vice Prime Minister Mykhailo Fedorov to ICANN on February 28, 2022 and to RIPE-NCC on March 2, 2022, https://www.icann.org/en/system/files/correspondence/fedorov-to-marby-28feb22-en.pdf and https://www.ripe.net/publications/news/announcements/request-from-ukrainian-government.pdf
2. RIPE-NCC Letter to Ukrainian Vice Prime Minister Mykhailo Fedorov, March 10, 2022, https://www.ripe.net/publications/news/announcements/response_to_ua_gov_-_10march.pdf; and ICANN Letter https://www.icann.org/en/system/files/correspondence/marby-to-fedorov-02mar22-en.pdf.
3. See, for example, Madhumita Murgia and Anna Gross, "Inside China's Controversial Mission to Reinvent the Internet," *Financial Times*, March 27, 2020, https://www.ft.com/content/ba94c2bc-6e27-11ea-9bca-bf503995cd6f.
4. ITU-T TSAG, Study Period 2017, Contribution 83, "New IP, Shaping Future Network," submitted by China Mobile Communications Corporation, China Unicom, Huawei Technologies Co., and the Chinese Ministry of Industry and Information Technology, September 10, 2019, https://www.itu.int/md/T17-TSAG-C-0083.
5. ITU-T TSAG, Study Period 2017, Contribution 83, "New IP, Shaping Future Network," submitted by China Mobile Communications Corporation, China Unicom, Huawei Technologies Co., and the Chinese Ministry of Industry and Information Technology, September 10, 2019, https://www.itu.int/md/T17-TSAG-C-0083.
6. See, for example, Emily Taylor, Kate Jones, and Carolina Caeiro, "Technical Standards and Human Rights: The Case of New IP," in *Reclaiming Human Rights in a Changing World Order*, Chatham House 2022.
7. Réseaux IP Européens Network Coordination Centre (RIPE-NCC), "Response to "New IP, Shaping Future Network" proposal," statement to the ITU-T, February 2020, https://www.ripe.net/participate/internet-governance/multi-stakeholder-engagement/ripe-ncc_tsag_new-ip.pdf.
8. Ibid (RIPE-NCC), p. 1.

9. See Madeline Carr, *U.S. Power and the Internet in International Relations: The Irony of the Information Age,* Palgrave MacMillan 2016, for a treatment of state power or Blayne Haggart, Matasha Tusikov, and Jan Aart Scholte, eds., *Power and Authority in Internet Governance: Return of the State?* Routledge 2021.
10. Newt Gingrich Tweet, March 14, 2014, https://twitter.com/newtgingrich.
11. L. Gordon Crovitz, "America's Internet Surrender," *Wall Street Journal*, March 19, 2014.
12. These STS perspectives are exemplified in, for example, Susan Leigh Star, "The Ethnography of Infrastructure," *American Behavioral Scientist,* Vol. 43, No. 3, 1999, pp. 377-391; Langdon Winner, "Do artifacts have politics?" *Daedalus,* Volume 109, 1980, pp. 121–136; Bruno Latour, "Where are the Missing Masses? The Sociology of a Few Mundane Artifacts," *Shaping technology/building Society: Studies in Sociotechnical Change*, 1992, pp. 225-258; Geoff Bowker and Susan Leigh Star, *Sorting Things Out: Classification and its Consequences*, MIT Press, 1999; Janet Abbate, *Inventing the Internet*, MIT Press, 1999; Laura DeNardis, *Protocol Politics, the Globalization of Internet Governance*, MIT Press, 2009; Andrew Russell, *Open Standards and the Digital Age*, Cambridge University Press, 2014. A comprehensive description of STS infrastructure studies work is included in Francesca Musiani, "Infrastructuring Digital Sovereignty: a Research Agenda for an Infrastructure-based Sociology of Digital Self-determination Practices," *Information, Communication and Society*, Volume 25, Number 6, 2022, pp. 785-800.
13. Laura DeNardis, "Hidden Levers of Internet Control: An Infrastructure-based Theory of Internet Governance," *Information, Communication & Society*, Volume 15, Number 5, 2012, pp. 720–738.
14. Francesca Musiani, Derrick L. Cogburn, Laura DeNardis and Nanette S. Levinson, eds., *The Turn to Infrastructure in Internet Governance*, Palgrave Macmillan, 2016; see in particular the Introduction by DeNardis and Musiani.
15. See, for example, Jon Postel, RFC 791, "Internet Protocol: DARPA Internet Program Protocol Specification," September 1981, https://datatracker.ietf.org/doc/html/rfc791.

16. April Fools Day RFC released as Michael Welz, RFC 8774, "The Quantum Bug," April 1, 2020, https://www.rfc-editor.org/rfc/rfc8774.html#RFC6921.
17. April Fools Day RFC released as Julian Onions, RFC 1606, "A Historical Perspective on the Usage of IP Version 9," April 1, 1994, https://datatracker.ietf.org/doc/html/rfc1606.
18. Jon Postel, RFC 760, "DOD Standard Internet Protocol," January, 1980, https://www.rfc-editor.org/rfc/pdfrfc/rfc760.txt.pdf.
19. Thomas Hughes, "The Evolution of Large Technological Systems," in Wiebe E. Bijker, Thomas P. Hughes, and Trevor Pinch, *The Social Construction of Technological Systems*, MIT Press, 1987, p. 45.
20. For a discussion of how the term ecosystem dates as far back as 1935 with the ecologist Arthur Tansley, see Peder Anker, "The Context of Ecosystem Theory," *Ecosystems*, Volume 5, Number 200, 1935, pp. 611-613.
21. See, for example, Nanette Levinson, "Ideas, Institutions, and E-volution: The Internet Governance Ecosystem," paper presented at the Annual Meeting of the IAMCR Law Section, July 2007.
22. Thus, it is vital to highlight IP in terms of its impacts on its complex setting as well as the impacts of the complex setting on IP. For theoretical background, see for example, Ludwig von Bertalanffy, "The Quest for Systems Philosophy," *Metaphilosophy*, Volume 3, Number 2, April 1972, pp. 142-145.
23. See Laura DeNardis, Chapter 1 in *Researching Internet Governance: Methods, Frameworks, Futures,* MIT Press, 2020, p. 10.
24. A large body of interdisciplinary scholarship has addressed the public interest implications of technical standards. See, for example, Sandra Braman, "Internet RFCs as Social Policy: Network Design from a Regulatory Perspective," *Proceedings of the American Society for Information Science and Technology*, Volume 46, Number 1, 2009, pp. 1–29; Laura DeNardis, *Protocol Politics: The Globalization of Internet Governance*, MIT Press, 2009; Niels ten Oever, "Wired Norms," doctoral dissertation, 2022; Brenden Kuerbis and Milton Mueller, "Securing the Root," in Laura DeNardis, ed., *Opening Standards: The Global Politics of Interoperability,* MIT Press, 2011; Corinne Cath and Luciano Floridi, "The Design of the Internet's Architecture by the Internet Engineering Task

Force (IETF) and Human Rights," *Science and Engineering Ethics*, Volume 23, Number 2, 2017, pp. 449-468; Niels ten Oever and Christoph Becker, "Infrastructural insecurity: Geopolitics in the Standardization of Telecommunications Networks," *Media International*, Australia, 2024.

25. Daniel J. Fuchs, "The Dangers of Human-Like Bias in Machine-Learning Algorithms," *Missouri S&T's Peer to Peer*, Volume 2, Number 1, 2018, https://scholarsmine.mst.edu/peer2peer/vol2/iss1/1.
26. Ksenia Ermoshina and Francesca Musiani, with a preface by Laura DeNardis, *Concealing for Freedom: The Making of Encryption, Secure Messaging, and Digital Liberties*, Mattering Press, 2022.
27. These technical characteristics of IP are presented in Laura DeNardis, *Protocol Politics: The Globalization of Internet Governance*, MIT Press, 2009.
28. Samantha Bradshaw and Laura DeNardis, "Privacy by Infrastructure: The Unresolved Case of the Domain Name System," *Policy and Internet*, Volume 11, Number 1, 2019.
29. See, for example, Julia Pohle, "The European Strive for Digital Sovereignty: Have We Lost Our Belief in the Global Promises of the 'Free and Open Internet'?" *Weizenbaum Journal of the Digital Society,* Volume 3, Number 2, November 20, 2023. See also Shawn M. Powers and Michael Jablonski, *The Real Cyber War: The Political Economy of Internet Freedom*, University of Illinois Press, 2015, who write about the myth of multistakeholderism.

CHAPTER 2

# A Radical Governance Innovation

There is no natural correspondence between borders and bits: there is a mismatch between the laws governing nations and the cross-border and decentralized way that information actually flows. This tension has historically complicated the question of who or what governs the Internet, crystallized at the turn of the twenty-first century in a French court case addressing the sale of Nazi memorabilia online. Citizens in France were able to purchase Nazi memorabilia on Yahoo!'s platform, despite the illegality of these purchases under French law. Yahoo! was sued because citizens were able to access this illegal content and merchandise, even though the company's servers were located in the United States under constitutional protections of free expression. The French court in the *LICRA v. Yahoo!* decision ruled that Yahoo! must block the ability of French residents from being able to purchase Nazi memorabilia on the platform.

Sovereignty is complicated in cyberspace, not only technically and legally, but also culturally. Only four years before the Yahoo! lawsuit, in 1996, John Perry Barlow, co-founder of the Electronic Frontier Foundation and former Grateful Dead lyricist, penned "A Declaration of the Independence of Cyberspace" warning governments that, "You are not welcome among us. You have no sovereignty where we gather."[1] Barlow was raising concerns about possible restrictions on free speech online



F. M. Alexander et al., *Geopolitics at the Internet's Core*, Information Technology and Global Governance,
https://doi.org/10.1007/978-3-031-89478-7_2

around a recently passed U.S. law called the Communications Decency Act (CDA). The U.S. Supreme Court unanimously overturned much of the CDA on First Amendment grounds in *Reno v. American Civil Liberties Union* (ACLU).

This dot-com era melee would have sweeping and lasting Internet governance legacies. Most notably, Section 230 of the CDA would remain, establishing immunity from liability for "interactive computer services" (information intermediaries such as social media companies) for the content posted by their users. Social media companies would not be held liable for information posted by others on their platforms. Section 230 would also establish a good Samaritan provision legally protecting these same companies when they do restrict objectionable content. This provision has helped shape a privatized, albeit contested, governance context in which platforms moderate content that would otherwise be legal. It has also immunized these same companies against lawsuits when someone is harmed on their platform.

Questions about who "controls" or governs the Internet—and the tensions between bits and borders and between private and public power—are just as complicated and politicized in layers of the technology farther removed from content. The Internet's infrastructure is subject to often conflicting regional regulations and simultaneously and centrally involves privatized governance decisions that shape conditions of speech, privacy, competition, and civility online. At the same time, many of the coordinating functions that keep the Internet operational are internationally and institutionally distributed and the technology itself crosses borders in many ways that transcend either traditional jurisdiction or private ordering.

The Internet Protocol can help reveal a great deal about this distributed "Internet governance" oxymoron that has come to be called multistakeholder governance. Pulling back the curtain on the technical architecture of IP helps make visible the cross-border digital infrastructure, concealed in plain sight, underpinning all of society. Similarly, pulling back the curtain on the functions of oversight and coordination over IP addresses helps demystify the structure and consequences of "multistakeholder Internet governance." These overlapping institutions and systems hold together much of the digital world.

What was once an esoteric area addressed primarily by government specialists, technical communities, and academics has now risen to the top of public policy agendas. This is because even the most abstract areas of technical coordination and design have direct implications for national security, economic stability, and human rights. This chapter uses IP infrastructure as a lens to examine the many layers of multistakeholder governance and surrounding geopolitical tensions. Examining this intersection of the IP ecosystem and multistakeholder governance helps elaborate three core themes that serve as the scaffolding of this book: the politics of technical design; the co-opting of infrastructure as a proxy for geopolitical power; and the ongoing tensions between the so-called multistakeholder model of governance versus the more nation-state-centered frameworks of digital or cyber sovereignty.

## The Internet Protocol as a Lens into Internet Governance

The Internet, built upon a series of voluntary standards and processes, has always required coordination and governance. But views about *who* is doing the governing and what is being governed have often been oversimplified or just grossly incorrect. Discussions about who should be in charge are typically oversimplified and reduced to calling out "the government," "the United Nations," "ICANN," or in some places "GAFAM," (short for Google Apple Facebook Amazon and Microsoft). None of these actors individually govern the Internet, in part because there is not merely one technical object of governance. Rather an entire ecosystem of infrastructure from protocols to interconnection points to names and numbers and platforms makes up the Internet. And there is also not simply a single coordinating function that alone keeps the Internet running. The development and performance of the vast ecosystem of functions necessary to keep the Internet operational, and the establishment of public policy around this infrastructure is collectively called global Internet governance.

The word governance dates back to the fifteenth century and refers to "the act or process of governing or overseeing the control and direction of something" (Merriam-Webster Dictionary). Over the years the who or the institution doing the process of governing (and the what is being governed) have changed markedly. In the early days of the Internet's predecessor network, ARPANET, the "who" and the "what" largely entailed a U.S. federally funded defense-oriented research innovation, with individuals such as early Internet pioneers Vinton Cerf, Jon Postel, and others designing protocols and coordinating critical resources.

As the network rapidly globalized and privatized, and as the U.S. Department of Commerce assumed a key role in the administration of critical Internet resources, questions about control followed. One arena for debate, and one serving as a marker recognizing a more global orientation, was the first phase of the United Nations World Summit on the Information Society (WSIS) which, in the Declaration of Principles of the 2003 Geneva Action Plan, articulated that "the international management of the Internet should be multilateral, transparent and democratic, with the full involvement of governments, the private sector, civil society, and international organizations."[2] The Action Plan also called for the creation of a Working Group on Internet Governance (WGIG, pronounced Wig-Ig) to, among other things, create a working definition of Internet governance. In 2005, the group crafted a working definition of Internet governance as follows:

"the development and application by governments, the private sector, and civil society, in their *respective roles*, of shared principles, norms, rules, decision-making procedures, and programmes that shape the evolution and use of the Internet."[3] (italics added).

Contention over the scope of Internet governance directly shaped this definition, arising in the historical context of global political concern over American oversight of names and numbers, and global interest in transferring this authority to a more international body such as the United Nations' International Telecommunication Union. The definition provides important insights: that numerous actor classes have a role in Internet governance; that each has a "respective role" and not an equivalence; and that the scope of governance includes development and not only use of the Internet.

The United Nations-facilitated working definition focuses largely on *institutions* and therefore has some limitations. The technical architectures of Internet governance themselves, as well as market forces, embed power relations and shape sociotechnical structures. But the WGIG definition and associated discussions mainstreamed the terms "global Internet governance" and "multistakeholder governance." Google Trends documentation of searches for the term "global Internet governance" shows a remarkable take-off in its use in 2006, the same year as the inaugural multistakeholder United Nations Internet Governance Forum (IGF) was held in Athens, Greece. Much of this initial global governance discussion centered on names and numbers and tensions over U.S. government stewardship.

It would be another ten years before U.S. government stewardship of critical Internet resources transitioned to a more global system when the U.S. government contract with ICANN expired on October 1, 2016 and the Affirmation of Commitments was terminated on January 7, 2017, completing ICANN's formal evolution to a global, independent, multistakeholder organization. This is only one epoch in the larger history of Internet governance, but one that serves as a benchmark in the evolution of multistakeholder governance approaches.

The dramatic movement in network governance from points of government-centric authority over telecommunication systems to a more multistakeholder and global one around the Internet echoed changes in the broader governance context worldwide. In 1992, the United Nations Earth Summit in Rio (with Nitin Desai, who later became the U.N. Secretary-General's Special Adviser for the World Summit on the Information Society (WSIS) and then the first Chair of the Internet Governance Forum) featured for arguably the first time the inclusion of stakeholders beyond national governments and international organizations. A similar pattern existed in the health arena.

In 1998, health experts at the World Health Organization (WHO) called on governments to catalyze a massive campaign to protect against infectious diseases. Realizing that governments alone did not have the expertise (or the funding) to deal with such complex, cross-border patterns of infection, donor governments decided not to go the United Nations route but rather to create a new institution, the Global Fund. Set up as a Swiss foundation, international in scope, the Global Fund was to be "a partnership between governments, civil society, the private sector, and people affected by the diseases."[4] The Global Fund's initial 2002 Governing Board began with members that included non-state actors and intergovernmental organizations.[5]

These other global policy arenas, around the environment and health, share much with Internet governance: involving cross-border, complex interactions and impacts; requiring technical or scientific expertise; involving power panoplies; and mediating geopolitical dynamics. To disentangle Internet governance for a technical and geopolitical examination, this book adapts an infrastructure-based framework of Internet governance taken from the authors' previous work,[6] with an emphasis on how the Internet Protocol uniquely traverses every layer of Internet governance. The following sections divide the functions of infrastructure coordination and regulation into seven categories, all intersecting with some dimension of the Internet Protocol.

## Administering Critical Internet Resources

Because of the technical requirement that domain names, IP addresses, and Autonomous System Numbers be globally unique, someone has always had to manage the distribution and allocation of these resources. And the Domain Name System (DNS) has served in the vital role of translating between domain names and IP addresses. This system requires numerous areas of coordination. Someone has to ensure the global uniqueness of each address. Someone has to decide how addresses are distributed around the world. Someone is responsible for maintaining the mapping of names and numbers for each top-level domain. This may sound straightforward, but control over IP addresses has been a contentious issue as the Internet has grown, the history of which is described in this book.

The actors involved in this administrative and policymaking function are vast and kaleidoscopic. In the contemporary era, address distribution is done hierarchically, with the Internet Corporation for Assigned Names and Numbers (ICANN) having the authority for global coordination of what is called the "IANA functions." This legacy phrase "IANA functions" refers to coordination of unique numbers, including IP addresses, and the root zone file. The root zone file serves as the master file recording the definitive mapping of top-level domains into IP addresses for each domain.

An affiliate of ICANN called the Public Technical Identifiers (PTI) allocates IP addresses to regional organizations for further allocation or assignment. These so-called Regional Internet Registries (RIRs)—such as AfriNIC in the African region, ARIN in North America, and others—in turn distribute addresses to local Internet registries or directly to network operators and others. There are also registrars, like GoDaddy, that assign domain names, and even domain name dispute-resolution providers that resolve domain name trademark disputes. DNS registry operators are responsible for maintaining the authoritative mapping of names and numbers in the domain they oversee. In short, even this one area of digital coordination over unique names and numbers encompasses a large number of coordinating tasks and involves numerous institutions, many of them private, not-for-profit organizations.

## Setting Standards for the Internet

The Internet Protocol and related standards, including those involved in securing IP and the DNS, emerged from a technical engineering community eventually known as the Internet Engineering Task Force, or IETF. The standards within the Internet Protocol ecosystem and surrounding are primary examples, but there are many others. Technical standards-setting is a core Internet governance function. Shared rules for enabling interoperability structure all dimensions of information exchange ranging from encryption, compression, formatting, encoding, authenticating, and error detection and correction, among many others.

How Internet governance works has been profoundly shaped by both the core Internet protocols and especially the institutional and procedural norms of the IETF. The IETF, responsible for core Internet Protocols, is one of the many institutions setting digital standards. The World Wide Web Consortium (W3C) establishes standards (called Recommendations) for the Web, such as HyperText Markup Language (HTML) and Extensible Markup Language (XML). The International Telecommunication Union (ITU) sets telecommunication and many other areas of digital standards. The Institute of Electrical and Electronics Engineers (IEEE), the International Organization for Standardization (ISO), the American National Standards Institute (ANSI), and countless other standards bodies and consortia work on standards that surround core technical specifications collectively constructing the digital world.

## Securing the Internet's Core

Cybersecurity governance is a critical area of Internet governance, and one overlapping with every other task of digital coordination. Institutions from banks to government agencies to universities invest heavily in securing their own internal systems, protecting data, and complying with the security and privacy regulatory contexts in which they exist. Large media companies, content intermediaries, and network operators secure their own networks and also sell cybersecurity services and products. As such, cybersecurity is highly privatized.

Governments also have a multifaceted role in securing the Internet and broader digital ecosystem. Most governments have a national cybersecurity strategy that includes protection of critical infrastructure and security standards for various sectors. While this varies from country to country, governments establish and enforce laws relating to cybersecurity, ranging from data protection laws to cybercrime to critical infrastructure protection. Most countries have numerous agencies or entities addressing cybersecurity in their respective areas. In the United States, for example, cybersecurity responsibility is distributed across multiple agencies. The Department of Homeland Security's Cybersecurity and Infrastructure Security agency (CISA) seeks to reduce risk in America's cyber infrastructure. The FBI's Cyber Division investigates cybercrime. The National Institute of Standards and Technology develops frameworks and guidelines for best practices in cybersecurity. The United States Cyber Command in the Department of Defense (DoD) carries out military cyber-operations. Many other entities have differing responsibilities from the NSA's intelligence function and the White House's various coordinating roles to individual agencies that oversee specific sectors, such as the energy grid, and local and state governments.

Governments also carry out incident response and coordination, including the operation of some Computer Emergency Response/Readiness Teams (CERTS) or Cyber Security Incident Response Teams (CSIRTS) that disclose known vulnerabilities and instructions for vulnerability mitigation. These are often public–private collaborations.

At the international level, the United Nations' First Committee has cybersecurity governance in its domain within two multilateral working groups: first the older and more limited in membership, Group of Governmental Experts (GGE) related to information technology and security norms that ended its work in 2021; and then the Open-Ended Working Group (OEWG) that began in 2019 focused on cybersecurity, with membership open to all UN Member States. Geopolitical tensions within the OEWG shape most discussions, often with one set of nations calling for a new treaty and new norms and another set of nations focused on implementing currently agreed-upon cyber norms, and also raising questions about involving non-state actors in the discussions. Additionally, regional organizations play important roles in facilitating cybersecurity governance and capacity-building.

In addition to cybersecurity governance discussions focusing on cyber defense and improving stability and security, some governments also have an interest in weakening Internet security for intelligence gathering and cyber law enforcement functions and for stockpiling knowledge of vulnerabilities for cyber offense.

The Internet arguably has a shared infrastructure core in addition to the operation of private networks and the overlay of agency coordination and regulatory constraints on this infrastructure. This core includes systems of routing and interconnection, virtual resources such as IP addresses, and the DNS. Securing this shared infrastructure is a central task of cybersecurity governance, and one involving the design and coordination of trust architectures such as public key cryptography.

As Chapter 7 will explain, specialized institutions called Certificate Authorities (CA) perform the critical—and sometimes problematic—task of validating the digital certificates that authenticate the validity of everything online from websites to email addresses and the integrity of documents. The Internet Protocol and its surrounding architecture are intertwined with these cybersecurity governance tasks in numerous ways: securing the Domain Name System against DDoS attacks; authenticating DNS queries; designing IPsec protocols that help encrypt communications over IP networks; using VPNs designed to cloak one's IP address; or securing inter-domain routing communications that advertise sets of IP addresses reachable via a network.

## Interconnecting Networks

It is hopefully obvious that the Internet is not one network but a network of networks that interconnect and use shared protocols. Networks are responsible for advertising to neighboring networks the IP addresses reachable through their networks and maintaining a consistent global routing policy. The institutions operating these networks are a mix of large telecommunication providers (e.g., Korea Telecom, AT&T), large Internet platform companies (e.g., Google, Facebook, Weibo), and specialized networks such as Content Delivery Networks (e.g., CDNs, such as Akamai) and Web hosting service networks (e.g., Amazon Web services). Network operators make private contractual agreements to conjoin networks, either bilaterally or at Internet Exchange Points (IXPs). Some of these IXPs, such as the Deutsche Commercial Internet Exchange (DE-CIX) or the London Internet Exchange (LINX), connect hundreds of network operators.

Each network—technically each autonomous system—is a routing domain that announces to adjacent networks the IP addresses that are reachable through the system. Networks use an internal protocol called an interior gateway protocol to make decisions about how to route packets based on IP address within each network. Routing between networks uses an exterior routing protocol called Border Gateway Protocol.

A variety of public interest concerns arise around interconnection. How are IXPs distributed around the world to bring access and network interconnection globally? They have historically been more concentrated in the West but have expanded internationally over time. The technical and financial arrangements these network operators make with one another collectively establish global economic conditions around access and competition. On what terms do networks agree to connect and exchange traffic, and what are the financial arrangements they make? Who pays and who doesn't? What is the role of IXPs in government attempts to enact surveillance and censorship? The system of network connection among private networks requires trust and has historically been an area of security vulnerability. How secure is this handoff of data across the borders between networks?

In some digital domains, governments have tried to impose various restrictions and economic conditions on interconnection. For example, the 2012 ITU World Conference on International Telecommunications (WCIT) in Dubai revisited an international telecommunications treaty known as the International Telecommunication Regulations (ITRs). In addition to a proposal from India calling for an elevation of ITU standards by making them mandatory, governments debated whether or not to expand the scope of the voice telephony accounting rate regime to the Internet.[7] This would create a multilateral regulatory structure over the Internet. These discussions were highly divisive and ultimately split the ITU between 89 governments wanting greater multilateral control over the Internet and 55 countries wanting to preserve the status quo of private-sector-led multistakeholder governance.[8]

Similar debates over interconnection arrangements have continued over time, such as efforts initiated in 2022 by the European Telecom Network Operators (ETNO) Association to have the European Commission apply the so-called sending party pays (also called fair share) model as a means of extracting revenues from Internet platforms to pay for network infrastructure in Europe.[9]

## Policymaking by Private Intermediaries

Private companies are a powerful force in every area of Internet governance, whether setting standards or securing private technical infrastructure. Many of these governance functions are not immediately visible to Internet users. Private companies also enact governance in more direct ways, such as moderating (or not moderating) content, making decisions about where to invest, operate and provide services, and through business models and terms of service that make decisions about speech, privacy, security, and access. The decision of Amazon's hosting service—Amazon Web Services, or AWS, to deplatform an entire social media company over speech that violated its terms of service, exemplifies this considerable power.

Because IP addresses touch end users and are globally unique, they have also become de facto identifiers intertwined with policy issues ranging from enforcement of copyright to individual privacy. A range of private companies including social media companies, hosting services, and all manner of financial and transactional intermediaries collect personal data and also metadata like IP addresses. Revenue models based on targeted online advertising rely upon this collection of IP addresses and other metadata. Private companies also sell this data to "data brokers" and others.

In addition to this direct shaping of conditions of speech and privacy, private intermediaries also serve as the means for governments to carry out policy. When law enforcement agencies seek to identify someone, they request the necessary information from platforms, network operators, and other intermediaries. When governments enact surveillance, they do so largely through private infrastructure. When governments seek to enforce intellectual property rights online, they do so via private intermediaries such as DNS resolution services, search engines, financial and transactional intermediaries, and content hosting providers. Governments also delegate censorship practices to the private sector.

## Governing by Usage and Markets

Internet governance is, on its surface, distinct from the question of how one "uses" the Internet, even while overlapping with usage issues in important ways.[10] But usage contexts and implementation decisions create constraints or opportunities that essentially serve as a de facto form of governance. For individual users, consider market choices, political voting choices, entrepreneurship and innovation, participation in technical institutions, digital literacy, cybersecurity choices, advocacy and activism, Internet boycotts, hacking, and circumvention of censorship. In many nations, citizens have always been a critical actor in and around Internet governance in its most broad definition.

Sandra Braman explains that "'Internet governance' includes uses (and users), decision-making by general-purpose policymaking entities (e.g., geopolitical governments) and by those specific to the Internet (e.g., ICANN), and decision-making and structurational actions by private and public sector entities, daemons and humans, through informal and formal, transient and fixed, means."[11]

The Internet Protocol, and especially IPv6, helps demonstrate how usage and users include large private and public institutional Internet users, highly influential as market-force implementers of technological systems. For example, standards development is meaningless without standards implementation and adoption. The private companies that implement standards in their products, and the users and networks that adopt IPv6 exert influence on the digital ecosystem and attendant characteristics. Even if a standard is developed, and even if a standard is implemented in a product, adoption and usage choices shape the overall technological infrastructure. Usage contexts are another force shaping "governance" of the Internet.

## Regulating and Policymaking by Governments

The term "private-sector-led multistakeholder Internet governance" can sometimes obfuscate the significant role of governments in overseeing every aspect of the digital economy and society. As the LICRA v. Yahoo! Ruling from 2000 established, sovereign governments have long exerted influence over Internet users and companies in their jurisdictions, and even beyond. They have done so via regulation of telecommunication systems (both national and international), investment and regulation of broadband access, global competition policy and antitrust levers, intellectual property rights enforcement, privacy policies such as the General Data Protection Regulation (GDPR) in the EU, and national security policies such as those related to the protection of critical infrastructure. Specific regulations such as Section 230 of the CDA in the United States and the European Union's Digital Services Act (DSA) have shaped, and continue to shape, the conditions that enable corporations to moderate content or have immunity from liability for the user content they host or organize.

Government involvement in the Internet has also acted in direct tension with the principles of openness, inclusion, and universality that have been aspirational principles for an idealized "free and open Internet." Whether systems of censorship or surveillance or regulatory efforts around localizing data within national borders, governments routinely use the Internet as a proxy for some other goal, such as social control or intelligence gathering. This tension has existed not only in the practice of Internet governance but even in discussions. At the 2009 Internet Governance Forum in Sharm El Sheikh, Egypt, United Nations security officers entered a meeting room during a session of the Open Net Initiative to remove—at the behest of an unnamed UN Member State delegation—a poster mentioning the Great Firewall of China as an Internet filtering system. A day later, a UN spokesperson said this involved enforcing the "no poster" policy. News media from around the world covered the incident, highlighting the incongruity between a multistakeholder forum dedicated to opening up access to the Internet, including ensuring Internet freedom, and the removal of a poster identifying one nation's Internet censorship policies.[12]

The interest and involvement of governments in the practice of Internet governance has only increased. An example is government intervention in the information and communication technologies underlying global supply chains (GSC) such as efforts to relocate semiconductor manufacturing within national or regional borders. The Internet Protocol has often been at the center of sovereign interest, whether Ukraine's request about withdrawing IP addresses from Russia during Russia's war on Ukraine or China's evolving interest in a "new IP."

In short, governments are, of course, powerful actors in the multistakeholder governance ecosystem through a combination of national and regional regulations, international agreements, participation in multilateral and multistakeholder institutions, and efforts to either protect or disrupt speech, privacy, competition, and security online, often by turning to the private sector to carry out enforcement or otherwise co-opting infrastructure for political mediation.[13]

## Multistakeholder Governance and Digital Sovereignty Tensions

Multistakeholder governance is not a goal in itself but, as the many coordinating functions above suggest, a descriptive reality of how the underlying infrastructure of the Internet is successfully administered. Unlike postal services and telephony, with technology oversight conducive to nation-state control, the arrival of the Internet with its networked and fractal architecture catalyzed over time radical governance innovations. Governments do not control the Internet. Nor do corporations. Nor does ICANN or the IETF. In fact, no single actor controls the Internet. Technical design is part of governance. Infrastructure is co-opted as a proxy for political power.

Despite how policymakers and the press sometimes monolithically discuss Internet oversight, the layers of coordination described above also help to portray this collection of overlapping functions necessary for security, interoperability, interconnection, content moderation, and the management of a global address space. Nation-state borders themselves do not reign in the Internet Protocol; governance paradigms calling for nation-state control rarely work when applied to a complex and global set of architectures that characterize IP.

In sum, the Internet Protocol has disrupted historic approaches to nation-state control and multilateral coordination and catalyzed the arrival of complex and distributed multistakeholder governance arrangements. Collectively, the totality of this oversight is usually called "multistakeholder Internet governance."[14]

Not every layer of Internet governance is multistakeholder. Some of these functions are carried out by a single stakeholder group, such as the technical community or governments or the private sector. Other functions involve coordination across stakeholders. ICANN and the IETF are arguably examples of institutions that are inherently—if imperfectly—multistakeholder. ICANN, in particular, is an example of an organization that procedurally and institutionally incorporates stakeholder perspectives. It does so, in part, through its three Supporting Organizations (SOs) responsible for policies in their respective areas, including the Address Supporting Organization (ASO), the Country Code Names Supporting Organization, and the Generic Name Supporting Organization, as well as four advisory committees. The advisory committees include the Governmental Advisory Committee (GAC), the Security and Stability Advisory

Committee (SSAC), the Root Server System Advisory Committee, and the At-Large Advisory Committee (ALAC).

While the balance of powers distributed across many actors has been a critical success factor for the Internet, it is also important to not romanticize or uncritically valorize this system.[15] Multistakeholder governance can mean the privatization of governance, raising questions of legitimacy and consent of the governed. There are also not shared principles and views of the multistakeholder model across nations (and even within nations). In many parts of the world, such as China, claims to support multistakeholder governance do not at all embody democratic values or openness but is deployed as a mechanism for carrying out censorship of media and citizens. Versions of digital sovereignty, as well as multistakeholder approaches, shaped both by historical/cultural and geopolitical views, have popped up over time and become reinvigorated.

Geopolitics has not disappeared. Indeed, it is intricately connected with IP-related governance issues whether it is differing views on digital sovereignty or differing approaches to where Internet governance decisions should be made or even differing stances on domains for cyber security decision-making. Governments, whether democratic or dictatorial, are realizing more and more that technical design yields power (both in geopolitical and related economic realms). This shift to a cyber sovereignty footing is even apparent in the national security realm where efforts in the United States and Europe related to secure IP address routing and root server security, respectively, have been initiated in top-down work programs that run counter to existing multistakeholder processes, institutions, and principles. Chapter 9 covers these episodes in some detail. The multistakeholder model is also sometimes a cover for advancing the interests of dominant companies and industries with an enormous stake in governance arrangements. United Nations discussions have increasingly deployed the term to move the dial of oversight further to governments and away from the technical community and private industry.[16]

The values in tension in how governance is distributed and carried out over multiple actors parallel the social construction of other Internet principles, such as openness. This openness at both the infrastructure and governance level have shaped the Internet's success and growth while this same openness has always been contested and resisted in many ways. The Internet has never been completely open, or completely multistakeholder. Even at the content level, history has been replete with restrictions on freedom of expression, from authoritarian government systems of censorship and filtering to the resurgence of proprietary social media systems that do not interconnect. Much of the world lives in countries where speech is highly censored. Laws around the world severely limit what is often called the "free and open Internet," cracking down on journalism and a range of what is considered objectionable speech such as insulting a monarch or posting a tweet critical of a religion. Private company business models based on openness—sometimes called surveillance capitalism—monetize people through maximum personal data collection and tracking.

In the same way that openness in theory and architecture has often been an ideal but never fully achieved in practice, multistakeholder governance—or even "multistakeholderism" as an ideology or dominant discourse, is just as politicized and just as contested. Structures of technical governance are not fixed. Many contemporary-era dynamics, including the global COVID-19 pandemic, war, and China's social credit and censorship regime, have solidified increasing government power. Like democracy, the radical innovation of multistakeholder technology governance is problematic and messy, yet still works and serves to create a balance of powers that has helped shape the success and reach of the Internet.

Tensions between the multistakeholder coordinating system around the Internet and national sovereignty have become a feature of digital governance. Contemporary international relations practices are grounded in the idea of nation-states and mutually recognized sovereign rights within their territorial borders. The concept dates back to 1648 and the Peace of Westphalia which ended the Thirty Years War in Europe and ultimately shifted and solidified the organizing premise of governments towards territorial sovereignty. The Internet Protocol and its core design principles are not organized around territorial borders. Packets take the most efficient route to reach their destination, and other systems of Internet architecture and governance cross borders and are distributed and decentralized in ways that do not sync up with national borders. This, however, has not prevented nation states from attempting to impose borders around technology to assert digital sovereignty.

While government exploitation or attempted coercion of the Internet Protocol is not new, calls framing the efforts as governments simply asserting their widely accepted sovereign rights in the digital world have increased over time. For some countries, this is grounded in the notion of the need to ensure and protect a more centralized and concentrated role of government in all aspects of society. For others, primarily European countries, they define digital sovereignty as an attempt to place the Internet user in the driver's seat, with regulatory efforts focused on shifting power away from companies and toward consumers. In either shade of digital sovereignty, the actions are based on states reaffirming or asserting their authority over the Internet as a means to achieve national policies that can be attempts to empower the state or favor national champions, or worse, to control people. According to this principle, "sovereignty depends on more than supranational alliances or international legal instruments, military influence or trade agreements": it depends on innovation ecosystems that are owned, controlled, and operated at local, national, or regional levels, "able to increase states' technical and economic independence and autonomy."[17]

Digital sovereignty strategies have landed on the political agenda of many states and supranational institutions. This priority is manifested by a number of diverse state-centered initiatives ranging from Russia's Internet sovereignty initiatives and the Great Firewall of China to Europe's Digital Services Act (DSA) to many efforts around the world to force data to remain within national borders (i.e., data localization). These initiatives contribute to flesh out particular "state profiles" in the current digital regulation landscape: China as the long-term digital sovereign; Russia as the more recent yet strong-willed authoritarian; the United States as the de facto sovereign as the home of the majority of the world's largest Internet platforms; India and Brazil as strong opposers of U.S. surveillance; and Europe as the promoter of a comprehensive regulatory framework, based on a strong human rights legal framework, in support of its wish for digital independence.

Behind these scenarios, more nuanced than generalized above, are a number of controversial and crucial issues related to the practice of Internet governance, at both the national and global levels. Is the fragmentation of the Internet a threat, or a response to the shortcomings of the Internet governance *status quo*? Is there a difference between how authoritarian and democratic states think about their digital sovereignty? Who are the key actors affected by the push for digital sovereignty? How do decision-makers worldwide make sense of the "digital sovereignty" label, and operationalize it, when different state actors use it to describe substantially different paradigms and processes (and often, different actors operating *within* each state, governments, parliaments, civil society organizations, technical operators)? Can a digital self-determination agenda be pushed by nation-states while preserving the global dimension of the Internet and its multistakeholder institutions, as well as civil liberties? Indeed, depending upon the answers to these questions, digital sovereignty dynamics appear as the foremost threat to multistakeholder governance of the Internet.

Even the nomenclature around issues of sovereignty has many shades, with "technological sovereignty" or "Internet sovereignty" used in certain contexts, "cyber sovereignty" used in still others, and "digital sovereignty" or "digital nationalism" deployed elsewhere. Yet each of these reflects the underlying tensions between bits and borders and power struggles among the many actors with a stake in the outcome of each conflict.

## The Centrality of IP in Internet Governance

What is clear, however, is that the design, administration, and geopolitics of the Internet Protocol ecosystem traverse every lever of Internet governance and debate about digital sovereignty. IP is a standard, established by a standards-setting institution. IP addresses are critical Internet resources requiring global coordination. Securing IP communications is a critical success factor for cybersecurity. Information intermediaries use and collect IP addresses in support of business models based on highly personalized online advertising. Networks that interconnect advertise to each other collections of IP addresses reachable through their regions. The DNS resolving domain queries into IP addresses is a central lever of blocking access to websites that violate intellectual property rights. Debates over redesigning or co-opting IP have become a feature of geopolitics.

This entanglement of IP across all layers of Internet governance is, in part, a sign of just how inherently overlapping these functions are. It is also an indication of the centrality of the Internet Protocol to how the Internet actually works and the coordination required to maintain its operation, security, and success. The design, administration, coordination, and even co-opting of the Internet Protocol are core parts of the Internet governance system. In this regard, the term "geopolitics at the Internet's core" does not only refer to the centrality and politics of the technology—IP—itself, but also the centrality of the governance of this technology and the ways in which infrastructure governance power struggles have followed the protocol from almost its inception.

## Notes

1. See UN World Summit on the Information Society, "Declaration of Principles," paragraph 48, December 12, 2003, https://www.itu.int/net/wsis/docs/geneva/official/dop.html.
2. John Perry Barlow, "A Declaration of the Independence of Cyberspace," Davos, Switzerland, February 8, 1996, https://www.eff.org/cyberspace-independence.
3. United Nations Working Group on Internet Governance, "Report of the Working Group on Internet Governance," Château de Bos, 2005, https://www.wgig.org/WGIG-Report.html.
4. The Global Fund's description of partnerships from its public-facing website "Partnerships" page, https://www.theglobalfund.org/en/.
5. Bernhard Reinsberg and Oliver Westerwinter, "The Global Governance of International Development: Documenting the Rise of Multi-stakeholder Partnerships and Identifying Underlying Theoretical Explanations," *The Review of International Organizations*, Springer, Volume 16, Number 1, January, 2021, pp. 59–94.
6. Laura DeNardis, *The Global War for Internet Governance*, Yale University Press, 2014; Also, Francesca Musiani et al., eds., *The Turn to Infrastructure in Internet Governance*, Palgrave MacMillan, 2016 and Laura DeNardis et al., eds., *Researching Internet Governance: Methods, Frameworks, Futures*, MIT Press, 2020.
7. Rohan Samarajiva, "A WCIT Proposal Primer: What Participants Need to Know for Dubai," LIRNEAsia, November 2012, https://lirneasia.net/wp-content/uploads/2012/11/LIRNEasia_Briefing_A_WCIT_Proposal_Primer_11_12.pdf.
8. Mike Masnic,"Who Signed the ITU WCIT Treaty…And Who Didn't," TechDirt, December 14, 2012, https://www.techdirt.com/2012/12/14/who-signed-itu-wcit-treaty-who-didnt/.
9. Fiona Alexander, "What's Old is New Again: Is Retrograde Telecom Policy Returning to Europe?" Center for European Policy Analysis, May 12, 2022, https://cepa.org/whats-old-is-new-again-is-retrograde-telecom-policy-returning-to-europe/.

10. See Dmitry Epstein, Christian Katzenbach, and Francesca Musiani, "Doing Internet Governance: How Science and Technology Studies Inform the Study of Internet Governance," *Internet Policy Review*, Volume 5, Number 3, 2020.
11. Sandra Braman, "The Irony of Internet Governance Research," in Laura DeNardis et al., eds., *Researching Internet Governance: Methods, Frameworks, Futures*, MIT Press, 2020.
12. See, for example, Jonathan Fildes, "UN Slated for Stifling Net Debate," BBC, November 16, 2009, http://news.bbc.co.uk/2/hi/technology/8361849.stm.
13. For elaboration of regional Internet governance, please see Jamal Shahin, Sophie Hoogenboom, Carlota Morais, and Mauro Santaniello, "Regional Digital Governance," in *Handbook of Regional Cooperation and Integration*, Edward Elgar Publishing, 2024, pp. 108–122.
14. Joseph Nye describes this as a regime complex in his application of regime theory to understanding Internet governance. He adopts an institutional lens, but this chapter helps bring infrastructure to the center of this model. See Joseph Nye, "The Regime Complex for Managing Global Cyber Activities," Global Commission on Internet Governance Paper Series No. 1, Centre for International Governance Innovation/Chatham House, 2014.
15. Mark Raymond and Laura DeNardis, "Multistakeholderism: Anatomy of an Inchoate Global Institution," *International Theory*, Volume 7, Number 3, 2015, pp. 572–616; Jeanette Hofmann, "The Multi-Stakeholder Concept as Narrative: A Discourse Analytical Approach," in Laura DeNardis et al., eds., *Researching Internet Governance: Methods, Frameworks, Futures*, MIT Press, 2020.
16. Mark Raymond and Justin Sherman, "Authoritarian Multilateralism in the Global Cyber Regime Complex: The Double Transformation of an International Diplomatic Practice," *Contemporary Security Policy*, October 22, 2023, pp. 110–140.
17. See Francesca Musiani, "Infrastructuring Digital Sovereignty: a Research Agenda for an Infrastructure-based Sociology of Digital Self-Determination Practices," *Information, Communication & Society*, Volume 25, Number 6, 2022, pp. 785–800.

CHAPTER 3

# Technical Design as Governance

What if an Apple iPhone user was unable to send an email or text to anyone using an Android phone? Though hard to imagine through the hyper-interconnected prism of the twenty-first century, in the quite recent past there was little or no interoperability between computers and devices made by different companies. As a result, corporate networks were largely unable to interconnect with one another, with several different proprietary architectures delineating a heavily fragmented landscape and causing problems for both suppliers and customers of networking equipment. In the contemporary era, proprietary protocols are an ongoing concern around the Internet of Things and around closed social media platforms that do not interoperate. But prior to the selection of the TCP/IP protocol suite as a de facto global standard, there was almost no interoperability at all.

The decision to engineer interoperability between different systems was a choice. It was both a technical and socioeconomic choice, which would privilege competition over monopolies and access to knowledge over proprietary enclosure. Attempts to solve the problem of proprietary protocol architectures and fragmentation arose as a core issue in a long-running (1970s to 1990s) debate, sometimes called the "protocol wars." Actors in the telecommunications and networking space gradually recognized that an open and interoperable standard was needed for a number



F. M. Alexander et al., *Geopolitics at the Internet's Core*, Information Technology and Global Governance,
https://doi.org/10.1007/978-3-031-89478-7_3

of sociotechnical and socioeconomic reasons: for connection, for innovation, for competition, and for access to knowledge (even before the World Wide Web rose to prominence in the 1990s). Networks were unable to communicate with one another; there was a vital need to fill this gap with a common, universal standard based on the most robust technology.

Technical and sociopolitical decisions are intricately entangled; societal contexts shape technical design and design reciprocally co-constructs societal conditions. Why, historically, have encryption technologies been regulated as part of weapons and munitions in export control policy? The strength of encryption and especially its key length—essential design choices—are a politically charged subject at the heart of many tensions between technology and society. Law enforcement and intelligence agencies require weaknesses in encryption to access information and carry out important government functions. In contrast, the ability to secure commercial and financial transactions, protect individual privacy, and protect communications of journalists and political dissidents requires strong encryption. Designers have tried to navigate these values tensions in their design of cryptographic technologies, all while allowing for political guardrails such as key strength restrictions and export controls.[1] Secure messaging tools, while created by technical design communities, are the result of political choices made inside and outside of these communities.

Standards and protocols—of which encryption standards are a foremost example—have long been a central concern for science and technology studies and historians of technology.[2] Understanding the underlying theoretical lenses of these scholarly approaches can help provide insights into the broader geopolitics of technology. Standards and protocols as coordination technologies act as mechanisms of ordering and interfacing not only between devices, but also between technologies and the stakeholders involved in their development.[3]

The TCP/IP suite delivers content over the Internet, specifying how data should be bundled into packets, where it will be transmitted, and how it will travel and where it will go. The DNS offers a grammar through which this content is accessible, in particular by translating the domain names which are familiar to us (.com, .fr) into entirely numeric IP addresses which are the unique identifiers of the resources on the network. Both TCP/IP and DNS standards, as designed, therefore have implications for Internet users' access to online resources, both the ability of data packets to successfully reach their destination, and the ability for

Internet users to reach resources they want without having to memorize long and unintuitive number sequences. These same technological affordances allow them to be used as tools or means of control, and possibly as weapons by actors who wish to obstruct access.

Design also runs into tension with implementation and adoption. Once entrenched, standards can become difficult to change or replace. The IPv4 standard, designed at a time prior to the massive growth of the Internet, has had great staying power, despite the availability of a newer standard, IPv6, designed to increase the number of available addresses.[4] Part of the slow deployment is attributable to the lack of native interoperability between the two IP standards.[5] In the case of the IPv4 protocol in particular, adherence to the standard is self-reinforcing but also wrapped up in the context of which companies, actors, and regions first used the Internet.

Standards are part of the broader context of technical infrastructures, often contested sites in which power relations materialize.[6] The body of research that adopts an infrastructure-based perspective to study these issues increased significantly in the opening decades of the 2000s. Technical governance processes are often understood as a set of ongoing and contested processes. Studies of controversies and studies of infrastructures have been mobilized as conceptual and methodological tools to account for this co-construction of digital power arrangements by both social and technical activities.[7] This increasingly appears as an effective way of approaching the problems that constitute the field of Internet governance.

The digital sovereignty controversy addressed in the previous chapter is, in part, a design question because of the bits and borders dilemma. What is designed into systems—both at the physical (submarine cables, data centers, Internet Exchange Points) and logical (algorithms or protocols) level—constrains or enables the political overlay of sovereignty, or not. The label "digital sovereignty" takes concrete shape today via a number of macro and micro "infrastructures of control," which institutional and other actors seek to co-opt as proxies of their authority; in return, this reshapes their identities and the territories in which they operate.[8]

Historians and social scientists have written many Internet design histories, using a range of lenses. This book focuses on the Internet Protocol ecosystem itself and related technologies which form only a portion of the histories. Even here, many lenses and perspectives apply.

Focusing on the history of the Internet Protocol, Haigh, Russell and Dutton argue that those early pioneers and designers of IP, "engineers and policymakers who built and promoted digital networks, were not seeking to build a commercial network that spanned the globe: their efforts were primarily local, educational and experimental." They further explain that discovery "pathways were influenced by many actors, including users, making decisions in a variety of specific political, economic, and social contexts."[9]

Townes, who also specifically focuses on the history of TCP/IP, argues that the "development and spread of TCP/IP was deeply influenced by the specific political context from which it emerged–namely, the US and its allies during the Cold War, which comprised a relatively open political space. The U.S. government put tremendous stock in technological knowledge, and gave the producers of that knowledge–academics–relative freedom to pursue it. The result was network technologies with those freedoms embedded–TCP/IP."[10] IP itself was possibly on the periphery at the start, eclipsed by the possibilities of other approaches. Yet, as this chapter will explore in more detail, IP "stuck". Townes points out that some writers use a security-rooted lens, viewing the U.S. Department of Defense's motivation for funding this work as "render(ing) its communication systems impervious to nuclear attack...the network was never intended to serve operational purposes."[11] Campbell-Kelly and Garcia-Swartz further highlight historical particulars as well as an economic framework in explaining the rise of TCP/IP.[12]

While these histories are messy and complex with IP moving from the periphery to becoming central despite its non-centralized design or perhaps particularly because of it, it is the values embedded in its initial design, along with some serendipity that presages its continuity and staying power. The following case studies help illustrate this historically specific and contextual politics in design and adoption choices around the Internet Protocol.

To complement this broad and well-established framework analyzing the politics of design, this chapter brings together three examples around the Internet Protocol. The first case describes the early 1990s selection of TCP/IP, versus the competing Open Systems Interconnection (OSI) protocol effort, as the set of standards that would form the basis of the modern communication system. The second case study delves into the politics of the next-generation Internet, the design and selection of a revised protocol—IPv6—to meet the demands of a commercializing and globalizing Internet. The final case involves the privacy implications of the design choices around the Internet Protocol ecosystem. Taken together, these cases both establish the co-construction of politics and technology at the core of the Internet and provide insights into the trajectory of choices that have helped to solidify the importance and dominance of IP in the digital economy.

## The Selection of TCP/IP over OSI

As late as the early 1990s, it was not clear what would eventually prevail as a unifying network standard overcoming proprietary architectures. A number of alternatives were emerging, and along with them clashes and tentative alliances among corporate, academic, and governmental approaches, as well as among different cultures. Some of these discussions occurred contemporaneously with broader debates over what we now see as Internet governance visions, including that of a more open Internet not governed exclusively by traditional nation-states.[13] However, pragmatically, a large majority of actors recognized the need for universal standards to interconnect all the many different networking environments that did not yet easily interconnect.

In 1977, the International Organization for Standardization (ISO) launched the Open Systems Interconnection (OSI) effort to standardize how different computer systems could communicate or interoperate. Agreed at ISO in 1982, the basic "reference model" of the OSI was officially published in 1984. This work attracted enthusiasm, including from the European Commission and a collection of European computer networking manufacturers (from Bull to Olivetti) organized in order to develop a common policy, referred to as the "Group of Twelve." Bull had been one of the first to announce an architecture which would eventually give way to the OSI model with its Distributed System Architecture, or DSA,[14] in mid-1979. Beginning in 1982, additional European manufacturers followed. Having the backing of some key industry players, engineers, and governments, the assumption globally was that OSI would be the standards framework for what we today call the Internet.

Interest in OSI was not limited to Europe. In 1990, the U.S. government required that government-procured products conform to OSI specifications. The Department of Defense viewed OSI as a global inevitability and the National Institute of Standards and Technology

(NIST) endorsed it. In addition, leading U.S. computer companies such as Digital Equipment Corporation (DEC) supported OSI.

However, these commitments proved insufficient as the OSI approach lost steam in the United States. First, "OSI had become much too complicated […]."[15] While TCP/IP was a tangible, working set of standards, OSI protocols had may layers with relatively limited deployment. For Vinton Cerf, it was essentially the slowness of the standardization process that was damaging."[16] The OSI effort essentially became bogged down in bureaucratic maneuvering of procedures at ISO and conflicting visions. The enduring lack of tangible, implementable protocols took the wind out of the OSI sails.[17]

At the European level, some countries, while publicly committed to OSI, also pursued national efforts to connect to the Internet. As an example, while the Europeans proposed the creation of a European research network based on OSI, named Cosine, national solutions emerged in several countries based on the TCP/IP standard (JANET in Great Britain, DFN in the Federal Republic of Germany, SURFNET in the Netherlands, and others). In addition, after having initiated the examination of OSI within the framework of the International Network Working Group, the engineers who were part of the "Internet" team kept on working on the definition of OSI.[18] Historian of technology Janet Abbate adds a geopolitical dimension, noting that the competing TCP/IP protocol suite that originated in the United States without official standards body involvement may have made that protocol less acceptable at the time.[19]

Shielded from most of the pressure that OSI faced, the U.S. DoD's Defense Advanced Research Projects Agency (DARPA) was developing a competing specification using a more streamlined design. The Internet Protocol began proliferating around government and academic networks. The standards body's "Request For Comments" system, initiated by Steve Crocker,[20] created an informal and flexible collective thinking system that allowed prompt reaction and agile feedback.

While some corporations and governments continued to argue about OSI in ISO, the press for networking interoperability continued unabated, as computer networks rolled out at national levels and as working solutions rather than primarily conceptual frameworks were urgently needed. This led many around the world to move forward with deployment of the Internet Protocol in conjunction with the Transmission Control Protocol, which became known as "TCP/IP."

In 1990, the European consortium had to recognize the effectiveness of TCP/IP. The Internet was already diffusing in Europe, thanks to the EUNET network which was based on the Unix operating system and TCP/IP. While the establishment fought for control and the right to set the rules in a bureaucratic and politicized international standards organization, the Internet Protocol, grounded in the idea of permissionless innovation and best effort deployment, emerged as the winner of the original Internet standards war of the late twentieth century.

The true winner in the standards-focused foundational controversy between OSI and TCP/IP in the late 1980s and early 1990s was the Internet as we know it today. A number of factors contributed to this, including the development of a complete IP suite and several partnerships with computer manufacturers and telecommunications companies that allowed for TCP/IP to be incorporated into various operating systems. While OSI first developed some momentum around a universal interoperability framework of networking standards, whether valid or not, it was TCP/IP, due to coming into widespread use on multi-vendor networks, that eventually took shape as the core component of the emerging Internet.

The fact that TCP/IP became the rising standard for connecting previously disparate islands of networks had several implications. First, government top-down mandates were not the decider, setting the stakes for a norm of standards-setting that would take root over time: a multistakeholder and bottom-up engineering culture based on what works and what can be expeditiously developed.

Second the fact that the majority of participants in the IETF, the home of TCP/IP, were Americans, as well as American company representation, solidified the early perception of American-dominated control over standards. And third, the controversy stabilized some foundational values for the future of Internet governance: ISO procedures were perceived as somewhat closed, especially by the technical community, while a consensus-based and more participatory approach (although still among "trusted insiders"), that would eventually become the norm in the IETF, succeeded.

This brief case study illustrates the early-stage unpredictability of winners, the limitations of multilateral institutional standards strategies, and the importance of working standards and working code over conceptual frameworks.

One takeaway of this foundational design controversy is that, even when there is a "winner," elements of the discarded alternatives may endure. One legacy of the OSI vs. TCP/IP saga was the retention of the seven-layer OSI framework as a conceptual model—albeit not a perfect one—for understanding how Internet standards work and interact. To this day, while actual OSI protocols did not gain traction, the model itself is still widely used as a reference for documentation and for teaching. Components of the OSI effort would also reappear in the options for the next-generation Internet Protocol selection process discussed next.

## The Expansion Struggle: Selecting IPv6 and Rejecting Kings[21]

Protocol problems can arise from success, and they did with IP. Even before the introduction of the World Wide Web and before the founding of Google, Internet engineers recognized that IP would need to be upgraded to accommodate the network's rapid growth and internationalization. In the very early, 1980 pre-Web days of the Internet, the decision to design a protocol that provided for 4.3 billion unique addresses was incredibly optimistic and demonstrated tremendous vision for the network. However, concerns emerged around 1990 that the 4.3 billion Internet addresses available under the Internet Protocol design—called IPv4—would not meet expected demand as the Internet expanded commercially and globally. To place this concern in its historical context, in 1990 there was no Amazon, Facebook, Google, Netflix, TikTok, Wikipedia, or Yahoo!. Smart phones were not on the horizon and this was seventeen years before the introduction of the iPhone. Far less than 1% of the world's population—fewer than 1.5 million—were actually online, and most people were not aware of "the Internet." Tim Berners-Lee had just developed the Web and there was not yet a browser to speak of, or Web content to search. But the Internet was expanding internationally. Engineers had the foresight to anticipate the need for more addresses. The rapid 1990s growth of the Internet, both because of the dot-com rise of commercial networks and the globalization of users, was staggering and proved them correct.

Growth and internationalization of the Internet were not the only factors raising concerns about the possibility of future Internet address scarcity. Another contributor to projected scarcity was internal to the technical design and administration of the protocol itself. When information is sent over the Internet, it is contained in "packets" or digital envelopes that also contain administrative overhead such as the Internet addresses of both the originating and destination devices. Routers read the destination address and then consult routing tables to make a determination about how to most expeditiously direct each packet to its destination. If routers had to read (i.e., process) all 32 zeros and ones of each address in all packets, it would take up far more processing power and time than reading a portion of each address. Internet engineers responding to this network efficiency concern decided to simplify the routing process by dividing addresses into a network segment (called a network prefix) and host number. Routers would only have to read the network segment to determine which network to route the packet to, with the host segment processed at the terminating network.

As part of this routing efficiency decision, the widely deployed Internet Protocol—IPv4—would create "three classes" of network addresses: Class A, Class B, and Class C. "Class A networks" used addresses that reserved the first eight bits for the network prefix and the remaining 24 bits for the host number. This provided more than sixteen million host numbers, calculated as $2^{24}$. Routers would only have to read the network prefix of each address, saving space in the global routing tables and speeding up the processing time for routers to "read" each unique address. Class A address assignments were massive groupings of more than sixteen million addresses. Class B (with a network segment of 16 bits) and Class C assignments (with a network segment of 8 bits) included roughly sixty-five thousand and two hundred fifty-six unique addresses, respectively.

Because of these network groupings—derived from a rational engineering efficiency decision—IPv4 addresses were in turn distributed in large groups known as "Class A" or "Class B" or "Class C" allocations and assignments. The technical requirement that each address be globally unique prompted the requirement that a central authority had to allocate these blocks of IP addresses for use by networks and end users. Otherwise, there would be the technical issue of two entities using the same address, causing a cascade of network problems.

There has been considerable Internet governance attention to the matter of who should have the responsibility for assigning and allocating addresses (eventually known as the Internet Assigned Numbers Authority, or IANA, functions). But the question of who received these addresses, and how many addresses, is also of public interest, one complicated by the approach of allocating large blocks of addresses in the early days of the Internet.

Many organizations—such as large network operators or large companies—required more than the roughly sixty-five thousand addresses available in a Class B allocation. They opted instead for a Class A allocation of more than sixteen million unique addresses that could be assigned to devices in the network.[22] Because of this large number of Class A blocks, many addresses were allocated, and therefore not available to assign to other institutions, but ultimately, not actually being used.

In other words, a collateral public interest issue was that many addresses were distributed in large blocks that might not have been needed, yet that took them out of circulation for others, creating resource scarcity. During the commercial growth of the Internet, the organizations which received the large Class A assignments of more than sixteen million unique addresses were not only large network operators. Stanford, MIT and other American institutions received early Class A assignments. American companies such as Hewlett-Packard, IBM, GE, Apple, and many others received these large allotments as well. Because the Internet was still largely an American institution in the 1980s and early 1990s, it is not surprising that U.S. institutions received these large allocations. But many never used the sixteen million unique addresses they received. Even in the twenty-first-century context, it is difficult to imagine many universities simultaneously using sixteen million Internet addresses.

Regardless of the reason for anticipated address scarcity, concern about "running out of Internet addresses" became one of the most pressing engineering and public policy concerns in the history of the Internet. These virtual resources were necessary precursors for the international growth of the Internet, for opportunities to innovate and develop new services, and use the Internet, and for access to networks and digital resources around the world.

The next-generation Internet Protocol's (IPv6) design, crafted to address these concerns, in hindsight, might seem straightforward. It expands the number of bits per address to 128, allowing for an Internet address space, meaning a total pool of available addresses, of $2^{128}$, or 340 "undecillion addresses." It is a number so large that even the vocabulary to discuss it is problematic. The easiest way to envision the magnitude of this number of available unique addresses is to picture 340 followed by 36 zeros.

At the heart of the process of envisioning, designing, and selecting IPv6 was the Internet Engineering Task Force. The direct trajectory of this engineering community harkens back at least to the 1970s when Internet pioneers Vinton Cerf, Robert Kahn, David Clark, and others informally launched a coordinating committee that would eventually create the IETF as a subsidiary organization in 1986. The IETF's mission is "to make the Internet work better by producing high quality, relevant technical documents that influence the way people design, use, and manage the Internet."[23]

The procedural norms of this institution have shaped the growth and success of the Internet over the years. One of these decisions was to make every IETF standard freely available for anyone to access. This electronic collection of documents—again the RFC series—has documented Internet standards since 1969. Anyone can make use of standards, implementing them in products, without requesting permission or having to pay royalties on this use. This decision to openly publish standards with no access or usage fees means that any developer of software and hardware services has been able to use these documents to ensure that its products are compatible and interoperable with products and services made by competitors.

The IETF's choice of the design of IPv6 was not obvious or without controversy. The selection of the standard that would become IPv6, as recounted in detail in the 2009 book *Protocol Politics: The Globalization of Internet Governance*, involved a contentious decision-making process that revived the OSI versus TCP/IP debate mentioned above, pitted companies against each other, raised concerns about "change control" and what institution would control protocol design going forward, and involved tensions between a top-down decision-making process versus grassroots, bottom-up engineering design. Because the selection of IPv6 predated widespread commercial and global use of the Internet and occurred behind the scenes in the Internet's technical community, the general public and the media were not aware of the battle and the immense consequences of the selection.

"We reject: kings, presidents, and voting. We believe in rough consensus and running code,"—the phrase that would become the de facto operating philosophy of the Internet Engineering Task Force, directly emerged from this protocol selection controversy.[24] MIT computer scientist David Clark, a prominent and respected contributor to Internet architecture and an insider in the Internet standards-setting community, gave a presentation at a meeting of the IETF called "A Cloudy Crystal Ball, Visions of the Future; Alternate Title: Apocalypse Now." In his provocative presentation, Clark described OSI as the "Standards elephant of yesterday" and identified a number of concerns about the Internet including standards leadership boards acting like "A House of Lords" and identified crucial Internet security concerns as "The problem we love to ignore."[25]

The twenty-fourth meeting of the IETF in Cambridge, Massachusetts, in July of 1992 was rife with concerns about the OSI-TCP/IP tension and controversy over the redesign of the Internet Protocol to expand the pool of available addresses.[26] Years before this high-spirited meeting of the IETF, a number of the pioneering engineers of the Internet, including David Clark, held a consensus assumption that the Internet, as designed and managed, would run out of IP addresses, a problem they sometimes described as address space exhaustion.[27] In 1990, even before the introduction of the World Wide Web, some in the IETF believed that, at the current assignment rate of IP addresses, there would be few left as early as 1994.[28]

Many of the discussions about address space exhaustion centered around the "Internet Architecture Board" (IAB), an umbrella organization tasked with formally approving Internet standards, managing the RFC publication process, and resolving technical issues not addressed in the IETF. In the early 1990s, the IAB was made up of less than a dozen people, primarily Americans such as Cerf and Postel and other early pioneers in the development of the Internet.

The question about how to accommodate international growth with more addresses existed within a broader set of concerns emerging in a globalization of the network. The IAB was interested in how to "acquire a better international perspective."[29] There was interest in the possibility of supporting more "international protocols," and holding Internet standards meetings outside of the United States. This was all in the context of legal restrictions on the export of encryption and the background question, and as described in the previous section, about whether standards advanced by the IETF or the OSI protocols facilitated by ISO, would become the interoperability glue that would finally enable seamless communications between products made by different manufacturers.

Recall the contemporary context of OSI v. TCP/IP tensions discussed in the previous section and how, even in the United States alone, government agencies and prominent corporations supported the OSI effort.

Even though TCP/IP was a tangible, working set of standards, and OSI protocols had relatively limited deployment, it was not at all clear which family of standards would eventually prevail (or whether they would co-exist in some way).

Selecting a new protocol for the Internet that originated in a different design community—primarily ISO—was an existential moment for the Internet, as well as Internet engineer design communities. In 1992, the Internet Society (ISOC) was formed to serve as an institutional umbrella organization for the IETF, and renamed the Internet Activities Board the Internet Architecture Board (IAB).[30] The question of how to institutionally internationalize loomed large in ISOC, including how to more formally work with global standards-setting bodies such as the ITU and have greater global participation and presence. Working in the background of a rapidly expanding Internet and associated institutions, IETF working groups discussed how to develop a new version of the Internet Protocol that would expand the available address pool, against the backdrop of a rapidly expanding Internet and associated institutions.

It was in this context of change, growth, and internationalization that the IAB made a controversial decision about the future of the Internet Protocol. It decided to aggressively promote and even select a replacement for the Internet Protocol that was considered part of the OSI protocol suite. The protocol was called Connectionless Network Protocol (CLNP) and would replace the Internet Protocol. "Many members of the community felt betrayed" by this decision; many were outraged and in "shocked disbelief," as evidenced by comments on the publicly available mailing lists of the IETF in the aftermath of the decision.[31]

This decision was controversial for several reasons. One part of the institutional reaction was about procedural control and institutional norms. The tradition of the IETF had always been one of bottom-up, working group-oriented design that would percolate up institutionally rather than a top-down decision dictating a specific design.

A possibly even greater concern related to the overarching global competitive tension between the IETF and ISO, and the accompanying tension between the two protocol suites, TCP/IP and OSI, which also existed in the background context of the largely American Internet rapidly becoming a global Internet. Other concerns surfaced about the influence of some then-dominant corporations with a stake in the outcome of the selection.

Hence the "Apocalypse Now" discussion at the July 1992 meeting of the Internet Engineering Task Force in Cambridge, Massachusetts and the solidification of the IETF's informal motto of "rough consensus and running code." The IAB officially retracted their proposal; the IETF continued pursuing and soliciting alternative designs for the new Internet Protocols; and Internet pioneer Steve Crocker led an institutional examination of standard-setting processes.

The solicitation of alternative proposals for the next-generation Internet Protocol resulted in many designs. This process yielded three finalist designs known by the acronyms CATNIP, SIPP, and TUBA, the latter of which was based on the ISO CLNP protocol. The IETF ultimately selected SIPP, based heavily on the prevailing IPv4 protocol; this was considered an incremental step because it was developed by IETF insiders. It solidified control of the new standard within the IETF rather than ISO or some other institution.

What seemed like a technical design problem was also an issue of power and change control. It is impossible in hindsight to understand what a different decision, and especially the move of design control from the IETF to ISO, might have meant for the Internet. The decision also took place, to some extent, outside of market forces. At the time, the technical community routinely thought of protocol design as primarily technical. Yet the preservation of power within the dominant Internet design communities was a primary and even explosive issue. Fast forwarding from the early 1990s IPv6 selection process, at a time when the IETF was comprised of American and European technical experts, until today when there are an increasing number of IETF technical experts from China, illustrates geopolitical recognition of the power of what might be seen by those outside of Internet design and governance discussions as an obscure standards body.

## Internet Addresses as a Privacy Concern

On June 13, 2023, IP addresses landed on the Today Show, an American morning broadcast television program on NBC. That day's segment highlighted privacy concerns around IP addresses on a new shopping app called TEMU.[32] A security expert on the show explained that IP addresses were being tracked, along with other information, even when not using the app. Personal information ranging from location and browsing history to political affiliation and sexual orientation could potentially be ascertained from this data collection (Fig. 3.1).

Landing as a topic on a major mass media morning show is an exception to how IP addresses have occupied a unique, albeit often concealed, place in the global privacy arena. Many of the most critical online privacy concerns center primarily around the content being transmitted, an issue framed in many policy discussions as data protection. Government surveillance of citizens, foreign surveillance, and data breaches are examples of this societal privacy concern around content. Other examples include the related privacy complication around mass data collection by social media platforms, network operators, and other corporate intermediaries. Protecting the content of a transmission, such as financial information, personal health data, or the body of an email, is only the top layer of an intricate, infrastructure-embedded system of identification that profoundly shapes the nature of privacy across the world.

The metadata surrounding content is also a privacy concern: timestamps about when a message was sent; port numbers and type of

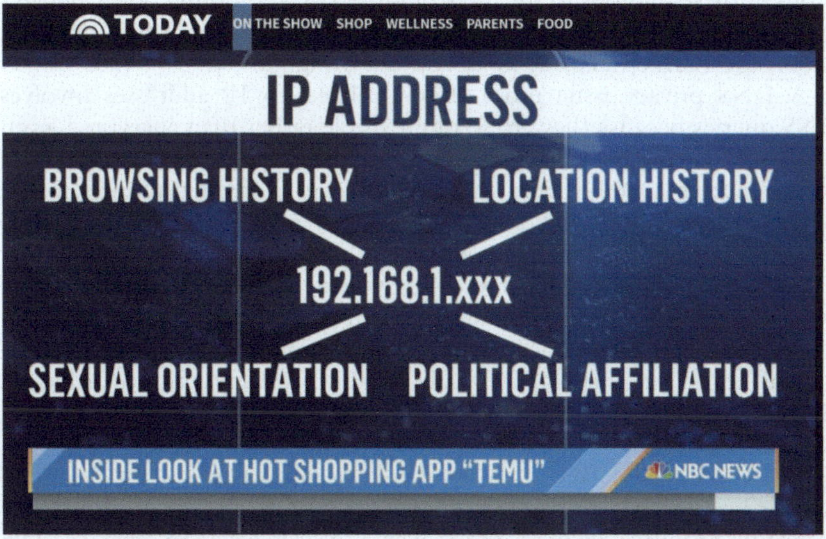


**Fig. 3.1** Screenshot of Today Show segment "TEMU: What you need to know about the hot shopping app," June 13, 2023

protocol used; cookies and history of websites visited; record of DNS queries; size of packet and duration of session; among other information that can raise privacy and identification concerns. Source and destination IP addresses are very much part of this metadata ecosystem and the Internet Protocol ecosystem writ large entangles with privacy in an equally important manner as content-based concerns.[33]

Some scholarly and policy attention around privacy has focused on the Domain Name System, and in particular the WHOIS system.[34] The WHOIS system is a freely available and searchable directory service that, since 1982, has provided information about the entities that use and manage domain names, including making public personal information (including name and address) about domain name registrants. Privacy concerns emerged over this system, with tensions between the need for identity disclosure to address public policy issues like cybersecurity research, cyberbullying, intellectual property rights enforcement, defamation, and law enforcement versus values of website anonymity for protecting registrant privacy and promoting freedom of expression. The European Union's General Data Protection Regulation (GDPR)[35] brought these tensions to the forefront in 2018, prompting policy debates and proposed revisions to address GDPR compliance, some ongoing within the ICANN ecosystem as of this writing.

A DNS privacy issue more closely related to IP addresses involves DNS queries because they are so often visible rather than encrypted, even when content itself is encrypted. Most instances of retrieving information online involve a DNS query that translates an individual request for an online resource into an IP address. DNS servers perform this specialized lookup function. These queries were largely designed to be unencrypted. The queries do not contain the content being retrieved, but the privacy concern is that the query lookup itself can provide sensitive data such as whether the individual is accessing disease information, addiction services, mental health support, or politically sensitive websites, all accessible via the network provider or other third party providing this DNS query resolution process.

The IETF has worked on a number of transport protocols to seek to standardize encryption of DNS queries to protect privacy (and improve security). Examples include: DNS over TLS (DoT); DNS over HTTPS (DoH); and DNS over QUIC (DoQ).[36] The DNS PRIVate Exchange (DPRIVE) Working Group of the IETF works on DNS privacy protocols and was chartered to "develop mechanisms to provide confidentiality to DNS transactions in order to address concerns surrounding pervasive monitoring."[37] Sometimes framed as "Privacy by Design," there has been increasing interest in and understanding of the role of engineering privacy directly into protocols through design choices.[38]

Historically, there have always been entanglements between IP design and privacy. The original design of the Internet Protocol could have embedded a physical identifier into the address, such as a unique Ethernet address (i.e., a MAC or Media Access Control address) associated uniquely with a physical Ethernet card in a computer or hardware inside of a mobile phone. In discussions in the IETF about how to generate a 128-bit unique IPv6 address, one alternative that emerged was to embed a computer's unique hardware address with the IPv6 address.[39] This approach was not selected but, if it was, would have allowed for easy tracing of any online activity back to a unique physical device and therefore a location and possibly person associated with that device. Instead, an Internet address is a logical address that is not inherently associated with a physical device.

Despite the choice to design IP addresses as logical (software-defined) addresses rather than physical identifiers associated with a physical device, they have nevertheless become part of privacy concerns online. Repeatedly used, static IP addresses can link directly to devices. An IP address, even one dynamically assigned, can be combined with other information, and may in many cases reveal someone's identity. For example, a government can make a request to a network operator to divulge the identity of which customer was accessing something online at a certain date and time. And the massive collection of information amassed by data brokers, especially in combination with artificial intelligence, can use IP addresses to make connections that identify people. As David Clark succinctly explains: "It is generally recognized that the current approach of using the IP address both as a locator and as an identifier was a poor design choice."[40]

Not surprisingly, IP address privacy continuously enters policy discussions. One example involves a dispute between U.S.-based hospitals and telehealth providers and the Department of Health and Human Services (HHS) regarding the application of the Health Insurance Portability and Accountability Act of 1996 (HIPAA) to hospital and provider websites. HIPAA includes Privacy, Security and Breach Notification Rules that are administered and enforced by HHS. Under the rules issued, individual IP addresses collected on pages related to specific health conditions are considered protected health information, meaning visitors to a hospital website must explicitly consent to this data being collected and passed onto any third parties.[41] The medical community objected and filed a legal complaint that targeted among other things that the rules "upended hospitals' and health systems' ability to share health care information with the communities they serve, analyze their own websites to enhance accessibility, and improve public health."[42]

The evolution of IP addresses and privacy is similar to the evolution of national ID numbers across the world that are used for identification purposes far beyond their original purpose. The complicated and often unsettled legal question is whether IP addresses are personally identifiable information. In the United States where there is not a comprehensive national privacy regulation, this question is addressed with varying degrees of clarity across a range of state law, administrative rulemaking in agencies, and through the Courts.

Despite having nothing to do with their technical purpose, IP addresses have landed on the center stage of global privacy concerns and will continue to occupy this place.

## The Legitimacy Question in Governance by Design

Technical design choices are a form of governance, as the three IP design topics highlighted in this chapter demonstrate. The selection of TCP/IP over the emerging OSI alternative underlines the importance of "working code" and the background context of geopolitics and industry competition. It also makes clear the institutional control battles among technical design communities that understand the stakes of both design and "change control." The selection of the standard that would become the next-generation Internet Protocol—IPv6—mediated similar institutional control questions but also raised questions about procedural governance conflicts between top-down versus bottom-up consensus driven processes. These two cases also illustrate that both the design and selection of a standard do not at all assure its eventual implementation. The forces and momentum behind OSI were strong and yet that protocol suite did not become the universal networking standard that would essentially become the Internet. The need for IPv6 and the implementation of IPv6 in standards was not sufficient to assure quick adoption, for a variety of reasons including lack of native backward compatibility with IPv4.

The privacy questions that arise within Internet Protocol design more directly illustrate the ways in which technical design co-produces public policy. While these three brief areas address different needs and raise different governance concerns—institutional control, procedural questions, and public policy formulation—the commonality is that design communities are also governance communities, even if not led by governments or mandated by governments or regulated by governments.

Technical communities enacting public policy can raise the question of legitimacy for some given that private or multistakeholder communities make these decisions as opposed to governments. It can be argued that expertise and institutional experience shape legitimacy. But legitimacy also derives from process, transparency, and openness. One relevant decision was to make every IETF standard freely available for anyone to access. Anyone can make use of standards, implementing them in products, without requesting permission or having to pay royalties on this use. This decision to openly publish standards with no access or usage fees means that any developer of software and hardware services has been able to use these documents to ensure that its products are compatible and interoperable with products and services made by competitors. Making these open standards available to read—as well as making standards-development processes open to any participant—also provides the transparency necessary for public accountability and the ability of various actors to weigh in on public interest implications of these standards. This open participation to multiple parties is an example of what has come to be called the multistakeholder model of Internet governance.

Barriers to participation certainly exist, whether cultural and language barriers, economic barriers such as lack of funding for the time required to participate, and others, but inclusion would not be possible at all without the procedural norms of open participation, open access, and open use. This attention to procedural openness and legitimacy has to remain central as various communities seek to exert control of the Internet Protocol or seek to replace it.

If design is governance, the process matters. And design going forward matters.

## Notes

1. Ksenia Ermoshina and Francesca Musiani, *Concealing for Freedom: The Making of Encryption, Secure Messaging, and Digital Liberties*, Mattering Press, 2022.

2. Technical standards are embodied in material arrangements but also in the meanings they generate. Standards are also a part of specific environments that include both certain physical forms and the ways in which they are used, and in their associated social and economic models. Sometimes this phenomenon occurs accidentally, as some seemingly minor decisions and actions condition and advance the resulting spatial and temporal effects.
3. For example, Galloway describes how TCP/IP and the DNS arise in the context of distributed forms of cultural production inherent in the contemporary economic and political context and the theoretically open way in which protocols are developed and in the control logic exercised by the protocols themselves. See, Alexander Galloway, *Protocol: How Control Exists after Decentralization*, MIT Press, 2004.
4. Laura DeNardis, *Protocol Politics: The Globalization of Internet Governance*, MIT Press, 2009.
5. In addition to economic, social and technical standardization mechanisms, there are institutional practices that serve to verify and certify standards. Allison Loconto and Lawrence Busch, "Standards, Techno-economic Networks, and Playing Fields: Performing the Global Market Economy," *Review of International Political Economy*, Volume 17, Issue 3, 2010, pp. 507–536.
6. See Francesca Musiani, "Infrastructuring Digital Sovereignty: a Research Agenda for an Infrastructure-based Sociology of Digital Self-determination Practices," *Information, Communication & Society*, Volume 25, Issue 6, 2022, pp. 785–800.
7. Complementary to the primarily institutional approaches that defined the Internet governance research agenda in its early days—and still figure prominently in it—such approaches examine the "agency" of technology designers, decision-makers, and users, as well as technical artifacts themselves, in a variety of historical and social contexts. These actors interact, in a distributed fashion, with other normative and legal systems on the Internet, with systemic consequences which can sometimes be unintentional. See Dmitry Epstein, Christian Katzenbach, and Francesca Musiani, "Doing Internet Governance: How Science and Technology Studies Inform the Study of Internet Governance," *Internet Policy Review*, Volume 5, Issue 3, 2020; Francesca Musiani,

"Science and Technology Studies Approaches to Internet Governance: Controversies and Infrastructures as Internet Politics," in Laura DeNardis, et al., eds., *Researching Internet Governance: Methods, Frameworks, Futures*, MIT Press, 2020, pp. 85–104.

8. See Francesca Musiani, "Infrastructuring Digital Sovereignty: a Research Agenda for an Infrastructure-based Sociology of Digital Self-Determination Practices," *Information, Communication & Society*, Volume 25, Number 6, 2022, pp. 785–800.
9. Thomas Haigh, Andrew Russell, and William Dutton, "Histories of the Internet: Introducing a Special Issue of Information and Culture," *Information and Culture*, Volume 50, Issue 2, 2015, p. 144, https://doi.org/10.7560/IC50201.
10. Miles Townes, "The Spread of TCP/IP: How the internet Became the Internet," *Millennium: Journal of International Studies*, Volume 41, Issue 1, July 11, 2012, p. 45.
11. Ibid., p. 43.
12. Martin Campbell-Kelly and Daniel Garcia-Swartz, "The History of the Internet: the Missing Narratives," *Journal of Information Technology*, Volume 28, Issue 1, 2013, pp. 18–33.
13. Exemplified in the mid-1990s by John Perry Barlow's "Declaration of Independence of Cyberspace" https://www.eff.org/cyberspace-independence, an early and provocative paper on the applicability of government in cyberspace. While this is a prominent and oft-cited example of cyber-exceptionalism, Barlow only wrote his declaration in 1996.
14. Distributed System Architecture, a layered network architecture proposed by Bull what would eventually give way to OSI: http://www.feb-patrimoine.com/english/distributed_systems_arch.htm.
15. Interview with M. Levilion, February 2003, by Valérie Schafer, quoted in her doctoral thesis and in Francesca Musiani and Valérie Schafer, "Le modèle Internet en question (années 1970–2010), *Flux*, Volume 85–86, Issue 3–4, 2011, pp. 62–71.
16. Judy O'Neill, an Interview with Vinton Cerf, Reston, online archives, Charles Babbage Institute, April 24, 1990.
17. Russell, 2013.
18. In 1972, a group of computer science researchers first formed an informal group to study and develop standards and protocols and consider the technical issues involved in connecting heterogeneous networks. This group became a subcommittee of the International

Federation for Information Processing later that year. Ideas developed by members of the group contributed to the original 1974 "Protocol for Packet Network Intercommunication" proposed by Kahn and Cerf.

19. Janet Abbate, *Inventing the Internet*, MIT Press, 1999, p. 173.
20. Internet pioneer Steve Crocker was, as a graduate student, part of the team that developed the protocols for ARPANET that form the basis of today's Internet.
21. For a detailed account of the design and selection of IPv6, see Laura DeNardis, *Protocol Politics: The Globalization of Internet Governance*, MIT Press, 2009.
22. Sue Kirkpatrick, Mary Stahl, and Mimi Recker, RFC 1166, "Internet Numbers," July, 1990.
23. https://www.ietf.org/about/mission/.
24. The phrase comes from David Clark's plenary presentation, "A Cloudy Crystal Ball, Visions of the Future," at the 24th meeting of the Internet Engineering Task Force in Cambridge, Massachusetts, July 1992, https://groups.csail.mit.edu/ana/People/DDC/future_ietf_92.pdf.
25. Ibid., (Clark 1992).
26. IETF, "Proceedings of the Twenty-Fourth Internet Engineering Task Force," Massachusetts Institute of Technology, Cambridge, July 13–17, 1992, https://www.ietf.org/proceedings/24.pdf.
27. Vinton Cerf, RFC 1120 "The Internet Activities Board," May, 1990; David Clark et al., RFC 1287, "Towards the Future Internet Architecture," December, 1991.
28. Scott Bradner and Allison Mankin, RFC 1752, "The Recommendation for the IP Next Generation Protocol," January, 1995.
29. Internet Activities Board, Meeting Minutes, January 8–9 1991, p. 41, https://www.iab.org/documents/minutes/minutes-1991/iab-minutes-1991-01-08/.
30. From RFC 3160: "After the Internet Society (ISOC) was formed in January, 1992, the IAB proposed to ISOC that the IAB's activities should take place under the auspices of the Internet Society. During INET 1992 in Kobe, Japan [June], the ISOC trustees approved a new charter for the IAB to reflect the proposed relationship [...]." As part of that reorganization, the Internet Activities Board was re-organized and re-named the Internet Architecture Board.

31. Laura DeNardis, *Protocol Politics: The Globalization of Internet Governance*, MIT Press 2009, p. 44, note 51.
32. Today Show Segment, "TEMU: What You Need to Know about the Hot Shopping App," June 13, 2023, https://www.today.com/video/an-inside-look-at-the-new-hot-shopping-app-temu-186079301604.
33. Samantha Bradshaw and Laura DeNardis, "Privacy by Infrastructure: The Unresolved Case of the Domain Name System, *Policy and Internet*, Volume 11, Issue 1, 2019.
34. See, for example, Stephanie Perrin, doctoral dissertation, "The Struggle for WHOIS Privacy: Understanding the Standoff Between ICANN and the World's Data Protection Authorities," University of Toronto, 2018, https://tspace.library.utoronto.ca/bitstream/1807/89738/3/Perrin_Stephanie_E_201806_PhD_thesis.pdf. See also, Milton Mueller and Mawaki Chango, "Disrupting Global Governance: The Internet Whois Service, ICANN, and Privacy," *Journal of Information Technology & Politics,* Volume 5, Issue 3, 2008, pp. 303–325; and Garth Bruen, *WHOIS Running the Internet: Protocol, Policy, and Privacy*, Wiley, 2015.
35. https://gdpr-info.eu/.
36. https://www.rfc-editor.org/rfc/rfc8484.html, https://www.rfc-editor.org/rfc/rfc7858.html, and https://www.rfc-editor.org/rfc/rfc9250.html.
37. Charter of the DPRIVE Working Group of the IETF, https://datatracker.ietf.org/wg/dprive/about/#autoid-1.
38. See, for example, Ann Cavoukian, "Privacy by Design," *IEEE Technology and Society Magazine*, Volume 31, Issue 4, pp. 18–19, 2012; Alissa Cooper et al., RFC 6973, "Privacy Considerations for Internet Protocols," July, 2013.
39. Laura DeNardis, "Privacy Design Choices," in *Protocol Politics: The Globalization of Internet Governance*, MIT Press, 2009, p. 77.
40. David Clark, *Designing an Internet*, MIT Press, p. 91.
41. See US Department of Health and Human Services "Use of Online Tracking Technologies by HIPPA Covered Entities and Business Associates," December 1, 2022, https://www.hhs.gov/hipaa/for-professionals/privacy/guidance/hipaa-online-tracking/index.html.
42. See American Hospital Association, "Hospital Associations and Hospitals File Lawsuit Challenging Federal Rule that Ties

Providers' Hands," November 2, 2023, https://www.aha.org/press-releases/2023-11-02-hospital-associations-and-hospitals-file-lawsuit-challenging-federal-rule-ties-providers-hands-their.

CHAPTER 4

# The Internet Address Space as a Geopolitical Space

Russian Internet pioneer, Alexey Soldatov, was sentenced to two years in prison by a Moscow court over "a deal to transfer a pool of IP addresses to a foreign-based organization."[1] Often referred to as the father of the Internet in Russia, Soldatov was involved in the founding of the Russian Institute for Public Networks (RIPN), which operated the Russian Internet backbone and was the first registrar for Russian domain names. Soldatov also served as Deputy Minister of Communications from 2008 to 2010. Yet in 2024, he was sentenced to two years for what was framed as abuse of power and embezzlement "through fraudulent activities involving IP rights" after RIPN decided to close and sought to transfer IP addresses to a Czech based company.[2] Critics, including Soldatov's son, immediately pointed to the vague nature of IP ownership rights in Russia and argued the proceeding was politically motivated.[3]

As the Electronic Frontier Foundation (EFF) stated, "We are deeply concerned that this is a politically motivated prosecution. Multiple reports indicate this may be true. Soldatov suffers from both prostate cancer and a heart condition, and this sentence would almost certainly further endanger his health."[4] EFF further noted some of Soldatov's other contributions to the global Internet, including facilitating the ICANN approval of using Cyrillic characters in domain names and pushing back against efforts to isolate the Russian Internet from the rest of the world.



F. M. Alexander et al., *Geopolitics at the Internet's Core*, Information Technology and Global Governance,
https://doi.org/10.1007/978-3-031-89478-7_4

No wars have been fought over IP addresses, but the distribution and control of these resources have become entangled in national and global political conflicts such as the Russian War on Ukraine and global digital sanctions against Iran. The allocation and administration of the IP address space has also been fraught with concerns about global accessibility and fairness, and marked sometimes by ad hoc instances of corruption, market manipulation, and malign personal gain.

There might be some merit to analogizing Internet addresses as "digital oil."[5] An analogy to the oil crisis of the 1970s sometimes cropped up when it became clear that the global pool of roughly 4.3 billion IP addresses (under the IPv4 standard) was rapidly depleting during the commercialization and globalization of the Internet. In the same way energy sources are finite, valuable natural resources necessary for functioning in the physical world, IP addresses, as designed, are finite, valuable resources necessary for participating in the digital world.

The technical design features of IP addresses have indeed created architectural affordances shaping their usage, distribution and governance, as briefly suggested in Chapter 1. Nearly every exchange of information over the Internet needs a globally unique IP address, making each a "critical Internet resource"—or CIR. As such, they have become a necessity for social and economic participation in the digital age. Because they were designed as a fixed (rather than variable) length binary number, the design creates a finite pool of resources. And because IP addresses create a globally unique number, even if only assigned temporarily, they can serve as a personal identifier. Some of these original design and governance features of the Internet Protocol, as well as exogenous shocks such as rapidly rising demand, have complicated the global distribution, availability, and deployment of these resources. Conflicts have arisen over IP addresses simply because they are a crucial resource for access to the Internet and therefore a site of economic and political struggle.

How are critical resources usually distributed? Resource distribution in other areas of the digital economy is often market-based. Buyers with the financial means purchase scarce materials and the distributional allocation is based on supply and demand. In other cases, legally constructed administrative procedures determine allocations. In the United States, for example, the FCC is responsible for allocating entire sections of electromagnetic frequency spectrum for commercial users as well as those at the local and state governments, while NTIA allocates spectrum for U.S. federal users. The International Telecommunication Union coordinates the allocation of satellite electromagnetic frequency and orbital slots. In other cases, some combination of market-based dynamics and regulatory oversight shapes distribution.

How IP addresses are distributed is unique. Allocations are neither market-based nor legally administered, nor a combination of the two. Yet they do have an explicit governance structure, one that has evolved over decades. A combination of technical design choices, administrative allocation decisions, and the historical trajectory of how the Internet has grown geographically has contributed to an uneven distribution in which American universities received, in the early days of the Internet, millions more addresses than entire regions in the developing world.[6]

Understanding the history of the IP address space is critical for understanding the present. The day American President Donald Trump left office after his first presidency, and indeed in the minutes before the transition to President Joe Biden, a portion of the Internet's addressing system—175 million IP addresses—came alive when announced by a young Florida company called Global Resource Systems. Why was a large portion of the Internet's address space activated via a Florida company right before President Biden took office and was the timing just coincidental? These addresses, assigned to the Pentagon and previously dormant, were now "alive" in the sense that they were advertised as reachable via the network—in Internet governance parlance technically called an autonomous system (AS)—run by this Florida company. What was technologically most notable about this development was the massive scale in that roughly one out of every twenty-five Internet addresses (under the traditional IPv4 standard) was suddenly advertised to the global Internet via this company. It took months before the *Washington Post* managed to run an article entitled, "Minutes before Trump left office, millions of the Pentagon's dormant IP addresses 'sprang to life.'"[7]

As respected technical expert Geoff Huston summarized, "The world of IPv4 addresses is a relatively obscure backwater of the Internet… So it came as a bit of a surprise to see a headline in the Washington Post about IPv4 addresses."[8] Huston suggested that the sudden advertisement of such a huge swatch of IP addresses was most likely related to network defense, essentially enlisting "the routing system to make it more challenging for others to use these addresses to mount hostile attacks on systems located within their networks."[9]

The Pentagon clarified that this was a pilot effort designed to identify vulnerabilities and improve cyber defense, possibly even for threat intelligence purposes or to detect unauthorized uses (a technique usually called a "Honeypot").[10] Eight months later, the Department of Defense retook control of the 175 million IP address, saying that the security pilot had ended.[11]

This one instance of IP addresses in the news helps unfurl some questions about the IP address space: why was so much of the IPv4 address space essentially dormant while so many regions could have used these; what historical trajectory led to the Pentagon controlling such a large swath of the Internet; what was the nature of the private corporation advertising these addresses from its network; and what is the connection between IP addresses and cyber defense?

This chapter explains the technical architecture and governance of the IP address space and explores associated economic and political tensions via three examples: IP addresses and their politics in Russia's war on Ukraine; court cases addressing misappropriation of Internet addresses in the African region; and IP address entanglements in political sanctions against Iran. Taken together, these controversies help explain the geopolitical stakes of the IP address space and foreshadow that institutional and geopolitical controversies over allocation and control of these virtual resources will likely continue.

## Decoding IP Addresses and the IP Address Space

Navigating geopolitical currents in the digital era is not possible without understanding the systems of technology and technological governance underlying contemporary conflicts. From STS scholars to computer scientists such as David Clark and his control point analysis, understanding societal implications or even the actors and processes involved requires opening the black box of technical architecture.[12] What exactly is the "Internet address space" and what are the technical and historical factors that have contributed to the politicization and contention over these finite virtual resources? This section provides a very brief technical background helpful for understanding IP addresses and the collective global IP address space.

Everything begins with a single IP address. An individual's ability to use email or access an online banking system requires unique binary addresses that virtually locate the origination and destination points of the information exchange. The ability for a company to become an Internet service provider is not possible without a pool of IP addresses to assign to customers, whether temporarily for a session or more permanently.

The long-dominant Internet address standard, IPv4, specifies that each Internet address is made up of a globally unique, fixed-length 32-bit number, such as:

00010011 00101000 10000001 00100001

In everyday usage, or at least for those who deal directly with Internet addresses, these binary addresses are usually written in an easier-to-use, shorthand "dotted decimal" notation such as 19.40.129.33. Longer IPv6 addresses are represented in hexadecimal, such as FDDC:AC10:8132:BA32:4F12:1070:DD13:6921. Those interested in understanding how binary numbers convert to dotted decimal or hexadecimal notation are invited to consult the Technical Appendix.

In short, the nomenclature around IP addresses involves different numbering systems: binary, decimal, and hexadecimal. Computing devices use binary numbers but humans use decimal or hexadecimal numbers as a shorthand notation for managing these numbers. There is nothing preordained about humans using the decimal system—a numbering system based on ten numbers (0, 1, 2, 3, 4, 5, 6, 7, 8, 9)—in math and in day-to-day life except perhaps because humans have ten fingers. But that is the dominant numbering system in use. Elementary school children learn that a number in decimal involves multiples of ten: a 1s place, a 10s place, a 100s place, and so forth so that the number 364 deconstructs as $3(100) + 6(10) + 4(1) = 364$. By adding new place-holders, these ten numbers can be combined into an infinite collection of numbers. This is the well-understood Base-10 system.

The binary numbering system—or Base-2—works exactly like the Base-10 system but, instead of ten numbers, it uses only two numbers, 0 and 1. Binary therefore involves multiples of two (rather than multiples of ten) and thus has a 1s place, a 2s place, a 4s place, an 8s place, a 32s place, a 64s place, a 128s place, and so forth so that a binary number such as 0111 deconstructs into the decimal number 7 as follows: $0(8) + 1(4) + 1(2) + 1(1) = 7$.

The hexadecimal (hex) numbering system—or Base-16—has sixteen unique characters. Given that there are only ten unique numbers in the everyday decimal system (0 through 9), hexadecimal adds letters of the alphabet to count higher (0, 1, 2, 3, 4, 5, 6, 7, 8, 9, A, B, C, D, E, and F). Because of the long length of IPv6 addresses (128 bits, or 0s and 1s), hexadecimal is used as shorthand notation.

One other nomenclature convention necessary for understanding IP address governance is a "slash" or /. Sometimes an IP address appears as 192.0.10.0/24 or 126.0.0.1/8. An IP address traditionally has had a network ID component and a host ID component. The network ID is the first part of the address that identifies a specific network and the host ID is the second part that locates a specific host (or computing device) on that network. Historically, routers have only read the network ID part of the address in order to consume less processing power than if it had to read the entire address.

The length of the network part of the address determined how many available hosts could be assigned on that network. If the network component is 8 bits, that leaves 24 bits to assign to hosts, or $2^{24}$ or more than 16 million hosts. This would be represented by a /8 after the address. If the network component is 16 bits, this would leave 16 bits to assign to hosts, or $2^{16}$ or roughly 65,000 hosts on that network and would be represented by a /16 after the address. A /24 after an address means that the fixed network prefix is 24 bits, leaving 8 bits to assign to hosts, $2^8$ or 256 hosts on that network. Because routers have historically only read the network prefix, this technical feature shaped the assignment of IP addresses into large blocks, in some cases even assigning 16 million addresses to a single organization, discussed later in this chapter.

What is the "IP address space?" This section has, thus far, discussed an individual IP address—its length, function, and its shorthand notation and other nomenclature conventions. These IP addresses—such as the origination address and the destination address, are inserted into the packets that are transmitted over the Internet and used to find virtual locations online. The totality of all IP addresses cumulatively available for allocation or already assigned is called the IP address space.

The Internet address space has evolved over time. Network addresses—then for ARPANET—are mentioned in the very first RFC, RFC 1, "Host Software," authored by Internet pioneer Steve Crocker, then at UCLA, in 1969, roughly contemporaneously to the first ARPANET nodes connecting, including the UCLA node. RFC 1 specifies that the destination code for each node be five bits long. Five binary digits provides a total address pool of $2^5$ or 32 unique codes: 00000, 00001, 00010, 00011, etc.[13]

Expanding the number of available addresses over time involved expanding the length of the address as the network grew. By 1981, the address length grew to 32 bits in a standard that would be codified in RFC 791, "Internet Protocol: DARPA Internet Program Protocol Specification."[14] Because the specification states that origination and destination Internet addresses should be 32-bits long, this allows for $2^{32}$ unique addresses or roughly 4.3 million addresses.

This pool of roughly 4.3 billion available addresses is the IPv4 address space, the theoretical and mathematical upper bound of unique addresses available under the standard. The later IPv6 standard expanded the size of each address to 128 bits, allowing for a total address size of $2^{128}$ or 340 undecillion addresses, meaning 340 followed by 36 zeros. This is the massive IPv6 address space.

IP addresses would have no meaning if not inserted into packets so that information transmitted over a network can reach its destination. One of the critical standardization functions of the Internet Protocol is its specification of packet header formats. When information is transmitted over a packet-switched network such as the Internet, it is broken up into packets and sent over the network via various routes determined by routers. Each packet includes the "payload" or information to be sent, such as the contents of an email, and also a header which contains the source and destination IP addresses along with other administrative data. In the Internet context, a packet is also called a datagram. Some of this additional administrative information includes bits related to error detection and correction, payload length, and version of protocol.

## From the "Legacy IP Address Space" to a Global System

In early Internet history, as the size of the address space grew, Jon Postel was responsible for keeping track of and assigning Internet identifiers.[15] In addition to tracking the allocation of IP addresses to ensure their global uniqueness, he was also responsible for the publication of protocol parameters and maintaining the database keeping track of the allocation of generic and country-code top-level domain names. The performance of these three tasks maintained the stability of the Internet and became known as the Internet Assigned Numbers Authority (IANA) functions. Postel was a pioneer in a number of areas of Internet architecture and governance, serving as the editor of the Request for Comments series documenting Internet standards, and helping to design many foundational Internet standards, among other contributions. For many, Jon Postel was IANA and Vint Cerf later described Postel as the Internet's "North Star."[16] Postel worked at USC's Information Sciences Institute, where Joyce Reynolds, in the 1980s, also became involved in day-to-day administration of number assignment, as well as other functions such as the editing of the RFC process. The functions they performed continued to be called the IANA functions.

In the contemporary Internet governance structure, a hierarchical system of institutions manages the Internet address space, again a term that describes the pool of available IP addresses, both IPv4 and IPv6 addresses. The IANA functions are now performed by the Public Technical Identifiers (PTI) group within ICANN, created as part of the IANA stewardship transition.[17] PTI has authority for allocating Internet addresses to regional organizations for further distribution. ICANN—via its IANA function—delegates large reserves of Internet addresses to what are called "Regional Internet Registries," which have been founded at different times during the rapid growth and globalization of the Internet. These include:

- AFRINIC—African Network Information Centre (African region)
- APNIC—Asia–Pacific Network Information Centre (Asia–Pacific region)
- ARIN—American Registry for Internet Numbers (Canada, United States, and several Caribbean and North Atlantic islands)
- LACNIC—Latin America and Caribbean Network Information Centre (Latin America, Caribbean)
- RIPE-NCC—Réseaux IP Européens Network Coordination Centre (Europe, Middle East, central Asia)

These regional institutions are responsible for allocating and assigning addresses in order to ensure globally unique distribution and to maintain accurate records of IP address registration. They charge a fee to perform this task. For example, "ARIN charges an initial transaction fee for the registration or transfer of Internet Protocol (IP) addresses and Autonomous System Numbers (ASNs), and an annual fee for ongoing registration services."[18] The RIRs publicize the fee schedules on their websites. For example, APNIC charges membership and annual fees based on the number of addresses registered.[19]

The regional Internet registry system rolled out in pieces as a response to increasing recognition and concern about how addresses are allocated globally. Several IP network operators in Europe came together to found RIPE-NCC's predecessor organization RIPE in 1989, and engage in shared learning and technical coordination. Originally, RIPE did not engage in the distribution of IP address space. It was not until 1992 when, as RIPE described it, the need arose and it added to its functions allocating IP addresses. RIPE-NCC was then formally established as the first regional Internet registry, founded in 1992. Next came APNIC in 1993, ARIN in 1997, LACNIC in 2002, and AFRINIC in 2005. In 2003, the existing RIRs established the Number Resource Organization (NRO) to serve as a coordinating body across the five institutions.[20]

Will there be another regional Internet registry, either by dividing existing RIRs territorially or for some new area such as a deep-space Internet? Procedurally under the modern ICANN system, organizations can not just set up shop and launch a new regional Internet registry. There is a process of accreditation by ICANN. The MoU for ICANN's Address Supporting Organization (ASO, closely linked to the NRO) stipulates that ICANN has the authority to approve the establishment of a new RIR, subject to specific criteria. These criteria, developed by the ASO (with direct involvement of what were then three RIRs), were accepted by ICANN's Board of Directors in June of 2001, prior to the accreditation of LACNIC and AFRINIC under these terms.

The criteria for evaluating applications for an organization to be recognized as an RIR include operating in a large geographical region, having broad support of the relevant Internet service provider community, and adhering to a number of governance principles and procedures around equal treatment of organizations, as well as policies in support of the global registry system, such as "Conservation of IP address space and aggregation of routing information."[21]

Governments have periodically raised concerns about geographically fair access to Internet resources, including IP addresses, as well as fair representation in oversight of address distribution. These concerns have arisen at UN meetings, including the World Summit on the Information Society (WSIS) process as well as at a variety of ITU meetings. Concerns have included the legitimacy of the Internet technical community's processes and criteria for the establishment of RIRs.

Arguing that Internet number management and allocation have a sovereignty component and given the historical role of the ITU with respect to the allocation of traditional telephone number country codes, some governments requested that the ITU become an RIR.[22] Under this model, Country Internet Registries (CIRs) would be established and given IP numbers to allocate for use within their borders. ITU staff at the time argued that "conceptually, this is similar to what is currently done by ITU for telephone numbering resources and for spectrum and satellite orbits and other registry functions."[23]

In 2009, the ITU established an ITU-T IPv6 working group, with the rationale of facilitating the deployment of IPv6 in the developing world. The working group's terms of reference specifically included an assignment "to further study the possibility for ITU to become another Internet registry, and propose policies and procedures for ITU to manage a reserved IPv6 block."[24] After three years of meetings and online discussions, including the direct and active engagement by ICANN and the RIRs, who were invited as expert participants at the request of countries that supported the existing system, the group concluded its work with a focus on capacity-building and did not recommend the ITU become an RIR.

All of the RIR institutions are private, non-profit entities, neither purely market-based nor under government control, but supported financially by their membership ranging from large telecom providers to small local Internet registries.

Regional Internet registries then allocate addresses to other address-distribution organizations, such as national Internet registries (NIRs), local Internet registries (LIRs), Internet service providers, and network operators, who in turn assign addresses to the end user institutions that rely upon these globally unique binary numbers to connect to the Internet. Under prevailing nomenclature, to "allocate" an IP address is to distribute it to another organization, such as an Internet service provider, for further assignment to end users. To "assign" an Internet address is to distribute it for use (rather than further allocation). The system is hierarchical and also regional in that the ICANN system allocates addresses to RIRs who allocate or assign addresses in their respective regions.

Collectively, these regional organizations are responsible for the administration of Internet numbers. Understanding their procedures, rules, and organizational norms requires some history of how the IP address space unfolded around the world. This system controlling the global distribution of valuable Internet numbers is remarkable in that it does not materially encompass governments. It is regional, but does not involve regional governments. The overall institutional system even opposes stronger government involvement. As the NRO explains in its position on Internet governance:

> Some governments and intergovernmental organizations have sought to play a stronger role in governing its use and ensuring that it is "properly" regulated. This approach has been resisted by the Internet community at large, which maintains that imposing governmental controls would inevitably stifle this highly effective network. Governmental oversight structures may have negative impacts such as slowing Internet innovation, subordinating technical decisions to political criteria, and increasing bureaucracy.[25]

This resistance to government oversight does not suggest the complete absence of government participation, but rather a more multistakeholder model that includes private industry, the technical community, governments, and civil society. The address-distribution institutions are concerned that political criteria will factor into technical and administrative decisions, if governments were more intricately involved. This may be true, but it is also true that political factors (and economic factors) also shape decisions of participatory and multistakeholder institutional formations, as addressed in this chapter.

Concern about how Internet addresses are distributed, including uneven regional distribution, long predates the formation of RIRs and eventually ICANN, as well as predating the development of IPv6. There could have been many ways to distribute Internet addresses, ranging from a market approach of selling them to handing them out based on merit or demonstrated need, among many other approaches. The history of Internet number allocation began as a first come, first served process. Because the Internet originated and initially grew in the United States, assignment of blocks of IP addresses was concentrated in the United States.[26]

In addition to address distribution initially concentrated in the United States, the IANA team distributed large blocks of addresses to end user organizations for technical reasons. As Chapter 3 explained, distributing addresses in fixed blocks known as Class A, Class, B, and Class C networks reflected the engineering rationale of simplifying the routing process and optimizing network efficiency. As described, a router would only have to read the first section—the prefix—of each 32-bit address rather than process the entire number, which would be read on the destination network correlated with the block of addresses. A Class A block of more than 16 million addresses ($2^{24}$) required only reading the first eight bits of the address. In other words, the first eight bits were the network prefix and the remaining 24 bits were the host number, providing 16 million unique addresses, calculated as $2^{24}$. If routers only had to read the first eight bits rather than the entire 32 bits, this both sped up router processing time and saved space in global routing tables. Similarly, a Class B block of roughly 65,000 ($2^{16}$) required reading the first 16 bits; and a Class C block or 256 ($2^{8}$) required reading the first 24 bits.

The choice for end user organizations then was between 256 or 65,535 or 16,777,216 addresses. Imagine a financial institution estimating a need of 600,000 IP addresses under this address class system. It would have viewed 65,535 as an insufficient amount to meet needs into the future so would opt for the 16,777,216 Class A block, more than sixteen million more than necessary, but the only option to meet anticipated needs.

Many of the recipients of 16 million or more addresses in this legacy IP address space before 1990 were government, military, university, or corporate research institutions involved in the early development or use of the Internet. This included AT&T Bell Labs, Bolt Beranek and Newman (BBN), General Electric, Hewlett-Packard, IBM, major universities, and many U.S. government agencies.

A number of Internet RFCs over decades document the allocation and assignment of these large blocks of addresses to institutions. For example, RFC 1166 "Internet numbers" published in 1990 is a snapshot of Class A, B, and C number assignments at the time. Some of the 44 Class A assignments of 16 million plus addresses were allotted to the tech companies of the time such as AT&T, DEC, HP, IBM, and Xerox, American universities including MIT, Carnegie Mellon, and Rutgers, and military networks.[27]

In the early 1990s, the Internet Engineering Task Force engineered a new system to address these unnecessarily large address distributions while still promoting routing efficiency. Known as classless inter-domain routing (CIDR),[28] this system eliminated the IP address class system, allowing routers to read any size network prefix, but also using route aggregation techniques so that a single router table entry could still represent thousands of address routes. Each packet would notify the router of the length of the network segment it should read, referred to as a "bit mask."

The IETF's RFC explaining the rationale for CIDR helps hint at the technical community's underlying philosophy about IP addresses as a shared public resource for the common good: "The IP address space is a scarce shared resource that must be managed for the good of the community. The managers of this resource are acting as its custodians. They have a responsibility to the community to manage it for the common good."[29]

In this same 1990s timeframe predating the RIRs and ICANN, IANA handed out addresses directly to organizations, a procedural condition that contributed to the evolution of regional differences in the IP address pool.

The term "legacy space" refers to the cumulative pool of IP addresses handed out prior to the formation of the RIR system. This legacy space is estimated to be one-third of the cumulative IPv4 address space, although some of this space—if unused—has been voluntarily relinquished and formalized into the RIR system.

Based on data directly from the NRO, the chart below depicts the distribution of IPv4 addresses managed by each RIR(Fig. 4.1).

In short, late twentieth-century contexts ranging from the rapid commercialization and growth of the Internet in the United States to the technical and institutional decision to have a universal IP address space and to assign addresses in large blocks—were at play in regionally constraining the IPv4 address space. The Internet Architecture Board (IAB), at the time Internet Activities Board (before June 1992), identified the asymmetrical geographical distribution of addresses as a critical problem to solve in the context of the Internet's rapid global growth.[30] Meeting the global demand for internet addresses became a key principle.

Throughout Internet history, there has been interest in moving to more of a market-based system of buying and selling Internet addresses, also amid concern about ad hoc black markets increasingly arising. Despite these discussions, the RIRs have generally adhered to the philosophy that address space should not be considered property[31] even while, in effect, once an organization holds a block of IP addresses it is arguably irrevocable unless voluntarily relinquished by the organization.

In 2012 the U.S. government, through NTIA, issued a first and only government policy statement on IP number principles, in part in the context of pressure to move to a market system of buying and selling

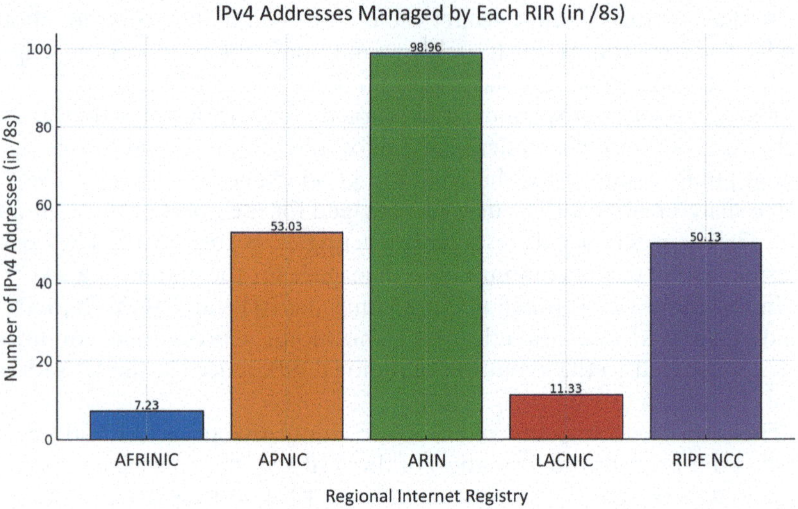


**Fig. 4.1** IPv4 addresses managed by each RIR (in /8 s)

addresses rather than allocating in a non-market approach. The "United States Government's Internet Protocol Numbering Principles" recognized the acute need to assure adequate numbers for those who needed them and asserted: "Consistent with the policies developed through the current multistakeholder model, the USG believes that all IP numbers are allocated for use on a needs basis and should be returned to the numbering pool when no longer needed."[32]

The history of IP addresses does also, however, include the rise of IP address transfer markets. The RIRs introduced their own policies for facilitating these largely commercial transfers beginning with RIPE-NCC in 2008. The RIRs publish policies for these transfers on their websites and also openly publish a record of each transfer. There is growing academic literature—especially from the perspective of institutional economics—that has analyzed IP address markets, black markets, the controversial commodification of the address space, and institutional policies about transfer markets.[33] The story of IP address allocation over time is much longer and more complex even than described here. But this section is sufficient to explain how IP addresses are largely allocated in the contemporary context and the history and evolution of this process, and how these serve as a background context for contentious flashpoints over control and ownership of IP addresses.

The larger question is how do binary numbers and institutions that distribute these numbers land in the center of geopolitical struggles, whether born of government action or private actors. The following three case studies help elucidate some of these points of power around IP addresses and the stakes of this politicization.

## The Politicization of IP Addresses in Russia's War on Ukraine

The politicization of Internet addresses (and also the DNS) crystallized, even for those far outside of the Internet's technical community, in the immediate aftermath of Russia's 2022 invasion of Ukraine. Emblematic of the turn to infrastructure as a proxy for geopolitics, Russia had long targeted Ukrainian critical infrastructure, including energy systems and communication networks. An hour before the invasion, Russia hacked into American satellite company Viasat's consumer satellite broadband service, disrupting several customers in Ukraine and tens of thousands of broadband customers beyond Ukraine's border.[34] The United States, the European Union, and other partners, publicly attributed the attack to Russia and shared its assessment that Russia targeted the satellite communication network to disrupt Ukrainian command and control capability.[35]

Russia was also disrupting some of its own media via a government crackdown on social media usage within the country and the criminalization of independent journalism. For example, Russia cut off citizen access to Facebook. Meta's President of Global Affairs at the time, Nick Clegg, posted that "Soon millions of ordinary Russians will find themselves cut off from reliable information, deprived of their everyday ways of connecting with family and friends and silenced from speaking out."[36]

A digital iron curtain around Russia also originated from outside the country. Some of this response involved government sanctions. For example, the Council of the European Union quickly imposed sanctions on state-controlled media outlets Russia Today (RT) and Sputnik for engaging in "continuous and concerted disinformation and information manipulation actions targeted at the EU and neighboring civil society members, gravely distorting and manipulating facts."[37] This sanction targeting media disinformation and manipulation tracked with its sanctions in other sectors such as blocking a subset of financial transactions or banning Russian airlines from the vicinity of EU airspace.

Traditionally, sanctions have long been a staple in the foreign policy portfolio, although the originators, types, and targets can change over time. The traditional actor imposing sanctions has been national governments. Regional organizations such as the European Union also can and do enact sanctions. At the international level, the United Nations imposes sanctions (per the UN Charter's Chapter VII). Countries and regions can also either implement these UN sanctions or issue sanctions that are supplementary to a United Nations sanction. Sanctions can be targeted or comprehensive, with varying outcomes.[38] They can include withdrawing aid or relate to finance, travel contract cancellation, travel bans, arms embargoes, asset freezes, withholding cooperation such as delaying agreement ratification, or agreement withdrawals.

More recently there has been an ambiguity in the discourse about sanctions as they relate to the Internet given the role of the multistakeholder technical community in administering Internet resources and the role of private companies in owning and operating most communications platforms. While governments took action against Russia via traditional sanctions, tech companies pulled products and services from Russia, some of them responding to direct requests or appeals by either the Ukrainian government or by their own customers.

In a swift, historic, and massive wave, numerous technology companies also responded to Russia's invasion of Ukraine by withdrawing products and services from Russia without being required to by government-imposed sanctions regimes. Some companies, such as Apple and Samsung, halted sales of their products in Russia. Apple also limited Apple Pay and disabled the traffic and incident features on Apple Maps in Ukraine to try to help protect Ukrainians. Software and service providers from Microsoft to PayPal and Norton LifeLock to the dating app Bumble suspended services; even TikTok suspended livestreaming in Russia.[39]

One of the most high-profile actions related to the Internet Protocol came from network operators Lumen and Cogent, who essentially disconnected from Russia at network peering and Internet Exchange Points (IXPs). These two companies may not be household names in the same way network operators that sell access to consumers are, but they are a critical and central part of how the Internet works. Unlike Verizon, T-Mobile, and other Internet service providers that primarily sell access directly to end users, Lumen and Cogent are primarily Internet backbone providers selling services to large enterprises, including other network operators. They form part of the backbone of the Internet via hundreds of thousands of miles of fiber-optic cable and other transmission facilities that carry the bulk of Internet traffic between edge networks and exchange traffic with each other at large IXPs.

Lumen physically disconnected its network from Russia, including withdrawing peering agreements to carry traffic originating in other networks. The company cited concern about security threats originating inside of Russia.[40] Cogent cited similar concerns, as well as an aversion to carrying disinformation originating in Russia.

This widespread withdrawal of products, networks, and digital services to Russia prompted a group of civil society organizations to write a cautionary letter about the collateral damage. They specifically called out the impact on Russian citizens' access to the Internet for organizing resistance and for accessing independent journalism and information that counters the Russian disinformation campaign. Even while condemning the invasion in the strongest possible terms, the organizations called out concerns about removing the ability to download apps that could be used to circumvent blocking and censorship by the Russian government. The signatories included Access Now, the Center for Democracy and Technology, the Electronic Frontier Foundation (EFF), the Wikimedia Foundations, and numerous other groups doing work at the intersection of technology and society.[41]

Whether or not one agrees with these private initiatives, no one could have predicted the massive, swift, collective self-initiated action of cutting off technology products, services, and networks to Russia by so many technology companies. Still others, notably Cloudflare, made a different decision and decided not to withdraw services to Russian citizens. While directly helping to protect Ukraine against cyberattacks and monitoring patterns of Internet traffic in Ukraine, as well as complying with required government-imposed sanctions, Cloudflare made a decision to not cut off Russia:

> We have received several calls to terminate all of Cloudflare's services inside Russia. We have carefully considered these requests and discussed them with government and civil society experts. Our conclusion, in consultation with those experts, is that Russia needs more Internet access, not less.[42]

The calculations about whether or not to terminate digital services in Russia after it invaded Ukraine reflect how values are often in tension in Internet governance decisions. On one hand, withdrawing access to technology in Russia could impede the ability of Russian citizens to access and use technologies of resistance, such as Tor, Virtual Private Network apps, or encrypted messaging. Conversely, cutting off technology potentially applies pressure points within Russia or can block Russian military communications or cyber attacks.

While all of these technologies in question—from network backbone providers to cloud computing—depend upon the IP ecosystem, IP addresses themselves became a flashpoint in the war. Ukrainian Minister of Digital Transformation, Mykhailo Fedorov, submitted request letters to both ICANN and RIPE-NCC, asking them to rescind or revoke DNS resources and IP addresses in use by the Russian Federation. If granted, the requests would effectively remove official sites and eliminate Russian government connectivity to the global Internet. The requests were an attempt to use technical infrastructure as a political proxy, with private and public forces alike co-opting infrastructure for a geopolitical objective having nothing to do with the core function of that infrastructure.

The Ukrainian Minister's letter to ICANN made three specific requests: 1. Revoking several top-level domains operating in Russia including .ru (the Latin alphabet country-code top-level domain, or ccTLD, for Russia), .рф (the cyrillic alphabet ccTLD), and .su (the legacy ccTLD that had been designated for the Soviet Union); 2. Helping to revoke the SSL certificates associated with those domains; and 3. Shutting down two DNS root servers located in Russia.[43]

ICANN declined Ukraine's requests to restrict the Russian Federation's access to the Internet, staking out a position against the politicization of technical infrastructure and explaining that "globally agreed policies do not provide for ICANN to take unilateral action to disconnect these domains."[44] ICANN also explained that it would not be able to actually revoke SSL certificates, which originate from third-party authorities.

ICANN's other objection to the requests was concern about the long-term effects of such actions on trust in the Internet and in the multistakeholder system of Internet governance. "Our mission does not extend to taking punitive actions, issuing sanctions, or restricting access against segments of the Internet – regardless of the provocations. ICANN applies its policies consistently and in alignment with documented processes. To make unilateral changes would erode trust in the multistakeholder model and the policies designed to sustain global Internet interoperability." ICANN did however, in a show of support, allocate USD $1 million in emergency financial support for continued access to the Internet in Ukraine.[45]

The Ukrainian request for action from RIPE-NCC added a fourth Internet technical infrastructure request: "Withdraw the right to use all IPv4 and IPv6 addresses by all Russian members of RIPE NCC," also to "help to save the lives of people in our country."[46] RIPE-NCC declined the Ukrainian request for several reasons:

> We regret to inform you that we cannot comply with this request. We do not have a mandate to take such actions, and as an organisation governed by community-developed policy and Dutch law, we cannot take such action unilaterally. We further believe that Internet number resource registrations should not be used as a means to enforce political outcomes, and that doing so would have serious implications for the Internet, not just in the Russian Federation but also for the rest of the world.[47]

Whether or not one agrees with the decision of this technical coordinating body to decline Ukraine's request, the questions arising for many were "who is RIPE-NCC" and "on what basis is their legitimacy to decide whether Russia stays connected to the Internet?" Understanding the history and contemporary structure of the global system for allocating IP addresses sheds light on this question.

The actions of ICANN and RIPE-NCC with respect to the Ukraine requests were consistent with their respective bylaws. Leaders in both organizations made these decisions without needing to consult their stakeholders. In each case, this was possible given the clear, stakeholder-developed and agreed-upon processes and rules.

If either ICANN or RIPE-NCC had made a different decision, it would have strayed from its respective bylaws and mission and possibly resulted in a variety of unintended consequences. First, such a deviation would have fueled long held criticisms that multistakeholder Internet governance institutions are captured by Western democracies, particularly the United States. Second, cutting off an entire country would have furthered Internet fragmentation and opened the door to similar requests being made with no clear standards for assessment. And third, trust in the Internet technical community would have also been eroded.

Taken together such consequences could have inadvertently legitimized authoritarian approaches.

While the relevant technical Internet governance institutions were determining how best to address these Internet access-related requests, the topic of the Russian invasion of Ukraine simultaneously surfaced in debates at the ITU. The ITU's Telecommunications Standardization Sector was in the midst of its quadrennial administrative conference to, among other things, elect new leadership and adopt new study group questions for the next four-year work cycle.

Deferred from the previous year due to the global COVID-19 pandemic, the typically uncontroversial and pre-orchestrated process for allocating leadership positions in the ITU-T study groups and sector advisory group was uncharacteristically challenged. Ukraine, supported by a coalition of western allies, made a formal request to remove the Russians under consideration from the candidate list. The request triggered a multi-day debate which culminated in a vote. With 102 countries present and eligible to vote, the Russians were eliminated from the leadership slate by a nearly 2 to 1 vote. Over 50 countries voted to deny the Russians any leadership roles, just over 20 to let them assume the roles, and 28 countries abstained. A similar vote during this period occurred at the UN Human Rights Council. In a special emergency session of the General Assembly, 93 countries voted to suspend Russia's membership in the Human Rights Council. Twenty-four countries objected and 58 abstained. Immediately after the vote, Russia withdrew its membership.[48]

## AFRINIC's IP Address Controversy

AFRINIC, the regional Internet registry overseeing IP addresses for the entire African continent, was placed "in receivership" in September of 2023.[49] This shocking development for a major institution of Internet governance was the culmination of years-long disputes and controversies over IP addresses. A receivership is a court-appointed mechanism usually relegated to companies in financial distress or mismanaged, and often put in place to allow creditors to recover funds owed to them. While different from bankruptcy proceedings, to say the least, being placed into a receivership is not a good development and usually follows a period of controversy and destabilization for an institution. This section will address the challenges that led AFRINIC to this unusual negative development, and how they illustrate that the IP address space is a political and economic space.

For years, AFRINIC, the newest of the five RIRs, had been embroiled in controversies involving contractual disputes concerning resource appropriation, mismanagement, and corruption involving a top employee, and all with speculation about wider geopolitical strategies looming in the background. As John Curran, President and CEO of ARIN, had written in ARIN's comment on part of AFRINIC's situation in 2021, AFRINIC was involved in "litigation with a company known as 'Cloud Innovation' operating out of the Seychelles and under control of an individual named Lu Heng (who resides primarily in Hong Kong)" and "received 6.2 million IPv4 addresses from AFRINIC in four different installments" with the majority of these addresses used outside of the African continent.[50] In other words, an accusation involved the payment of registration fees to AFRINIC for the use of IPv4 addresses and then profiting on these addresses by offering them in a secondary market for IPv4 addresses outside of the African continent.

The Cloud Innovation litigation—which involved extensive court cases and even the freezing of assets—was only one of many AFRINIC controversies related to IP addresses. A former AFRINIC top employee, Ernest Byaruhanga, was alleged to have misappropriated IPv4 internet addresses to private companies he himself (and family members) owned and then those companies sold these addresses to other parties. Instead of being used by African organizations and citizens, they ended up in non-African entities and were sold mainly to non-African entities. AFRINIC, after conducting its own internal inquiry, fired Byaruhanga in December 2019 and referred the allegation to the Mauritius police. As AFRINIC CEO Eddy Kayihura announced on the AFRINIC mailing list:

> As an update on the matter relating to the WHOIS database alleged fraudulent manipulation; the case was reported to the Central Criminal Investigation Division of the Mauritius Police Force on Tuesday 10 December 2019 for further investigation and action. In addition, given the serious nature of the allegations, a disciplinary hearing was held on 13 December 2019 after which Management decided to summarily dismiss Ernest Byaruhanga with immediate effect on grounds of very serious professional misconduct.[51]

In March of 2019, the Supreme Court of Mauritius, after receiving information from the U.S. Federal Bureau of Investigation, ordered AFRINIC to investigate possible corruption related to the selling of IPv4 addresses.

Following receipt of the order from the Mauritius Supreme Court and allegations of address misappropriation, AFRINIC conducted its own internal audit and published a lengthy report, "AFRINIC WHOIS Database Accuracy Report," in 2021.[52] The Report examines "the rightful custodianship of Legacy IPv4 resources, falling under the jurisdiction of AFRINIC."[53] AFRINIC received these legacy addresses from other RIRs, (who were covering the Africa region before AFRINIC's accreditation in 2005).

According to AFRINIC's own internal audit, the Report reveals that 2,371,584 IPv4 addresses were "misappropriated from AFRINIC's pool of resources and attributed to organizations without any justification."[54] Of these, 1,799,168 were compromised legacy addresses. Additionally, the ownership of 936,704 legacy IPv4 addresses was still in dispute as of the report date. AFRINIC was able, however, to reverse any "unsubstantiated" changes to 467,968 legacy addresses.

Tied to its investigation efforts, AFRINIC also put in place in June 2019 a fraud and corruption policy, followed by the institution of an independent whistleblower platform in June 2020. In sum, the AFRINIC 2021 report documents the findings of the internal audit, the alleged misconduct of the former AFRINIC official, and subsequent steps taken by AFRINIC.[55]

The AFRINIC Report illustrates well a number of interrelated themes. The first is the market or economic element of IP addresses and what the report describes as the scarcity of IPv4 addresses on the African continent; a second thread is the technical history, the existence of legacy IPv4 addresses in AFRINIC's purview; both intersecting with another thread, an individual in a knowledgeable position involved in corrupt practices. With regard to economics or market elements, IPv4 addresses have become more valuable. At the same time, AFRINIC was allocating and assigning addresses with costs well below the going prices in other regions.[56]

Regarding geopolitical questions, these controversies and court cases raise several issues. First, does any region itself have a legal or moral obligation to serve Internet address requests for that particular region only[57] or, as the Hong Kong business person has argued during this controversy, is the Internet global and thus, there is no problem with his company,

Cloud Innovations, purchasing internet addresses then subsequently sold to non-African entities, as AFRINIC and RIRs are "just bookkeepers?"[58]

Further, is there a norm or value that in a region where there are significant inequalities regarding access to the Internet itself let alone domain names, Internet addresses allocated to that regional internet registry should remain in that specific region? The 2007, 2016, and 2020 AFRINIC bylaws do state that its membership is open to: "(i) any Person who is geographically based within, and providing services in the African region, and who is engaged in the use of, or business of providing, open system protocol network services; (ii) or any other Person who is approved by the Board or the members."[59]

Beyond the geopolitical, between March 2021 and September 2022, Cloud Innovation Ltd. filed numerous actions with the Mauritius Supreme Court. Additionally, a related company from Hong Kong called Larus filed four cases of its own against AFRINIC.[60] These actions caused severe challenges for AFRINIC. Contractual disputes and ensuing litigation had notable short-term impacts on AFRINIC, as their assets were temporarily frozen and there was a question at one point about whether they could continue to operate,[61] with ICANN and other RIRs stepping in to offer help until their assets were unfrozen.[62]

On September 22, 2022, AFRINIC issued a press release from then CEO Eddy Kayihura in which he said "The pioneers of the Internet built this system in a manner that would prevent capture and we ought to strive to keep things as such."[63] Soon thereafter he had to leave the CEO role because AFRINIC did not have a properly constituted board[64] that could renew the CEO's contract. As of early 2024, AFRINIC still has no CEO, and it continues to face financial challenges resulting from the myriad court actions.[65]

Recognizing these very serious challenges as well as the vital role for AFRINIC as an Internet registry for the Africa and related region, on 26 March 2023, the NRO wrote to alert ICANN and the greater community about the ongoing governance challenges at AFRINIC.[66] They argued for a program that would involve: "raising awareness and increasing the involvement of AFRINIC's community in its governance model; hosting dedicated events, or collocating with existing community events, aiming to raise awareness of AFRINIC and its governance; ensuring high levels of community participation in these events and membership participation in the election; identifying capable and experienced candidates to serve on the AFRINIC Board; and, reducing opportunities for capture by any single interest group."[67] This call for an effort to strengthen AFRINIC governance reflects a capacity development model, highlighting the AFRINIC community and its participatory roles. It also underlines the connections between ICANN and the RIRs.

In sum, the recurring theme of this complex and ongoing cross-national and cross-regional case highlights the imbricated roles of individuals, corrupt or honorable; economics; law; technology and geopolitics, all intimately connected to Internet infrastructure properties, histories, markets, and policies.

## IP Addresses at the Core of Iranian Geopolitics

The IP ecosystem has often been entangled with the global politics and tensions around Iran. Iran itself has received considerable global attention over its Internet shutdowns throughout the years, often in response to widespread citizen protests. One of the most extensive outages, in November 2019, took down the majority of Internet connectivity for days.[68] A similar nationwide outage for most of Iran's roughly 84 million citizens in 2022 followed widespread protests over the death of women's rights activist Mahsa Amini after her arrest for protesting mandatory hijab wearing.[69] These widespread disruptions, addressed in Chapter 6, involve a confluence of technologies ranging from the DNS to cutting off mobile phone access.

IP addresses, more specifically, have been drawn into legal actions related to state-sponsored terrorism. In 2014, Iran's ccTLD and associated IP addresses were the subject of litigation in the United States. Based on an earlier court decision which had found Iran guilty of the 1996 bombing death of Ira Weinstein, his family began legal proceedings to seize Iranian assets. Legal action was initiated against ICANN to begin the transfer of Iran's ccTLD and associated IP addresses to the Weinstein estate.[70] ICANN opposed these requests and the litigation continued over a two-year period, involving multiple court actions and an Amicus Curiae brief filed in support of ICANN's position by the Obama Administration. Ultimately the plaintiffs' requests were denied by the U.S. Court of Appeals, with the Court quoting the Obama Administration filing that to transfer these critical Internet resources "would be devastating for ICANN, for the [current] model of Internet governance, and for the freedom and stability of the Internet as a whole."[71]

IP addresses have been more directly implicated by sanctions around Iran, sometimes being frozen for Iranian entities covered by political sanctions. Because RIPE-NCC is the regional Internet registry covering Europe and the Middle East, it is responsible for Iran. RIPE-NCC is also incorporated in the Netherlands and therefore subject to Dutch law and European Union sanctions regulations that involve: "Financial restrictions, which consist of freezing of funds and economic resources belonging to designated persons and entities; and a prohibition on making funds and economic resources available to such persons and entities."[72]

Notably, in the context of sanctions freezing or withholding IP addresses, IP addresses in this context are considered to be economic resources, deemed as such by the Dutch Ministry of Foreign Affairs. As RIPE-NCC explains, "Accordingly, we are prohibited from making new Internet number resources available to any sanctioned persons or entities. We are also required to freeze any resources they already have."[73] RIPE-NCC publishes "quarterly transparency sanctions reports" that detail its actions to comply with EU sanctions requirements.[74] Freezing the registration of IP addresses, in practice, prohibits the sanctioned entity from transferring IP addresses or autonomous system numbers or acquiring new ones. Financial payment transactions, including those that RIPE-NCC receives, have also been caught up in these geopolitical sanctions.

RIPE-NCC has had to lawfully comply with sanctions, while also expressing its general view that geopolitics should not disrupt communications and that it should not take a position in political disputes. From a public statement released as early as 2014, "The Executive Board of the RIPE NCC believes that the means of communication should not be affected by political discussions or disputes."[75] Over time, RIPE-NCC has sought a blanket exemption for sanctions involving Internet number resources, but Dutch and EU authorities have not agreed and IP addresses have been effectively frozen.

IP addresses are also used to identify transactions, financial or otherwise, that violate U.S. sanctions against Iran. The United States imposed sanctions against Iran for the first time in November 1979, following the seizing of the U.S. Embassy in Tehran, and subsequently in the 1980s (more precisely in 1981 and 1987) as a result of Iran's actions in the Persian Gulf, the country's uranium enrichment program, and terrorism support. Sanctions beginning in 1979 obviously predate the modern global Internet, which has both complicated and enabled sanctions.

The Office of Foreign Assets Control (OFAC) within the U.S. Treasury Department administers a variety of sanctions programs that restrain trade and asset transfers with Iran.[76] OFAC has acknowledged, as early as 2004, the role that IP address blocking plays in sanctions compliance: "A number of Internet-based financial service companies already developed Internet Protocol (IP) address blocking procedures. These companies use publicly available data to maintain tables of IP addresses based on geographic region. Users attempting to initiate an online transaction or access an account from a sanctioned country are blocked based on their IP address."[77] IP addresses are at the center of these tensions between political sanctions and access to knowledge and basic online services.

Sanctions against Iran also sometimes carve out exceptions, such as technologies related to the ability of Iranian citizens to circumvent Iranian government censorship. As the Congressional Research Service summary of U.S. Iranian sanctions explains: "Beyond humanitarian exemptions, the U.S. Treasury has issued general licenses to authorize otherwise prohibited transactions for specific purposes, including the provision of telecommunications services and equipment to Iranians to circumvent their government's attempts to cut off internet access."[78]

The U.S. Treasury Department, through OFAC, also has directly sanctioned Iranian companies that are carrying out Internet censorship of citizens. One example is its designation of the network technology company "Arvan Cloud" and two top employees, all in close relationship to Iran's Ministry of Intelligence and Security (MOIS)—all as sanctioned entities for their roles in censorship in Iran.[79]

It is clear that IP addresses do, and are expected to, serve as part of geolocation-based enforcement of sanctions and blocking of transactions. As an example, a cryptocurrency and virtual currency exchange platform Kraken, incorporated in Delaware, settled with the U.S. Treasury Department for USD $362,128. The settlement summarized the violation: "Due to Kraken's failure to timely implement appropriate geolocation tools, including an automated internet protocol (IP) address blocking system, Kraken exported services to users who appeared to be in Iran when they engaged in virtual currency transactions on Kraken's platform."[80]

The "world's first blockchain forensics team," CipherTrace (owned by MasterCard), regularly monitors sanctions-related IP usage across the Bitcoin blockchain, and interestingly, it "has detected more than 72,000 unique Iranian IP addresses linked to more than 4.5 million unique Bitcoin addresses. These Iranian IP addresses were either involved in direct cryptocurrency transactions or were used to query the blockchain to verify funds in cryptocurrency addresses that they control."[81] As a CipherTrace report explains well:

> Many of the tagged bitcoin addresses have been linked to multiple Iranian IP addresses, likely indicating the usage of mobile wallets connecting to multiple internet sources. IP addresses on mobile devices are constantly refreshed by service providers upon beginning new data sessions. These IP addresses are not directly visible on the blockchain, meaning banks, money service businesses or cryptocurrency exchanges do not have direct visibility into the link between a bitcoin address and users in a sanctioned country that query it. Iranian nationals are using Bitcoin to mine and liquidate funds as the country provides licensed mining operations with inexpensive electricity to power mining rigs. Mined funds can then be liquidated on the global market, often with no indication of which part of the world they came from, if the addresses are not checked for linked IP queries. (...) One likely explanation for this uptick in Iranian IPs is the abundant increase of Bitcoin mining by Iranian actors. Many of the new Iran-associated addresses interact with mining pools.[82]

Faced with this risk of supporting illegal and sanctioned activities such as the ones tracked by CipherTrace, companies might choose to overcorrect in preventing access to their services, a reaction that would affect innovation but also have important human rights implications.

In short, Iranian IP addresses are problematic business cards and also effective enforcement tools occupying a central place in the geopolitics of sanctions and the flow of information within the country. This unique geopolitical role is shaped by the technical architecture of IP, especially the network ID as a location proxy as well as the easy ability to filter transactions based on IP address.

## IP Addresses as a Proxy for Political Power

IP addresses are globally unique resources and are critical entry points into the digital world. It is thus perhaps unsurprising that the core issues surrounding IP addresses—the history of their production, their distribution, their allocation—have often been linked, both in the practice and in the scholarship of Internet governance, to the creation and development of ICANN, and the eventual IANA stewardship transition. This is in part due to the distributed and highly decentralized nature of the Internet number allocation ecosystem. The multitude of players involved in the use of a single IP number can be complex and varied (i.e., ICANN, Regional Internet Registries (RIRs), national Internet registries (NIRs), local Internet registries (LIRs), Internet service providers, and end user institutions). ICANN, initially, being the most public-facing of these players and, operating at a global level, made it a place for governments to focus attention. The fact that the U.S. government had a unique relationship and contract with ICANN only exacerbated those concerns, and that twenty-year control struggle from U.S. stewardship to multistakeholder governance is the subject of Chapter 5.

Yet, this chapter has clearly shown that there is a need to counter—or at least to expand—the narrative beyond ICANN and its relationship with the U.S. government. Indeed, IP addresses and the control dynamics surrounding them are fully global, and sometimes controversial, issues. Controversies over the IP address space, over the distribution and allocation of this finite and crucial resource, are about fundamental "digital rights" issues, such as the very access to the digital space at the global and regional levels; and they are often reactions to in-built or externally generated imbalances that could prevent such access. IP addresses are about political and economic power, and the actors wielding it. Conflict continues between a privatized system managed by the Internet technical community founded on a needs-based system and geopolitical concerns of global equality and government control.

The three cases examined in this chapter have shown the extent to which issues surrounding IP addresses vary greatly in nature and geographical scope; however, these cases unfold as examples of broader Internet governance problems, such as the finiteness of digital resources, the abilities of different groups and geographical regions to access them, and the extent to which architectural affordances are embedded in the technical design features of IP addresses. Such problems highlight the need to view IP addresses as a basic social and political resource for Internet users and hit at the very core of the overall theme of this book—technical infrastructure as a proxy for political power.

## Notes

1. Associated Press, "A Russian Internet Pioneer Is Handed a 2-year Prison Sentence by Moscow Court," July 23, 2024, https://apnews.com/article/russia-crackdown-soldatov-1515f320ea6e332574f38d0320a69b5f.
2. "Father of the Russian Internet Jailed for Transferring IP Addresses Abroad," bne IntelliNews, July 24, 2024,https://www.intellinews.com/father-of-the-russian-internet-jailed-for-transferring-ip-addresses-abroad-335171/.
3. Andrei Soldatov and Irina Borogan, "The Kremlin Jails the Father of Russia's Internet," Center for European Policy Analysis (CEPA), July 23, 2024, https://cepa.org/article/russia-jails-the-father-of-russias-internet/.
4. Electronic Frontier Foundation, "EFF Calls For Release of Alexey Soldatov, 'Father of the Russian Internet,'" September 4, 2024, https://www.eff.org/deeplinks/2024/09/eff-calls-release-alexey-soldatov-father-russian-internet.
5. As *The Economist* did in a widely cited article in 2017, in relation to data, https://www.economist.com/leaders/2017/05/06/the-worlds-most-valuable-resource-is-no-longer-oil-but-data.
6. Sue Kirkpatrick, Mary Stahl, and Mimi Recker, RFC 1166, "Internet Numbers," July 1990.
7. Craig Timberg and Paul Sonne, "Minutes Before Trump Left Office, Millions of the Pentagon's Dormant IP Addresses Sprang to Life," *Washington Post*, April 24, 2021, https://www.washingtonpost.com/technology/2021/04/24/pentagon-internet-address-mystery/.
8. Geoff Huston, "IPv4 in the Headlines," APNIC Blog, April 27, 2021, https://blog.apnic.net/2021/04/27/ipv4-in-the-headlines/.
9. Ibid., (Huston).
10. See, for example, Jon Brodkin, "Pentagon Explains Odd Transfer of 175 Million IP Addresses to Obscure Company," *Ars Technica*, April 26, 2021, https://arstechnica.com/information-technology/2021/04/pentagon-explains-odd-transfer-of-175-million-ip-addresses-to-obscure-company/.
11. Craig Timberg, "A Secretive Pentagon Program That Started on Trump's Last Day in Office Just Ended. The Mystery Has

Not," *Washington Post*, September 10, 2021, https://www.washingtonpost.com/technology/2021/09/10/pentagon-internet-protocol-addresses-trump/.
12. David Clark, "Control Point Analysis," in *Proceedings of 2012 TRPC Conference*, http://dx.doi.org/10.2139/ssrn.2032124.
13. Steve Crocker, RFC 1, "Host Software," April, 1969, https://www.rfc-editor.org/rfc/rfc1.txt.
14. Jon Postel, RFC 791, "Internet Protocol." September, 1981, https://www.rfc-editor.org/rfc/rfc791.txt.
15. National Research Council, "Signposts in Cyberspace: The Domain Name System and Internet Navigation," The National Academies Press, 2005.
16. Internet Society Press Release, "Internet Society Statement on the Death of Jon Postel," Reston, VA, October 1998.
17. The IANA stewardship transition is described in detail in Chapter 5.
18. From ARIN's published fee schedule, https://www.arin.net/resources/fees/.
19. From APNIC's published fee schedule, https://www.apnic.net/about-apnic/corporate-documents/documents/membership/member-fee-schedule/.
20. See, for example, "Open Letter to ICANN from the Regional Internet Registries," November 6, 2003, https://www.nro.net/open-letter-to-icann-from-the-regional-internet-registries/.
21. ICANN, "Criteria for Establishment of New Regional Internet Registries," accepted June 4, 2001, https://www.icann.org/resources/pages/new-rirs-criteria-2012-02-25-en.
22. See: ITU, Director TSB Report on WTSA Resolution 64 "IP Address Allocation and Encouraging the Deployment of IPv6," p. 3, specifically "Many developing countries had requested that the TSB become an additional registry for IP addresses so that countries could have the option of obtaining IP addresses directly from ITU. This request should be evaluated and its advantages and disadvantages should be reported in the study that the Director of TSB is instructed to present to Council 2009 (Resolution 64)," September 22, 2009, https://www.itu.int/md/S09-CL-C-0029/en.
23. See ITU, Director TSB Report on WTSA Resolution 64 "IP Address allocation and encouraging the deployment of IPv6",

p. 3, September 22, 2009, https://www.itu.int/md/S09-CL-C-0029/en.
24. See ITU-T IPv6 Working Group landing page, Terms of Reference, https://www.itu.int/en/ITU-T/others/ipv6/Pages/default.aspx, accessed July 5, 2025.
25. Number Resource Organization FAQ entry for "What is the NRO Position in Relation to Internet Governance," https://www.nro.net/about/nro-faq/#5, accessed August 2, 2023.
26. See, for example, Radu, Roxana. *Negotiating Internet Governance*, Oxford University Press, 2019.
27. Sue Kirkpatrick, Mary Stahl, and Mimi Recker, RFC 1166, "Internet Numbers," July, 1990, p. 6.
28. R. Hinden, RFC 1517, September 1993, Y. Rekhter and Tony Li, RFC 518, September 1993, and V. Fuller, T. LI, J. Yu, and K. Varadhan, RFC 1519, September 1993 all document classless inter-domain routing approaches. Note that V. Fuller and T. LI, RFC 4632, August 2006 obsoletes RFC 1519.
29. Yakov Rekhter and Tony Li, RFC 1518, "An Architecture for IP Address Allocation with CIDR," September 1993.
30. Vinton Cerf, RFC 1174, "IAB Recommended Policy on Distributing Internet Identifier Assignment and IAB Recommended Policy Change to Internet 'Connected' Status," August, 1990.
31. See ARIN 6.4.1. https://www.arin.net/participate/policy/nrpm/#6-1-introduction.
32. See https://www.ntia.doc.gov/blog/2012/united-states-government-s-internet-protocol-numbering-principles.
33. See, for example, Milton Mueller, Brenden Kuerbis, and Hadi Asghari, "Dimensioning the Elephant: an Empirical Analysis of the IPv4 Number Market," *Journal of Policy, Regulation and Strategy for Telecommunications, Information and Media*, Volume 15, Issue 6, 2013, pp. 6–18; Ioana Livadariu, et al. "On IPv4 Transfer Markets: Analyzing Reported Transfers and Inferring Transfers in the Wild." *Computer Communications*, Volume 111, 2017, pp. 105–19; Benjamin Edelman and Michael Schwarz, "Pricing and Efficiency in the Market for IP Addresses." *American Economic Journal of Microeconomics*, Volume 7, Number 3, 2015, pp. 1–23.
34. The disruption numbers come from ViaSat's own account and incident report of the February 44, 2022 attack on its systems:

Viasat Corporate News Release, "KA-SAT Network Cyber Attack Overview," March 30, 2022, https://news.viasat.com/blog/corporate/ka-sat-network-cyber-attack-overview.

35. Antony J. Blinken, Secretary of State, U.S. State Department press statement, "Attribution of Russia's Malicious Cyber Activity Against Ukraine," May 10, 2022, https://www.state.gov/attribution-of-russias-malicious-cyber-activity-against-ukraine/.
36. Nick Clegg, President of Global Affairs, statement via Twitter, March 4, 2022.
37. Council of EU, Press Release 207/22, "EU Imposes Sanctions on State-Owned Outlets RT/Russia Today and Sputnik's Broadcasting in the EU," March 2, 2022, https://www.consilium.europa.eu/en/press/press-releases/2022/03/02/eu-imposes-sanctions-on-state-owned-outlets-rt-russia-today-and-sputnik-s-broadcasting-in-the-eu/.
38. See, for example, Thomas Biersteker and Clara Portela, "EU Sanctions in Context: Three Types," *European Union Institute for Security Studies* (EUISS), 2015, https://repository.graduateinstitute.ch/record/293226?ln=en; and Peter Feaver and Eric Lorber, "The Sanctions Myth," *The National Interest*, Volume 138, 2015, pp. 22–27.
39. TikTok announced their sanctions on Twitter on March 6, 2022, https://twitter.com/TikTokComms/status/1500535437861048320.
40. See Lumen's question and answer publication about their decision, https://news.lumen.com/RussiaUkraine and Doug Madory, Blog "On Cogent", March 7, 2022, https://www.kentik.com/blog/cogent-disconnects-from-russia/#on-cogent
41. Civil Society Letter to Biden Administration regarding Russia Sanctions and Internet Access, March 10, 2022, https://www.accessnow.org/cms/assets/uploads/2022/03/Civil-society-letter-to-Biden-Admin-re-Russia-sanctions-and-internet-access_10-March-2022-1.pdf.
42. Statement of Cloudflare President Matthew Prince, "Steps We've Taken Around Cloudflare's Services in Ukraine, Belarus, and Russia," March 7, 2022, https://blog.cloudflare.com/steps-taken-around-cloudflares-services-in-ukraine-belarus-and-russia/.

43. Mykhailo Fedorov, Letter to Göran Marby, February 28, 2022, https://www.icann.org/en/system/files/correspondence/fedorov-to-marby-28feb22-en.pdf.
44. ICANN letter to Ukraine dated March 2, 2022, https://www.icann.org/en/system/files/correspondence/marby-to-fedorov-02mar22-en.pdf.
45. ICANN announcement, https://www.icann.org/en/announcements/details/icann-allocates-emergency-financial-support-for-continued-access-to-the-internet-06-03-2022-en.
46. Ukrainian Government, Letter to RIPE-NCC, dated March 2, 2022, p. 2, https://www.ripe.net/media/documents/Request_from_Ukrainian_Government.PDF.
47. RIPE-NCC, "RE: Official Request from Ukrainian Government to Help Stop Russian War," March 10, 2022, p. 1. https://www.ripe.net/publications/news/announcements/response_to_ua_gov_-_10march.pdf.
48. United Nations, "UN General Assembly Votes to Suspend Russia from the Human Rights Council," April 7, 2022, https://news.un.org/en/story/2022/04/1115782.
49. John Curran, Number Resource Organization letter on behalf of the NRO Executive Council, "re: Appointment of an Official Receiver for AFRINIC," September 14, 2023, https://www.nro.net/wp-content/uploads/NRO-re-Official-Receiver-for-AFRINIC-nrosigned.pdf.
50. John Curran, ARIN Blog, "AFRINIC and the Stability of the Internet Number Registry System," August 27, 2021, https://www.arin.net/blog/2021/08/27/afrinic-and-the-stability-of-the-internet-number-registry-system/.
51. Eddy Kayihura, AFRINIC CEO, "AFRINIC Updates" posting on AFRINIC Community-Discuss mailing list, January 17, 2020, https://lists.afrinic.net/pipermail/community-discuss/2020-January/003444.html.
52. Accessed on the AFRINIC website at https://afrinic.net/ast/pdf/afrinic-whois-audit-report-full-20210121.pdf.
53. AFRINIC 2021 Report, https://afrinic.net/ast/pdf/afrinic-whois-audit-report-full-20210121.pdf.
54. Ibid.
55. Ibid.

56. Milton Mueller, Vagisha Srivastava and Brenden Kuerbis, Blog post, "A Fight Over Crumbs. The AFRINIC Crisis," Internet Governance Project, August 19, 2021.
57. A rationale from the RIRs and the Internet community on why the addresses are given out regionally is outlined in the IETF RFC 1366, October 1992: "The major reason to distribute the registration function is that the Internet serves a more diverse global population than it did at its inception. This means that registries which are located in distinct geographic areas may be better able to serve the local community in terms of language and local customs [...] as other regions of the world become more and more active in the Internet, the IANA and the IR may choose to look for candidate registries to serve the populations in those geographic regions. [..] It is important that the regional registry is unbiased and widely recognized by network providers and subscribers within the geographic region. It is also important that there is just a single regional registry per geographical region at this level to provide for efficient and fair sub-allocation of the address space."
58. Associated Press news wire (reported in The Independent, UK version), "Africa Internet Riches Plundered, Contested by China Broker", October 1, 2021, https://www.independent.co.uk/news/south-africa-chinese-mauritius-uganda-china-b1930385.html.
59. See, for example, https://www.afrinic.net/finance?view=article&id=75:bylaws&catid=28&lang=en-GB.
60. Simon Sharwood, "Africa's Internet Registry Has Sometimes Needed Financial Assistance to keep operating, could fail, warns ARIN head", *The Register*, February 22, 2023 https://www.theregister.com/2023/02/22/afrinic_failure_warning_apnic_link/.
61. See, for example, https://afrinic.net/20210727-ceo-addresses-freezing-of-afrinic-financial-accounts.
62. See, for example, https://afrinic.net/20211015-update-on-legal-case-freeze-order-on-afrinic-bank-accounts-has-been-removed.
63. AFRINIC Press Release, September 22, 2022.
64. CircleID Reporter, "AFRINIC "In a Bad Situation" Has Not Been Able to Constitute a Board and Has No CEO," February 22, 2023, https://circleid.com/posts/20230222-afrinic-in-a-bad-situation-has-not-been-able-to-constitute-a-board-and-has-no-ceo.
65. Simon Sharwood and CircleID Reporter, supra note.

66. NRO to ICANN Letter, March 26, 2023, https://nro.net/wp-content/uploads/Letter-NRO-to_ICANN-Re-Engagement-AFRINIC-Community-signed.pdf.
67. NRO, "Letter to ICANN—Proposal to Re-engage the AFRINIC Community," March 26, 2023, https://www.nro.net/letter-to-icann-proposal-to-re-engage-the-afrinic-community/.
68. For an analysis of the Iranian 2019 shutdowns, see, for example, Article19, "Iran: Tightening the Net 2020: After Blood and Shutdowns," September 2020, https://www.article19.org/wp-content/uploads/2020/09/TTN-report-2020.pdf.
69. Freedom Online Coalition, "Joint Statement on Internet Shutdowns in Iran," October 20, 2022, https://www.state.gov/joint-statement-on-internet-shutdowns-in-iran/.
70. United States District Court for the District of Columbia, "Civil Action No. 02-1811 (RCL) Writ of Attachment on Judgment Other than Wages, Salaries and Commissions," June 24, 2014, https://www.icann.org/en/system/files/files/writs-subpoenas-24jun14-en.pdf.
71. United States Court of Appeals for the District of Columbia Circuit, "Opinion of the U.S., Court of Appeals for DC, Case 14-7193," p. 32, August 2, 2016, https://www.icann.org/en/system/files/files/litigation-haim-et-al-opinion-court-appeals-circuit-02aug16-en.pdf.
72. Athina Fragkouli, RIPE Labs, "How Sanctions Affect the RIPE NCC," November 18, 2011, https://labs.ripe.net/author/athina/how-sanctions-affect-the-ripe-ncc/.
73. Athina Fragkouli, RIPE Labs, "How Sanctions Affect the RIPE NCC," November 18, 2011, https://labs.ripe.net/author/athina/how-sanctions-affect-the-ripe-ncc/.
74. RIPE-NCC "Quarterly Sanctions Transparency Reports," multiple years, https://www.ripe.net/publications/ripe-ncc-organisational-documents/transparency-report/.
75. RIPE-NCC, "Executive Board Resolution on Continuity of Services to All RIPE NCC Members," October 21, 2014, https://www.ripe.net/publications/news/executive-board-resolution-on-continuity-of-services-to-all-ripe-ncc-members/.
76. See, for example, *Federal Register*, Volume 83, Number 214, November 5, 2018, Rules and Regulations, pp. 55269–55271.

77. U.S. Department of Treasury, Office of Foreign Assets Control, "Compliance for Internet, Web Based Activities, and Personal Communications," FAQ #73, April 13, 2004, https://ofac.treasury.gov/faqs/73.
78. Congressional Research Service (CRS), "U.S. Sanctions on Iran," July 20, 2023, https://crsreports.congress.gov/product/pdf/IF/IF12452#.
79. U.S. Department of Treasury Press Release, Office of Foreign Assets Control, "Treasury Sanctions Iranian Company Aiding in Internet Censorship," June 2, 2023, https://home.treasury.gov/news/press-releases/jy1518.
80. U.S. Department of Treasury, Enforcement Release, "OFAC Settles with Virtual Currency Exchange Kraken for $362,158.70 Related to Apparent Violations of the Iranian Transactions and Sanctions Regulations," November 28, 2022, https://ofac.treasury.gov/media/929541/download?inline.
81. CipherTrace, "Cryptocurrency Crime and Anti-Money Laundering Report, *CypherTrace Cryptocurrency Intelligence*, May 2021, p. 15. https://ciphertrace.com/wp-content/uploads/2021/05/CipherTrace-Cryptocurrency-Crime-and-Anti-Money-Laundering-Report-May-2021-051221b.pdf.
82. Ibid., pp. 15–17.

CHAPTER 5

# A Twenty-Year Control Struggle from U.S. Stewardship to Private Governance

One institution stands out in the context of these many examples of the geopolitics of Internet addresses. Whether in actions related to Internet addresses and the Russia-Ukraine war, or in the legitimacy assessment concerning a regional Internet registry, ICANN has played a central role in the IP ecosystem and served as a key institution in a highly geo-politicized context. Not surprisingly, ICANN has been the subject of a plethora of research, policy, and media attention, far too vast to highlight here.[1] Because of its key role in IP administration and because of the geopolitical importance of IP, ICANN has been at the core of numerous controversies related to its structure, its dependence on other Internet governance actors, and the scope of its mandate.

This chapter adds a perspective from first-hand, direct policymaking involvement in the trajectory that led to ICANN's role in the IP ecosystem, from its embryonic beginnings as a small, not-for-profit organization established in response to the U.S. government policy space, to its current status as a global, multistakeholder institution with more than 400 staff and offices in nine locations around the world.[2] The chapter tackles the early international discussions related to IP ecosystem resources and describes in detail the privatization process initiated by the U.S. government after rejecting intergovernmental based Internet resource coordination. It then details the concurrent international debates



F. M. Alexander et al., *Geopolitics at the Internet's Core*, Information Technology and Global Governance,
https://doi.org/10.1007/978-3-031-89478-7_5

which led to a shift away from the framing terminology of privatization and to that of multistakeholder governance. The chapter highlights that, without the World Summit on the Information Society and attending geopolitical overlay, ICANN might not have evolved into the radical governance innovation of multistakeholder Internet governance with respect to the administration of critical Internet resources, as described in Chapter 2.[3] Tracing this evolution over more than twenty-five years, as well as its deep embedding with other Internet institutions around the world including the mushrooming Internet registry industry, highlights the many dimensions of power in Internet addressing and the accompanying geopolitical and inter-institutional control challenges that ICANN has faced.

## Early International Discussions

As the commercial Internet began to flourish in the 1990s, companies and other stakeholders needed to develop their online identities. While IP numbers were then sufficiently available given the sheer number provided by the IPv4 standard, the domain namespace remained largely limited to the original general-purpose, top-level domains established in the mid-1980s in RFC 920.[4] These original gTLDs were .gov, .edu, .com, .mil, and .org and ccTLDs for countries based on ISO's two-letter country-code standard.

With a term or name only being able to be registered to one actor at the second level, "companyname.com," the first come, first serve approach that had been used to allocate names prompted a sense of scarcity and urgency. This set in motion discussions about the need to expand the sheer number of names, and prompted governance-related debates about how to choose them, who should choose them, who should operate the name registries to ensure global interoperability, and how they should be allocated on an internationally equitable basis. With only one commercial entity being able to use a name at the second level, trademark concerns were front and center.

Ultimately, the Internet Society (ISOC) and IANA created the International Ad Hoc Committee (IAHC) to develop a proposal to expand the name space. The sponsoring organizations selected the twelve members of the group. Internet technical experts were chosen from ISOC, IAB, IANA,[5] and the U.S. Federal Networking Council. The World Intellectual Property Organization (WIPO) and the International Trademark

Association (INTA) selected the trademark experts (reflecting increasing concerns with trademark legal issues) And, the ITU selected staff members to participate, reflecting that institution's past role in global telecommunications efforts.

The IAHC held a series of meetings culminating in a three-day conference in 1997 in which 80 organizations either signed or declared their intent to sign a new Memorandum of Understanding (MoU) related to the allocation and management of generic top-level domains. Under the proposed understanding, the ITU would serve as the global depository of the MoU and WIPO would administer an arbitration and mediation mechanism for disputes. The ITU issued a press release that heralded the agreement as a "restructure" of the Internet.[6] This early call for restructure would be the first of many efforts over the next 20 years, efforts that have persisted.

## U.S. Rejection of Proposal for Intergovernmental Leadership

While some U.S. stakeholders, including government officials, had participated in the IAHC process, the Clinton Administration rejected the idea of the global MOU and one grounded in an intergovernmental process. Just two months later, the White House released a "Framework for Global Electronic Commerce."[7] The *Framework* articulated five principles that were to become the foundation of U.S. government technology policy for the next twenty years, namely a light touch government regulatory approach with a strong commitment to private-sector leadership and industry self-regulation. This vision was in direct contrast with the centralized government-led system that the IAHC had proposed.

The *Framework* also laid out nine policy recommendations covering a range of issues including Internet tax and tariffs, intellectual property protection, technical standards, and privacy. It was accompanied by an Executive Order assigning a series of tasks to various U.S. cabinet agencies. With respect to the DNS, which included IP resources and the publication of the protocol parameters or IP standards, the Secretary of Commerce was directed "to support efforts to make the governance of the domain name system private and competitive and to create a contractually based self-regulatory regime that deals with potential conflicts between domain name usage and trademark laws on a global basis."[8]

The U.S. government had the ability to unilaterally issue this directive given the roles of the Defense Advanced Research Agency Project (DARPA) and the National Science Foundation (NSF) in funding the early development of portions of what is today's modern-day Internet, including TCP/IP. The Defense Information Systems Agency Network Information Center (DISA NIC) originally maintained the list of allocated IP resources among the various government grantees via the work of then graduate student Jon Postel. Postel also published a list of the protocol parameters (such as port numbers and codes that identify certain kinds of protocols) and Internet standards agreed upon by engineers. This would evolve into the Request for Comments (RFCs) series, or voluntary Internet standards agreed via the processes at the IETF. Internet Protocols require many unique codes and numbers—called protocol parameters—in order to successfully operate. Authoritative responsibility for these protocol parameters, which would evolve into a core responsibility of IANA, inadvertently later linked the IETF directly to the U.S. government in a manner not fully appreciated or understood at the time. The maintenance and publication of these combined lists or databases, along with other core IP address responsibilities, became known as the Internet Assigned Numbers Authority, or IANA.

As networks developed and expanded beyond government users, in 1991, the NSF assumed responsibility for the non-military portion of the Internet infrastructure. The NSF eventually entered into a Cooperative Agreement with Network Solutions to provide non-U.S. military registration services to the original top-level domains. This arrangement was the subject of a lawsuit. As a result, in 1999, the fee structure agreed to by NSF and Network Solutions was effectively declared an unconstitutional tax.[9]

With the existing U.S. government administered processes related to the allocation of IP resources facing a series of lawsuits, and issues of international fairness gaining prominence due to the IAHC process, the Clinton Administration's decision to issue the *Framework* and reject the IAHC outcome was not without controversy. The legitimacy of this step was not universally accepted, setting the stage for routine confrontations for twenty years between those that supported what was to become the ICANN administered multistakeholder model of DNS management, and those that pushed for oversight through the ITU.

## U.S. Privatization Process via NTIA

In 1997, the U.S. Framework for Electronic Commerce Executive Order delegated the U.S. Secretary of Commerce the task of privatizing the Domain Name System (DNS) in a way that would increase competition and facilitate international participation in DNS management. That job was given to the Department's National Telecommunications and Information Administration (NTIA). The day after the Executive Order was issued, NTIA published a request for comment seeking public input on a series of principles to evaluate future privatization proposals and specific questions on the operation of the DNS including the roles of the various actors as well as the trademark issues that had surfaced in the IAHC process.[10] A range of parties that included individuals, not-for-profits, and corporations filed a total of 430 formal comments.

The comments factored into NTIA's next step which was a discussion draft for "A Proposal to Improve Technical Management of Internet Names and Addresses," issued on January 30, 1998.[11] The discussion draft was published the following month in the U.S. Federal Register as a proposed government rule seeking public input, later known as the "Green Paper." The Green Paper laid out the path for the U.S. government to ramp down its role in the administration of Internet resources, called for the creation of a new not-for-profit corporation (later called "newco") to which the U.S. government role would move, and supported the creation of new top-level domains (TLDs), downplaying trademark challenges.

The Green Paper received 650 comments, including comments from stakeholders outside of the United States, which were considered in the formulation of NTIA's Statement of Policy on the Management of Internet Names and Numbers, or the "White Paper."[12] The White Paper, among other things, articulated principles for the new system of Internet resource management, confirmed that the DNS functions should be coordinated on a centralized basis, rejected calls to separate the management authority of domain names and IP numbers, and issued a call for proposals from entities wishing to be designated as "NewCo" to be the U.S. government's privatization partner. Five proposals were received, with ICANN, a new not-for-profit corporation organized under the leadership of Jon Postel, being chosen as it was the only proposal that met the criteria of the White Paper and that had requisite support.[13]

Consistent with Postel's proposal and ultimately reflected in ICANN's original 1998 bylaws, ICANN was to be comprised of a Board, three supporting organizations (i.e., address, domain name, and protocol) and three advisory committees (i.e., governmental, DNS root server system, and membership).[14] Each anticipated stakeholder group in this construct, including governments, would have a voice in the coordination of the global domain name system. Over time, ICANN's internal structures evolved into three supporting organizations (i.e., generic names, country-code names, and address) and four advisory committees (i.e., at-large, governmental, security and stability, and root server system).[15] The idea behind this multistakeholder model was based on bottom-up, open, and shared decision-making in which stakeholders would come together to develop policies that are then reflected as requirements in the registry and registrar contracts that ICANN administers.

On November 25, 1998, roughly eighteen months after the initial White House tasking, NTIA and ICANN entered into a Memorandum of Understanding (MoU) for the "DNS Project." The MoU laid out a series of tasks for both parties, the principles that would guide their efforts, as well as their respective roles and obligations that, once completed, would allow the U.S. government, via NTIA, to step away from its role in DNS administration.

While the parties and involved stakeholders undertook this process with a two-year time frame in mind, the entire process was much lengthier and more controversial. Over the next eight years the MoU would be amended seven times with the final amendment shifting the characterization of the relationship as a Joint Project Agreement (JPA) and establishing a mid-term review to give the appearance of progress.[16] As a legal matter, the MoU construct was a cooperation framework for a partnership, meaning that at any time either party could terminate the relationship and changes had to be mutually agreed upon.

To achieve the goal of privatization, the MoU tasked ICANN with expanding the namespace as well as transitioning the existing informal arrangements to administer and allocate domain names into formal contracts. Thus, ICANN would need to enforce these contracts under the envisioned self-regulatory scheme. ICANN's overtures to those they would ultimately regulate were not always warmly embraced. To demonstrate confidence and encourage constructive engagement by all parties, fifteen months after the MoU was signed, NTIA issued the IANA functions contract to ICANN. The original contract was sole sourced—i.e., given to ICANN without any consideration to other possible contractors—as a way for the U.S. government to confer legitimacy to ICANN.[17] Using a government contract to designate ICANN as the institution to provide direct services to third parties—what the contract did—was envisioned as a temporary measure. Full privatization meant that ultimately the IANA customers would develop their own direct legal arrangements with ICANN, negating the need for the NTIA-provided contractual backstop.

The IANA functions contract established a second legal arrangement between NTIA and ICANN, one that due to federal contracting rules placed NTIA in a formal decision-maker role. The use of a contract for the IANA functions, unlike the NTIA/ICANN MoU, gave NTIA the ability to exercise sole discretion over the performance of the IANA functions. For the first time coordination over assigning technical Internet protocol parameters and allocating Internet addresses (i.e., the distribution of IP number blocks to the regional Internet registries) was subject to U.S. government contracting rules. Because protocol parameters—codes and numbers—are necessary for so many Internet protocols, and communicated as part of the RFCs, this IANA function, in effect, linked not only IP resource allocation but also IETF standards to a single government in a structure that came with both real and perceived roles, responsibilities, and legal obligations, and resulted in misunderstandings which plagued all involved. The close linkage between IANA's protocol parameter assignment function and IETF prompted ICANN to have a separate memorandum of understanding with the IETF specifying how "IANA will assign and register Internet protocol parameters only as directed by the criteria and procedures specified in RFCs, including Proposed, Draft, and full Internet Standards and Best Current Practice documents, and any other RFC that calls for IANA assignment."[18]

The IANA contract was awarded to ICANN again in 2001, 2003, and 2006, largely unchanged except for the deployment of DNSSEC in the root in the fourth contract cycle.[19] However, in 2011, NTIA initiated for the first time a call for public input on the terms and performance standards of the IANA services by issuing first a request for comments and then a further notice of inquiry. With these steps, NTIA was allowing the actual customers of the IANA functions, as well as other relevant stakeholders, to have a direct voice in a U.S. government contracting process, which for this fifth cycle was to be a competitive bid. Stakeholder feedback led to accountability and transparency reporting, respect for local country laws, a company-wide conflict of interest policy, and structural separation of policymaking and implementation requirements being added to the scope of work. NTIA issued a public solicitation notice or request for proposal on November 10, 2011.

While U.S. federal contracting law prohibited the disclosure of who applied, ICANN did discuss with its stakeholder community its submission. Whether or not others applied is not publicly known, but it came as a surprise to some that on March 10, 2012, NTIA canceled the RFP stating "we are canceling this RFP because we received no proposals that met the requirements requested by the global community."[20] Even with the limitations of procurement law, NTIA deeming ICANN's proposal as insufficient was a rare public rebuke. The RFP, unchanged, was reissued the following month, and ultimately ICANN, with a changed proposal, emerged as the winner of the competitive bid with NTIA asserting: "the process used over the last year, and the resulting new contract requirements, are tailored to ensure respect for the relevant global multistakeholder policy processes."[21] This served as a clear indication that NTIA had asserted its role in an unusually public manner, albeit on behalf of the global Internet community.

## Final Steps and Shift to Multistakeholder Framing

As the NTIA/ICANN MoU, now JPA, faced expiration once again, NTIA sought input from interested stakeholders. It issued a Notice of Inquiry to assess the status of the transition of the U.S. government role to the private sector.[22] With a decade's worth of international forums (including that of the Internet Governance Forum) and consistent calls for the NTIA to move forward, NTIA and ICANN adjusted their MoU by co-signing on September 30, 2009, nearly eleven years after the first agreement, the Affirmation of Commitments.[23] The new construct was chosen as a way to show progress and ICANN's increasing maturity, but leave NTIA as a continued backstop. The title—Affirmation of Commitments—was an invention, chosen by looking for synonyms in a word processor. In an effort to build global support for this step, prior to the public announcement and release of the Affirmation, NTIA sent senior staff to five countries over the course of ten days (i.e., UK, France, Brazil, China, and Japan) to preview the new arrangement and engage in dialogue.

The Affirmation established a long-lasting framework for the private-sector-led coordination of the DNS, injected a clear obligation for ICANN to act in the global public interest, and included a commitment for the U.S. government to participate in ICANN processes. The agreement was operationalized through a series of review teams to be made up of ICANN community members and relevant outside experts. These teams were to routinely evaluate ICANN's executions of tasks and make recommendations for improvements on key areas such as accountability and transparency, stability and security, and the introduction of new generic top-level domains (gTLDs). Through the Affirmation review teams, NTIA had established a mechanism to share its oversight role as opposed to completely giving it up, with the NTIA Administrator named a permanent member of the Accountability and Transparency Review Team (ATRT).

After two cycles of the ATRT, continued enhancements were made to ICANN; however, tensions in the international community lingered regarding the role of governments in the allocation and management of Internet resources. The following section describes in some detail the geopolitical overlay of the twenty-year process, including how in 2012, the world split into two camps at the ITU World Conference on International Telecommunications (WCIT). The split caused the Obama Administration to consider what actions the United States could take to convince other governments to support multistakeholder Internet governance.

It was decided at a political level that the United States could demonstrate its clear and unwavering commitment to multistakeholder Internet governance if it was to finally complete the DNS project initiated with the 1997 Framework for Electronic Commerce. Intense internal U.S. government staff-level, interagency debates followed regarding the scope of the appropriate terms and conditions to attach and which method was best to ensure the continued stability and security of the DNS. Ultimately, NTIA announced on March 14, 2014, the final step in the privatization process—the path to terminate the remaining unilateral U.S. government relationship—the IANA functions contract.[24] However, NTIA would not just "give" the IANA functions to ICANN and terminate the contract, as many had expected for years, but rather it asked ICANN to convene global Internet stakeholders to develop a proposal. Characterized as the transition of the U.S. government's stewardship of the IANA functions,

NTIA called on ICANN to convene a process to develop a proposal with broad stakeholder support that would meet the following criteria:

- Support and enhance the multistakeholder model;
- Maintain the security, stability, and resiliency of the Internet DNS;
- Meet the needs and expectation of the global customers and partners of the IANA services;
- Maintain the openness of the Internet.

NTIA also clearly stated "that it would not accept a proposal that replaces the NTIA role with a government-led or an intergovernmental organization solution."[25]

Response to the announcement was mixed within the directly impacted community groups, with some ICANN participants demanding more change at ICANN and others calling on NTIA to retain the contract and, in fact, amend it to address outstanding ICANN policy issues. Paradoxically, all of those that had, for over a decade, called on NTIA to take this step, were expressing reservations about the change. Given the two ATRT cycles that had successfully occurred, NTIA and ICANN were surprised by the response. To address these concerns, a workstream was added to develop recommendations to further enhance ICANN's accountability. This workstream became a separate but integral track to what would be a two-part consolidated IANA stewardship transition proposal.

The U.S. Congress, which over the years had held routine NTIA oversight hearings on ICANN, was displeased to different degrees. NTIA received dozens of oversight letters, a few hearings were held, a Government Accountability Office (GAO) investigation was requested, and NTIA was mandated to provide quarterly status reports to Congress.[26] Congressional questions focused on whether NTIA had the legal authority to take such a step. With the entire privatization processes stemming from a 1997 Executive Order, there had never been legislative direction from the U.S. Congress. Rather, there had only been House and Senate resolutions supporting the multistakeholder model.

Did Congress need to have an up or down vote to approve the final proposal? Other questions were raised about whether U.S. government property was being given away as part of the transition. If so, legally, Congressional approval was required. Even those members of Congress that were supportive, were looking for safeguards and more information from NTIA.

While NTIA engaged in addressing the concerns of members of Congress, the ICANN community moved forward with two parallel processes. The first was the IANA Stewardship Transition Coordination Group (ICG) which tackled the actual performance and oversight structure of the IANA functions. The ICG asked each of the three primary IANA functions customers—the domain name customers through an ICANN working group, the numbering customers through the RIRs, and the protocol parameters customer through the IETF—to develop and submit a proposal for their respective service. Each of the groups used their own multistakeholder consultative process to develop standards and performance metrics for the IANA functions operator (IFO) to follow in performance of their respective function. In effect, three separate direct customer contracts replaced the NTIA stewardship arrangement. The ICG's proposal also called for the IFO to be structurally separate from ICANN so that the customers could, if performance levels ever degraded, run a process to select a different IANA functions operator.

The second parallel process was the ICANN Cross Community Working Group on Accountability (CCWG) which for its part developed a series of escalating community powers that effectively created a power sharing structure between the ICANN Board and the various constituency groups. Referred to as the "Empowered Community," it called for nine specific powers that ICANN supporting organizations and advisory committees could come together to trigger as tools to hold the ICANN Board and staff accountable. The powers ranged from rejecting budgets and operating plans and removing individual board members or the entire board to requiring community approval of Bylaw changes.[27] Two other recommendations emerged from this group: one for a standing independent review panel and another for the incorporation of elements of the Affirmation of Commitments into ICANN's Bylaws, including Accountability and Transparency Reviews as well as commitment to free expression and maintaining the openness of the Internet.

On March 6, 2016, ICANN submitted the consolidated stakeholder-developed proposal. When all was said and done, participants in the ICANN-convened process spent more than 800 working hours in meetings on the proposal, exchanged more than 33,000 mailing list messages, convened more than 600 meetings and calls and incurred legal fees of millions of dollars for proposal development. The first half of the two-part proposal was evaluated against the initially announced criteria and was also assessed against the Committee of Sponsoring Organizations (COSO) internal risk controls framework recommended by the US Government Accountability Office after a congressionally requested study to review the implications of the transition.[28] NTIA chose to have the second half of the proposal, the accountability enhancements called for by the ICANN community in reaction to NTIA's initial transition announcement, evaluated by a team of independent corporate governance experts. The governance experts were asked to examine the possibility of institutional capture within ICANN to address external criticisms that surfaced during the proposal development process. On June 9, 2016, NTIA announced that the proposal met the criteria, the COSO controls, and were consistent with the sound principles of good governance and published a complete assessment report.[29]

The transition continued to face a series of domestic political hurdles. Over the years, when U.S. domestic stakeholders in ICANN, ranging from intellectual property rights holders to law enforcement, did not get what they wanted, they would often go to Congress to put pressure on ICANN or NTIA. This had stoked intermittent Congressional interest over the years, with the 2014 NTIA announcement initially taking many in Congress off guard.

Strong reservations and doubts continued to be expressed by a handful of legislators, including Senator Ted Cruz who was running for the Republican presidential nomination at the time. He likened the effort to a Panama Canal type of giveaway of the Internet.[30] An acrimonious NTIA oversight hearing was held, where among other things, Senator Cruz threatened jail time for the NTIA staff involved.[31] Some in Congress also questioned the legality of the entire effort and whether or not NTIA was running afoul of the Property Clause of the Constitution and giving away U.S. government property. The GAO was asked to look into the matter and a negative finding could have brought the entire effort to a standstill. Ultimately on September 12, 2016, a full two years after NTIA's initial announcement, the GAO determined there were no property-related problems.[32]

The IANA stewardship transition then became entangled in the annual Washington, D.C. September budget fights over funding for the federal government. A handful of lawmakers demanded the Administration postpone the transition as a condition of continued government funding. Without reauthorization, the federal government would shut down on

Friday September 30, 2016. Coincidentally, this was the same day the IANA functions contract was set to expire. Eventually, on Wednesday September 28th, Congress agreed to what is called a clean continuing resolution which is status quo funding for the federal government. With no conditions added to the budget, yet another obstacle for NTIA to move forward with the stewardship transition was removed.

Having escaped the budget showdown process that Wednesday night, the staff at NTIA breathed a sigh of relief, only to come to work on the morning of Thursday September 29th to be told that the attorneys general (AGs) for Arizona, Oklahoma, Nevada, and Texas had filed a lawsuit to stop the transition. The four AGs claimed the IANA stewardship transition was an illegal giveaway of U.S. government property and if it occurred would limit free expression on the Internet. They argued for a temporary restraining order (TRO) to prevent NTIA from letting the contract expire. Note that this contract was not one for which the U.S. government was the customer for the services provided nor was any money involved.

With the IANA functions contract expiring the next day, a hearing was held in the Southern District of Texas U.S. in Galveston, Texas. After listening to the arguments of both sides and reviewing the amicus briefs provided by Internet stakeholders, Judge George C. Hanks Jr. ruled to deny the plaintiffs' application for declaratory and injunctive relief. At 12:01 a.m. on October 1, NTIA posted a simple one-line press release stating that the IANA functions contract had expired.[33]

For the world, the process was complete; and the U.S. government's unique role was removed. However, after twenty years and with little fanfare, the privatization process was actually completed the first week of January 2017, when NTIA and ICANN exchanged letters to mutually terminate the Affirmation of Commitments,[34] thus once and for all ending the U.S. government's unique role in the administration of the Internet resources.

## Geopolitics in the Wings

While public comment processes and stakeholder engagement at every turn defined the NTIA approach to the assignment, all of this was occurring in a world where the U.S. government's unique and historical role in the administration of the DNS system was increasingly under attack. As NTIA was kicking off its relationship with ICANN, world governments via the ITU agreed to the first ever resolution on the Internet Domain Name System.[35] Resolution 102 as it would be called was agreed to at the 1998 ITU Plenipotentiary Conference raising issues of global equality, asserting the role of national governments, and instructing the ITU Secretary General to take an active part in discussions.[36] The Plenipotentiary Conference is a treaty conference held every four years to consider updating the roles, responsibilities, and priorities of the ITU as well as elect the institution's leadership.

Initially proposed by Europe with France taking the lead role in the negotiation, this resolution would come to be the source of contentious debate every four years at ITU Plenipotentiary meetings. Debates were often driven by individual governments or regions who felt slighted or aggrieved in an ICANN process and had little to no impact on the NTIA deliberations. In fact, the need for NTIA, ICANN, and other ICANN supporters to spend time and resources to repeatedly and routinely defend against such external attacks slowed down the efforts to build ICANN and develop the necessary internal structures.

Disagreements over the administration of Internet resources were also a major flashpoint in the five-year World Summit on Information Society process. A UN summit held unusually in two phases because Member States could not agree where to meet, the first phase culminated in a 2003 meeting in Geneva, Switzerland. Throughout the various regional and global preparatory meetings of the first phase, questions about the legitimacy of ICANN were raised, often echoing discussions at the ITU where some countries continued to push for an intergovernmental approach to administer Internet resources. Of particular insult for some countries was the role that the U.S. government via NTIA had in approving changes related to their respective country-code top-level domains (ccTLDs, such as .kh for Cambodia or .fr for France) in the IANA functions-produced root zone file. And while the NTIA role was arguably clerical, the fact that the role even existed was reason enough for some governments to oppose ICANN.

These discussions fell under the rubric of Internet governance, a term for which there was not even an agreed definition. Reaching a stalemate and saved by the fact that there was a second phase of the Summit planned for Tunis in 2005, the issue was punted. The WSIS first phase Geneva outcome called for the creation of a working group on Internet governance (WGIG), involving all stakeholders. The WGIG was asked to define

Internet governance, identify the respective roles and responsibilities of all stakeholders involved, and make proposals for consideration in Tunis.[37]

So, while not directly impacting the NTIA decision-making process or changing the NTIA/ICANN relationship, or even using the word multistakeholder, the WSIS Geneva outcomes did for the first time globally legitimize the notion of stakeholders from the private sector and civil society having a role, not just governments.[38] This did trigger the shift away from the Clinton Administration coined privatization rhetoric to one of multistakeholder governance for the United States and others.

The second phase of WSIS was largely a repeat of the first phase, as more and more governments began to be concerned with the Internet given its growing economic and societal importance. Debates around Internet resource administration, intellectual property, Internet connectivity costs, and cybersecurity revealed continuing divides among Member States. However, unlike the Geneva phase where non-governmental stakeholders were routinely asked to leave negotiation rooms, the proceedings were more open, a reflection of the WSIS Geneva outcome, recognizing the roles of all stakeholders. Additionally, participants had the report of the intersessional multistakeholder WGIG to consider.

The WGIG, which was asked to tackle the three main areas of disagreement of WSIS Phase 1—the who, what, and how of Internet governance—addressed them in a largely overview manner, instead spending most of their effort coming up with proposals for new mechanisms.[39] While the idea of a global discussion forum was included, the majority of proposals called for major changes in the current U.S. government role. The Geneva based Ambassador soon to be managing the WSIS Phase 2 process came to Washington after the report's release and urged the Bush Administration to make clear its views so that expectations were calibrated appropriately heading into the negotiations. In response, NTIA issued a statement of four succinct principles that made clear that while the U.S. was always willing to discuss relevant issues, meaningful changes to the NTIA/ICANN relationship were off the table.[40] Catching even allies off guard given the lack of advance notification and coordination, the "U.S. Principles on the Internet's Domain Name and Addressing System" was seen by some as a Monroe Doctrine of the Internet.[41]

With the WGIG report and NTIA's DNS Principles, which rejected a majority of the recommendations, as an input to the process, the discussions continued and the unique role of NTIA was once again under a microscope. After intense debates and still no agreement on if or how to change the U.S. role via a UN effort, the United States agreed to the creation of the Internet Governance Forum (IGF) as a place to continue dialogue.[42] This compromise in 2005 allowed for the NTIA process with ICANN to continue while at the same time creating a space for all stakeholders to conduct dialogue on a host of Internet issues.

And while the WSIS Tunis process did not directly influence NTIA's decisions regarding its relationship with ICANN, the IGF's discussions that followed did. The IGF, by design, is not a negotiation forum, but rather a space for cross-stakeholder dialogue and sharing of views. With respect to NTIA's relationship with ICANN and its stewardship of the IANA functions, this environment allowed for honest, open and respectful airing of concerns, engaging NTIA and other parties in constructive dialogues. The 2006–2008 IGF's were sources of input into the NTIA thinking around the Affirmation of Commitments and the first articulation of ICANN decisions having a public interest component. Additionally, ICANN and stakeholders used input from the 2014–2015 IGFs in the process of developing the IANA stewardship transition proposal.

In December of 2012, the global community convened in Dubai for the ITU World Conference on International Telecommunications. The main purpose of the meeting was to update an existing quarter-century-old treaty focused on facilitating international telecommunications interconnection.[43] Previous iterations addressed issues such as international telephone accounting rates and private telecom operators' use of leased lines. Some countries saw this as an opportunity to modernize the treaty and proposed including Internet-related provisions. The discussions were politically fraught with a push by some to upend the multistakeholder model for critical Internet resource allocation as administered by ICANN and the RIRs.[44] Ultimately, the world split with 54 countries, including the United States, voting no and not signing, and 89 countries, including Russia and China voting yes and signing the treaty.

The 2013–2015 timeframe also marked, in addition to the IANA transition process, global responses to the Snowden disclosures regarding U.S. government surveillance. Following these 2013 revelations, then-President of Brazil, Dilma Rousseff, used her opening speech at the 2013 United Nations General Assembly to condemn U.S. government surveillance of electronic communications. She highlighted key principles including freedom of expression, privacy, and multistakeholder governance. Concern about U.S. government surveillance also dominated the subsequent discussions at the 2013 IGF in Bali, Indonesia. In response, the Brazilian Internet Steering Committee (CGI.br), working with other Internet governance stakeholders and institutions such as ICANN, planned a global, multistakeholder meeting, NETmundial, in Brazil to talk about the evolution of the Internet governance ecosystem.[45] Held in Sao Paulo, Brazil in April 2014, 1480 stakeholders from 97 nations participated. Stakeholders irrespective of their category (e.g., governments, private sector, technical community, civil society) lined up at microphones to make their interventions, including government representatives from Iran and Russia, and all participated in the negotiation of an output document.

The NETmundial meeting produced a set of principles and proposed a roadmap for the future of Internet governance.[46] From a process perspective, the NETmundial meeting was a multistakeholder negotiation, albeit toward a document. The output document criticized surveillance practices, called for the IANA stewardship transition process to extend beyond the ICANN community, and addressed human rights, privacy, and freedom of expression. The outcome document, however, did not meet the expectations of some civil society organizations, which criticized the final product as too weak on human rights.[47] Brazil, ICANN, and the World Economic Forum attempted to follow up the two-day meeting with a NETMundial Initiative, but without broader stakeholder buy-in, it proved unsuccessful. A NETmundial + 10 follow-up meeting happened in April of 2024 in Sao Paolo.

## Legacy and Impact

A striking characteristic about the transition of the stewardship of the IANA functions, given its controversy, was that life did not change for the average Internet user the day after the transition. The Internet continued to work. The institutions of technical Internet governance, those involved in the infrastructure layer, emerged strengthened and further entrenched in the IP ecosystem. The multistakeholder model (i.e., open, bottom-up, and participatory processes with shared decision-making), arguably a radical approach to technology governance, was almost globally embraced, at least at a surface level. And a more diverse set of global stakeholders became involved in what had been insular Internet governance debates as the issues surfaced on a broader international stage. Of course, cultural, linguistic, and resource challenges continued to impact global stakeholder participation.

Internet governance institutions established during this period included the creation of ICANN, the completion of five regional Internet registries, and the solidification of the IETF as the premiere Internet standards organization. The Internet Governance Forum, while not an institution of Internet governance but rather a multistakeholder dialogue, was also an outgrowth. Organically, more than 150 regional, sub-regional, and national IGFs emerged around the world. And, the long standing institutional fight between ICANN and the ITU was seemingly resolved when in 2019, ICANN became a Sector Member of the ITU's Development Sector.[48]

All was not completely sorted, however, as a government, stakeholder, or institution with designs on using the Internet Protocol as a lever of control periodically challenges the status quo. Geopolitical control tensions simmer just below the surface. Some lingering concerns have questioned the extent to which, as a California non-profit, ICANN remains under the jurisdiction of U.S. law. However, for ICANN to be similarly situated and have immunity akin to other international coordinating groups like the International Red Cross, a governmental overlay would need to have final say, a structure that would run contrary to the multistakeholder model. Others question the effectiveness of ICANN, pointing to the length of time it can take to resolve a problem or simply are unhappy if an outcome does not result in exactly what they want. There is also a periodic push to expand the remit of ICANN into content-control issues or seek unilateral solutions outside of the system. These tensions and the increasing turn to infrastructure, including the DNS, as points of control are addressed in Chapter 6.

Over twenty years, geopolitics shifted and influenced the initial goals and rhetoric of critical Internet resource management away from planned privatization to multistakeholder governance. This change and the accompanying broader global acceptance of the radical governance innovation is a notable outcome of the UN WSIS process. The ideas put forward in 2023 by UN Secretary General Guterres as part of the UN Global Digital Compact discussions clearly and unambiguously highlighted these questions.[49] Offering up a series of suggestions to answer what he called "strategic gaps in global governance arrangements" of the Internet, debates were once again triggered over whether multilateral processes where governments retain the ultimate decision-making authority as opposed to multistakeholder approaches which involve all stakeholders are best suited to address new digital challenges.[50] Multilateral institutions like the United Nations will claim they are embracing multistakeholder governance approaches, but in fact, are merely permitting a select and pre-approved set of stakeholders to express an opinion, but have no role in final decisions; making the process more akin to a multistakeholder consultation, not the multistakeholder innovation of Internet governance.

The WSIS + 20 review raised questions about whether this legacy would be maintained or whether control struggles would resurface and result in a different future outcome. Will this approach be widely accepted as an appropriate tool to solve broader digital challenges already being extensively discussed in the IGF or will there be a push for multilateral-only solutions?[51] The outcomes of ever-present renegotiation processes and their impact, if any, on the Internet Protocol ecosystem, are yet to be determined.

## Notes

1. See for example Derrick Cogburn, Milton Mueller, et al., "The U.S. Role in Global Internet Governance," *IEEE Communication Magazine*, December 2005, pp. 12–14; George Christou and Seamus Simpson, "Gaining A Stake in Global Internet Governance: the EU, ICANN and Strategic Norm Manipulation," *European Journal of Communication,* Volume 22, Issue 2, June 2007, pp. 147–164; Nicola Palladino and Mauro Santaniello, "IANA Functions, ICANN, and the DNS War" in *Legitimacy, Power, and Inequalities in the Multistakeholder Internet Governance*, Palgrave Macmillan, 2021; Richard Hill, "Internet Governance, Multistakeholder Models, and the IANA Transition: Shining Example or Dark Side?" *Journal of Cyber Policy*, Volume 1, Issue 2, 2016, pp. 176–197; Kevin McGillivray, "Give it Away Now? Renewal of the IANA Functions Contract and its Role in Internet Governance," *International Journal of Law and Information Technology*, Volume 22, Issue 1, Spring 2014, pp. 3–26; Milton Mueller, "Detaching Internet Governance from the State: Globalizing the IANA." *Georgetown Journal of International Affairs*, 2014, pp. 35–44.
2. ICANN announcement, "ICANN Publishes FY23 Annual Report and Audited Financial Statements" October 4, 2023, https://www.icann.org/en/announcements/details/icann-publishes-fy23-annual-report-and-audited-financial-statements-04-10-2023-en

and ICANN locations, https://www.icann.org/locations, accessed April 1, 2024.

3. The 1997 U.S. Framework for Electronic Commerce called for the "privatization of the management of the domain name system (DNS) in a manner that increases competition and facilitates international participation in its management." The subsequent Memorandum of Understanding between ICANN and NTIA used the same phrasing. It was only in 2006, after the WSIS discussions that the phrasing began to shift to "transition to the private sector" and then in the 2009 Affirmation of Commitments the wording "multistakeholder, private sector led" is used.
4. Jon Postel and Joyce Reynolds, RFC 920, "Domain Requirements," October, 1984.
5. In the early days of the DNS, the Internet Assigned Numbers Authority, or IANA, typically referred to a single person, Internet pioneer Jon Postel, who updated the series of interrelated databases that keep the DNS coordinated. In 2000, as part of the U.S. government's DNS privatization effort, the U.S. Department entered into a contract with the Internet Corporation for Assigned Names and Numbers (ICANN) to perform the IANA functions.
6. International Telecommunication Union, "80 Organizations Sign MoU to Restructure the Internet," May 1, 1997, https://www.itu.int/newsarchive/press_releases/1997/itu-08.html.
7. United States Clinton Administration White House, "The Framework for Global Electronic Commerce," July 1, 1997, https://clintonwhitehouse4.archives.gov/WH/New/Commerce/.
8. United States Clinton Administration White House, "Presidential Directive," July 1, 1997, https://clintonwhitehouse4.archives.gov/WH/New/Commerce/directive.html.
9. See Thomas v. Network Solutions, Inc. for a full discussion of the lawsuit, history of the NSF and Network Solutions relationship and the outcome of the case, https://caselaw.findlaw.com/us-dc-circuit/1211563.html.
10. NTIA, "Request for Comment on the Registration and Administration of Internet Domain Names," July 2, 1997, https://www.ntia.doc.gov/legacy/ntiahome/domainname/email/index.html.

11. NTIA, "A Proposal to Improve Technical Management of Internet Names and Addresses—Discussion Draft," January 30, 1998, https://www.ntia.doc.gov/legacy/ntiahome/domainname/dnsdrft.htm.
12. NTIA, "Management of Internet Names and Address—Statement of Policy," June 5, 1998, https://www.ntia.doc.gov/legacy/ntiahome/domainname/6_5_98dns.htm.
13. See the section "Private Sector Proposals Received in This Proceeding" for the five proposals submitted as "NewCo" as well the public comments received on the five proposals, https://www.ntia.doc.gov/legacy/ntiahome/domainname/background.htm.
14. ICANN, "Bylaws for Internet Corporation for Assigned Names and Numbers," ICANN, November 6, 1998, https://www.icann.org/resources/unthemed-pages/bylaws-1998-11-06-en.
15. ICANN, "How is ICANN Organized," accessed March 11, 2024, https://atlarge.icann.org/about/how-is-icann-organized.
16. See NTIA's archived website at https://www.ntia.doc.gov/legacy/ntiahome/domainname/icann.htm for the full record of the NTIA/ICANN MoU and subsequent seven amendments.
17. NTIA defined the IANA functions as: "(1) The coordination of the assignment of technical Internet Protocol parameters; (2) the administration of certain responsibilities associated with Internet DNS root zone management; (3) the allocation of Internet numbering resources; and (4) other services related to the management of the.ARPA and.INT top-level domains." See NTIA's IANA Functions Contract information page at https://www.ntia.doc.gov/page/iana-functions-purchase-order for the original 2000 sole source purchase order and subsequent amendments, the 2012 competitive bid and selection process and amendments, and the 2016 contract close out.
18. ICANN, "IETF-ICANN Memorandum of Understanding Concerning the Technical Work of the Internet Assigned Numbers Authority," June, 2000, https://www.icann.org/resources/unthemed-pages/ietf-icann-mou-2000-03-01-en.
19. NTIA, "Modification 5 to the IANA Functions Contract," July 13, 2010, https://www.ntia.gov/files/ntia/publications/modification5_icann_dnssec_implementation.pdf.

20. NTIA, "Cancellation Notice of the IANA Functions Request for Proposal," March 10, 2012, https://www.ntia.gov/other-publication/notice-cancelled-internet-assigned-numbers-authority-iana-functions-request.
21. NTIA, "Commerce Department Awards Contract for Management of Key Internet Functions to ICANN," July 2, 2012, https://www.ntia.doc.gov/press-release/2012/commerce-department-awards-contract-management-key-internet-functions-icann.
22. NTIA, "Commerce's NTIA Seeks Public Comment Regarding Expiration of the Joint Project Agreement with the Internet Corporation for Assigned Names and Numbers Set to Expire September 30, 2009," NTIA, April 27, 2009, https://www.ntia.doc.gov/press-releases/2009/commerces-ntia-seeks-public-comment-regarding-expiration-joint-project-agreement.
23. NTIA, "Affirmation of Commitments by the United States Department of Commerce and the Internet Corporation for Assigned Names and Numbers,"September 30, 2019, https://www.ntia.doc.gov/files/ntia/publications/affirmation_of_commitments_2009.pdf.
24. NTIA, "NTIA Announces Intent to Transition Key Internet Domain Name Functions," March 14, 2014, https://www.ntia.doc.gov/press-release/2014/ntia-announces-intent-transition-key-internet-domain-name-functions.
25. Ibid.
26. See NTIA, Reports to Congress on IANA transition at https://www.ntia.doc.gov/page/reports-congress-iana-transition.
27. ICANN, "Empowered Community," https://www.icann.org/ec.
28. U.S. Government Accountability Office (GAO), "Structured Evaluation Could Help Assess Proposed Transition of Key Domain Name and Other Technical Functions," August 2015, https://www.gao.gov/assets/gao-15-642.pdf.
29. NTIA, "IANA Stewardship Transition Proposal Assessment Report," June 9, 2016, https://www.ntia.gov/report/2016/iana-stewardship-transition-proposal-assessment-report.
30. Craig Timberg, "Contract Expiration to End U.S. Authority over Internet IP Addresses," *Washington Post*, September 30, 2016, https://www.washingtonpost.com/business/economy/contract-expiration-to-end-us-authority-over-internet-ip-addresses/2016/09/30/4610adbb-c039-4b92-8637-ebd15874cf12_story.html.

31. "Senator Cruz: This Internet Transition Poses Real Risks to Liberties of Americans," Office of Senator Ted Cruz, Video Link #3, September 14, 2016, https://www.cruz.senate.gov/newsroom/press-releases/2016/09/14/sen-cruz-this-internet-transition-poses-real-risks-to-liberties-of-americans.
32. U.S. Government Accountability Office (GAO), "Property Implications of Proposed Transition of U.S. Government Oversight of Key Internet Technical Functions," September 12, 2016, https://www.gao.gov/products/b-327398.
33. NTIA, "Statement of Assistant Secretary Strickling on IANA Functions Contract," October 01, 2016, https://www.ntia.gov/press-release/2016/statement-assistant-secretary-strickling-iana-functions-contract.
34. NTIA, "NTIA/ICANN Exchange of Letters," January 6, 2017, https://www.ntia.doc.gov/files/ntia/publications/ntia-icann_affirmation_of_commitments_01062017.pdf.
35. While the U.S. State Department leads and coordinates delegations to the United Nations, including the ITU, staff from agencies like NTIA, FCC, DHS, DOD, NASA, and DOJ serve on the delegations as subject matter experts, often serving as issue set lead negotiators. For issues related to Internet governance, including the domain name system, at the ITU and WSIS processes, NTIA plays that role.
36. ITU, "Resolution 102: Management of Internet domain names and addresses," Minneapolis 1998, https://www.itu.int/osg/spu/infocom/resolutions/res102.html.
37. World Summit on the Information Society, "Geneva Plan of Action—Section C6. Enabling Environment, 13b," December 12, 2003, https://www.itu.int/net/wsis/docs/geneva/official/poa.html.
38. Other stakeholders such as the technical community and academia would be explicitly called out in later WSIS related agreements.
39. WGIG, "Report of the Working Group on Internet Governance," June 2005, https://www.wgig.org/docs/WGIGREPORT.pdf.
40. NTIA, "U.S. Principles on the Internet's Domain Name and Addressing System," June 30, 2005, https://www.ntia.gov/other-publication/us-principles-internets-domain-name-and-addressing-system.

41. Associated Press, "U.S. Keeps Hold on Internet," *Wired*, July 1, 2005, https://www.wired.com/2005/07/u-s-keeps-hold-on-internet/.
42. WSIS, "Tunis Agenda for the Information Society," paragraphs 72–78, November 18, 2005, https://www.itu.int/net/wsis/docs2/tunis/off/6rev1.pdf.
43. WCIT-12: Conference Overview, ITU, accessed April 1, 2024, https://www.itu.int/en/wcit-12/Pages/overview.aspx.
44. Eli Dourado, "Behind Closed Doors at the UN attempted takeover of the Internet," *Ars Technica*, December 20, 2012, https://arstechnica.com/tech-policy/2012/12/behind-closed-doors-at-the-uns-attempted-takeover-of-the-internet/.
45. Francesca Musiani and Julie Pohle, "NETmundial: Only a Landmark Event if 'Digital Cold War' Rhetoric Abandoned," *Internet Policy Review*, Volume *3*, Issue 1, 2014, https://doi.org/10.14763/2014.1.251.
46. "NETMundial Multistakeholder Statement", April 23-24, 2014, https://netmundial.br/2014/netmundial-multistakeholder-statement/.
47. Electronic Frontier Foundation "Human Rights are Not Negotiable: Looking Back at Brazil's NETMundial," April 25, 2014, https://www.eff.org/deeplinks/2014/04/netmundial.
48. ICANN, "ICANN Submits Application to International Telecommunication Union for ITU-D Sector membership," February 28, 2019, https://www.icann.org/en/announcements/details/icann-submits-application-to-international-telecommunications-union-for-itu-d-sector-membership-28-2-2019-en.
49. United Nations Secretary General Antonio Guterres, "Our Common Agenda Policy Brief 5: A Global Digital Compact—and Open, Free and Secure Digital Future for All," May 2023, https://www.un.org/sites/un2.un.org/files/our-common-agenda-policy-brief-gobal-digi-compact-en.pdf.
50. Fiona Alexander, "Deja Vu: Is the UN Attempting to Take Over the Internet (Again)?" *Center for European Policy Analysis*, July 11, 2023, https://cepa.org/article/deja-vu-is-the-un-attempting-to-take-over-the-internet.
51. The 2023–2024 United Nations Open-Ended Working Group related to cybersecurity demonstrates this turn toward bracketed multistakeholder consultation: Nation-state delegations may veto

any non-state actor organization that wishes to be accredited to be involved in any multistakeholder consultations or involvement; further it is the nation-state members that make the decisions. See Nanette Levinson, "Inclusion Changes & Challenges at the United Nations: Reframing Emerging Cybersecurity Debates," *International Studies Association*, August 2023.

CHAPTER 6

# The Internet Protocol and Content Battles

Battles over control of digital content are central to most contemporary political and economic problems: national security and war, political censorship, intellectual property rights enforcement, foreign influence campaigns and coordinated inauthentic behavior, health disinformation, defamation, harassment, and hate speech. Often these battles are actually fought at the level of infrastructure.

On the same day as the Hamas terrorist attack against Israel on October 7, 2023, there were simultaneously online attacks targeting Israel-based websites. Cloudflare, a prominent network and content intermediary, reported that they detected and addressed significant DDoS attacks that began twelve minutes after the ground attack:

> Cloudflare systems automatically detected and mitigated DDoS attacks that targeted websites that provide critical information and alerts to civilians on rocket attacks. The initial attack peaked at 100k requests per second (rps) and lasted ten minutes. Forty-five minutes later, a second much larger attack struck and peaked at 1M rps. It lasted six minutes. Additional smaller DDoS attacks continued hitting the websites in the next hours.[1]

Cloudflare's account of the opening days and weeks of the ensuing Israel-Hamas war explained that targeted media and newspaper websites



F. M. Alexander et al., *Geopolitics at the Internet's Core*, Information Technology and Global Governance,
https://doi.org/10.1007/978-3-031-89478-7_6

accounted for more than 50% of these DDoS attacks, followed by software companies and government websites, similar to what the company observed in the aftermath of Russia's invasion of Ukraine.[2]

Such distributed denial of service attacks, involving billions and billions of online requests designed to incapacitate a target, often specifically exploit the IP ecosystem. These techniques, some detailed in Chapter 7, include HTTPS floods, TCP SYN-ACK floods, IPv4 UDP floods, and IPv4 ICMP floods, among others.

Network infrastructure and protocols such as IP might seem, on their face, far removed from the content-related issues playing out in social media platforms and other information intermediaries. In policy and practice, this is not correct. From the Domain Name System to BGP, deeper layers of Internet infrastructure are increasingly co-opted for, and even central to, the practice of blocking or otherwise disrupting content.

Some content-control battles involve unlawful material, but a complication for the private institutions that operate or manage cross-border technologies is that laws about what information is legal vary significantly across the world. One country's illegal hate speech is another country's protected speech. Some countries have *lese-majeste* laws criminalizing speech insulting a monarch. Still other countries have laws censoring certain types of political speech. The spectrum of illegal content online includes defamation, intellectual property rights infringement, disinformation, cyberbullying, harassment, incitement to violence, threats, and terrorist speech. Governments, in themselves, are not usually able to take down this information and thus have long turned to companies to enforce relevant laws.

Digital intermediaries also block information that is legal but that violates their own corporate policies and terms of service. These companies might, for example, delete information or sometimes entire accounts that violate their acceptable use policies on obscenity or incivility. The massive volume of content moderation that happens in practice far exceeds the capacity of human moderation, and thus often depends upon automated systems and artificial intelligence.

Regardless of the legal status of content, and regardless of whether content moderation decisions originate with the state or industry, the process and act of blocking information largely falls to the private-sector intermediaries that own and operate the infrastructure and therefore are capable of removing, blocking, or otherwise moderating content. Content hosting providers, web hosting companies, app intermediaries, security intermediaries, network operators, DNS resolution providers, financial transaction providers, and many other types of Internet intermediaries beyond social media platforms collectively serve as a powerful and problematic tool for blocking or redirecting content.

What does the IP ecosystem have to do with any of this? This chapter first addresses the broader context of how national security, intellectual property rights enforcement, law enforcement, censorship, and almost every other content-control concern has moved "down the stack" of technical architecture into infrastructure intermediation of all types. It then describes real-world cases of entanglements between IP and content control: DNS redirection for intellectual property rights enforcement; co-opting IP-related technologies for political censorship and kill-switch attempts; and IP infrastructure providers' involvement in government's human life and safety efforts. In doing so, the chapter lays out both the architectural points of control where content moderation occurs and the institutions of IP address governance—such as registrars, registries, network operators, ICANN, and DNS resolution providers—that are increasingly targeted as an entry point to attempt to exert content control.

What does it mean that the Internet Protocol ecosystem—a technical and institutional architecture never designed for content control, is now viewed and used by some as an intervention carrying out censorship and other forms of content blocking? The chapter concludes with an exploration of the implications of this turn to infrastructure for content control for the stability of Internet technical architecture and governance.

## The Turn to Infrastructure for Content Control

Private digital intermediaries, most visibly social media platforms, routinely remove content that is completely lawful but that violates the terms of service and acceptable use policies of these companies. For example, in the United States, social media companies remove information that is protected by the First Amendment of the Constitution, meaning the U.S. government cannot act, but which these companies deem as unacceptable for violating their terms of service. For example, Meta's community standards include a prohibition on describing "women as household objects or property or objects in general," speech that is legal but which the company prohibits under its standards.[3]

In early 2022, Meta removed from its Facebook platform the profile and account of Konfederacjia, a Polish far-right party, for spreading what the company believed constituted, under its standards, misinformation about COVID-19 but was described by the Polish government as exercise of freedom of speech by a "legally operating political party."[4] The content removal transparency reports companies like Google have published over the years also demonstrate that companies sometimes reject government requests to take down accounts or block content. Whether choosing to remove legal content, complying with government censorship requests, or pushing back against government requests to remove content, the contemporary era is marked by the privatization of governance in content moderation.

Questions about blocking, redirecting, or otherwise moderating content exist in a broader context in which deep layers of infrastructure and infrastructure intermediaries are increasingly co-opted.[5] Information intermediaries and infrastructure intermediaries alike are points of possible interception and potential moderation tools for all information in the digital public sphere.

The term "information intermediary" typically brings to mind social media platforms, content aggregation sites, search engines, generative AI platforms, and other technologies that serve as an immediate interface between content and humans. But intermediaries "down the stack" and further removed from human users create equally, if not more powerful mediation points for content control. Some of these include: application intermediaries such as the Apple app store; advertising systems; transactional intermediaries; content distribution networks; financial intermediaries; trust infrastructures; and hosting services. Acting as information intermediaries, Google and other companies offering search engines acknowledge that copyright removal requests are one of many variables factored into algorithmic ordering, such as not returning links to websites alleged to violate copyright or at least demoting these links in the search engine results.[6]

The turn to infrastructure in content control, including via financial intermediaries, has a well-established history. One notable example dates back to 2010 when WikiLeaks began releasing sensitive U.S. diplomatic cables into the public domain. In this so-called Cablegate incident, PayPal and other financial intermediaries made private decisions to disable the flow of funding to WikiLeaks for violating the company's acceptable use policy (Fig. 6.1).[7]

Further complicating the Cablegate example, EveryDNS, the DNS resolution service provider used by WikiLeaks decided to terminate their

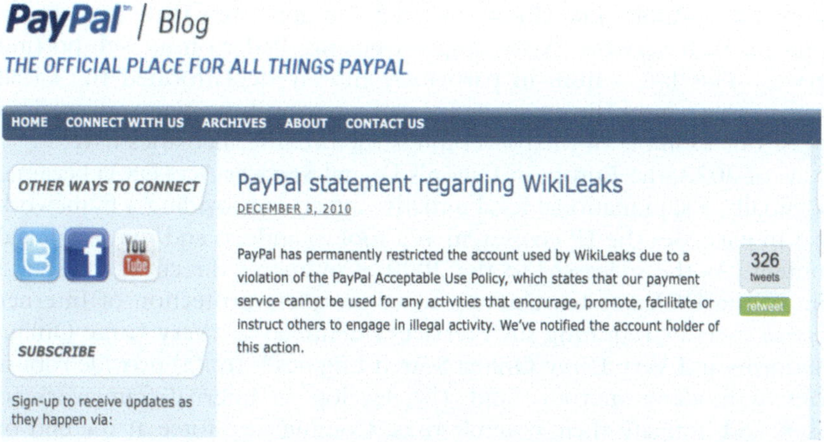


**Fig. 6.1** Screenshot of PayPal's 2010 announcement, via Internet Aarchive

services. As a result, the domain name used by WikiLeaks could no longer be reached. And while a sophisticated Internet user could still access the content by typing in the IP address 88.80.13.160 in the address bar, for the average user this content was unavailable until WikiLeaks established a new presence at wikileaks.ch.

Content control by infrastructural intermediaries can be more extensive in impact than moderation by content intermediaries. Social media company censorship and moderation—however necessary or controversial—can take a scalpel to each problem and remove a single post, a thread, or an account. Transactional intermediaries have the capacity to remove entire sites, platforms, or repositories.

A graphic example of this turn to infrastructure to control content followed the January 6, 2021 insurgency into the U.S. Capitol to prevent the U.S. Congress from their procedural count of electoral votes to certify the 2020 presidential election. Social media companies such as Facebook, Twitter, and YouTube removed specific information and accounts related to this event while Parler, a social media platform popular among far-right users, allowed a more unmoderated flow of political information, including the type of information other platforms removed for violating their terms of service related to the incitement of violence and hate speech. Parler was then essentially deplatformed from the Internet in many ways. Apple and Google deleted the app from their app stores. Amazon Web Services (AWS) stopped hosting Parler on its web hosting service. This last action, in particular, entirely deplatformed the social media service until the company located a new web hosting service. This is just one example of the power infrastructure intermediaries have.

As of 2023, the European Union's Digital Services Act (DSA) became, essentially, a supranational legal initiative aimed at providing a framework that in part uses the IP ecosystem as a tool to address and remove illegal content. As the successor to the 2000 eCommerce directive, the stated aim of the DSA was to achieve a more complete protection of Internet service users by requiring such services (identified as "Very Large Online Platforms and Very Large Online Search Engines") to: (a) provide robust content moderation tools; and, (b) develop an internal framework to assess and mitigate their systemic risks. Coming into force at the end of August 2023, the DSA has impacted a number of designated services, with companies starting to engage in risk assessment exercises and mitigation responses in regard to, for example, the promulgation of unlawful content through these services. Each European Union Member State would also be required to designate an independent "Digital Services Coordinator" with independent authority for insuring DSA compliance within their region.[8]

With the backdrop of Russia's invasion of Ukraine in 2022 and Hamas' terrorist attacks in Israel in 2023, the European Commission published a set of Recommendations on October 18, 2023 to address online illegal content. In presenting the Recommendation, EC president Ursula von der Leyen referred to a "*Hamas' terrorist attack [that has] led to an online assault of heinous, illegal content promoting hatred and terror,*" making clear that the regulatory content moderation concern was focused on terrorist organizations. The Recommendation prompted Member States to move ahead with the DSA well in advance of the February 2024 deadline, stating that "Where extraordinary circumstances—such as an international armed conflict or terror attacks—justify it, the Commission encourages Very Large Online Platforms and Very Large Online Search Engines to draw up incident protocols relevant to the specific incident."[9]

The free flow of information over the Internet might have been an ideal of many foundational technologies from the World Wide Web to TCP/IP. It still is an aspirational ideal. But Internet usage and governance has evolved, in practice, to a much more complicated and ideologically malleable ecosystem that is entangled with more concealed layers of infrastructure further removed from users. The IP ecosystem is no exception. While largely outside of public view and perhaps even further down the infrastructure stack, it too has been dragged into the content-control enterprise.

## Internet Protocol and Intellectual Property Rights

What does the DNS have to do with the World Cup of football/soccer? In December of 2022, special agents within the U.S. Department of Homeland Security ordered the seizure of 55 Internet domain names alleged to be violating copyright law by illegally streaming live World Cup games.[10] The normal DNS mechanisms that would point to these websites instead redirected viewers to a government message that the sites have been seized for copyright infringement.

The Domain Name System was never designed to be a content-control mechanism, but its co-opting for this reason has become a routine matter. The types of infringing sites blocked via the DNS span the spectrum of intellectual property rights (IPR) concerns. Some sites violate copyright by selling pirated movies or illegally sharing music. Other targeted sites unlawfully sell counterfeit pharmaceutical products protected by patents. Still others violate trademark protections, such as selling counterfeit luxury products.

Intellectual property rights issues also exist inside infrastructures of Internet Protocol governance themselves. Some technical standards are embedded with royalty-bearing patents. Search engine algorithms that order the information sphere are protected by trade secrecy laws. Conflicts over trademark rights arise over competing claims to a domain name, such as references to trademarked terms. Within generic top-level domains, disputes are adjudicated through a process known as the Uniform Domain Name Dispute Resolution Policy, or UDPR. Adjudication processes under the UDPR, agreed to by all ICANN-accredited registrars, are handled by one of many ICANN-approved dispute-resolution service providers, such as the World Intellectual Property Organization (WIPO).

In terms of protecting the intellectual property rights around content that flows over the Internet, the global regulatory architecture is very clear, even if sometimes socially contested. The ease and minimal cost of replicating and sharing intellectual property has made media piracy and other forms of infringement a significant public policy area in Internet governance. At the international level, the nations that are members of the World Trade Organization (WTO) are party to a multilateral agreement on intellectual property known as the Trade-Related Aspects of Intellectual Property Rights (TRIPS) agreement. At the domestic level, many nations have strong laws addressing online infringement, such as the Digital Millennium Copyright Act (DMCA) in the United States.

Approaches that involve directly bringing lawsuits or criminal charges against individuals who illegally download content have been problematic for the media companies and artists whose work has been infringed. Going after a teenager for accessing music or a mother for using a Prince song in a home video of their baby dancing has been both reputationally damaging and ineffective in stopping copyright violations.[11]

Infrastructure-based content protection measures have quickly become an alternative to targeting individuals, such as terminating the Internet access associated with people who repeatedly download or share copyrighted material from the Internet. IP addresses are often at the center of these mechanisms for blocking access to or carrying out law enforcement functions around intellectual property rights violations, especially via Internet Service Providers (ISPs). Content owners or other third parties notify ISPs of an IP address associated with a person alleged to have violated intellectual property rights. ISPs are usually able to determine the identity of the alleged copyright infringer by matching their records to the IP address and date and time information they receive from the third party.

Once a certain number of repeat violations are alleged to occur, the service provider will take some action, including possibly terminating an account. Over the years, these approaches, implemented in various parts of the Western world,[12] have been referred to as "graduated response" or "three-strikes laws" or, in the United States, "DMCA Repeat Infringer Policies." For example, Comcast's DMCA Repeat Infringer Policy for its Xfinity Internet access service states that: "Triggering steps under this policy may result in the following: a form of communication that requires you to log in to your account or call us; a temporary suspension of, or other interim measures applied to, your service; or the termination of you Xfinity Internet service as well as your other Xfinity services (but not Xfinity Mobile)."[13]

Similar copyright removal requests are made to other intermediaries, such as search engines, which remove or demote allegedly infringing sites based on URL. Content industries and the holders of patents, copyrights, trademarks, and trade secrets have shifted from targeting individuals to co-opting infrastructure to block access or take down infringing material.[14] A diverse array of Internet intermediaries intervene to block websites and other repositories that infringe upon intellectual property rights. Because these are illegal activities, and because of requirements under law, such as the DMCA in the United States, intermediaries take down, demote, or block this information. These intermediaries include Internet Service Providers, search engines, social media platforms, content hosting sites, and advertising, financial, and transactional intermediaries of all types.

The DNS and the institutions that administer the DNS have similarly landed in the center of intellectual property rights battles. Similar to blocking or demotion in a search engine, co-opting the DNS does not involve taking down actual content on a website. Instead, the content only appears to the user to be blocked because the domain name of the page or website has been seized or because a registry has redirected the query to another site, such as the law enforcement page shown in Fig. 6.2. Sometimes both the domain name seizure and redirection to a law enforcement site are simultaneously carried out, as in the case of the World Cup domain name seizures discussed earlier.

The process of a government using DNS-based IPR enforcement is multifaceted, but not a technically or legally difficult process, if the domain name registration or DNS resolution occurs in a company within the respective country's borders. The domain name can be transferred to the government, or simply forfeited. Or, the DNS query process itself can provide redirection from the site.

The process of DNS-based IPR enforcement becomes much more complicated when doing so would require a local DNS modification that would conflict with the Internet's universal name and number space. When the domain name of a targeted website is registered with a registrar in another country, or when the registry overseeing the domain is located in another country, this creates a jurisdictional challenge for governments seeking to block access to intellectual property infringing websites. Techniques that alter the mapping of names into numbers locally can block access to these sites but also create a complicated technical scenario in which the DNS becomes fragmented and possibly insecure.

**Fig. 6.2** Author screenshot of a U.S. Homeland security domain name seizure notification

A significant and widespread Internet boycott in December of 2011 and January of 2012 was entangled with DNS-based intellectual property concerns over DNS fragmentation. This boycott was extensive and striking:

> Thousands of web sites went dark or altered their opening screens to protest antipiracy legislation moving through the U.S. Congress. Wikipedia blacked out its popular English-language site for twenty-four hours, instead displaying a banner reading "Imagine a World without Free Knowledge." Reddit and thousands of other popular sites blocked access to their content. Google blacked out its famous doodle logo on its opening search screen. Internet advocacy efforts cumulatively gathered more than ten million petition signatures, and Congress was inundated with phone calls. This historic protest and mass Internet boycott was a response to two proposed bills, the Stop Online Piracy Act (SOPA) and the Preventing

Real Threats to Economic Creativity and Theft of Intellectual Property Act (PROTECT IP ACT, or PIPA).[15]

This antipiracy legislation had broad bipartisan support in the U.S. Congress, so what was it that prompted this boycott? Concerns included the proposed heightened criminal penalties for illegally downloading movies, possible intermediary liability, and increased law enforcement demands for search engines, network operators, and financial and advertising intermediaries to block or suspend services to infringing websites.

The legislation particularly alarmed the Internet's core engineering community, who issued a letter warning Congress that the proposed legislation would "risk fragmenting the Internet's Domain Name System" and "seriously harm the credibility of the United States in its role as a steward of key Internet infrastructure."[16] Engineers had also raised concerns about technical measures that might interfere with cybersecurity protections, and especially Domain Name System Security Extensions (DNSSEC).[17]

The technical concern involved the website redirection provisions of the bill requiring local service providers to block and redirect traffic to infringing websites by altering the authoritative record of how to universally resolve names into numbers. Ultimately, the Obama Administration issued a statement opposing the bills as drafted in part due to concerns about disrupting the underlying architecture of the Internet and undermining Administration priorities such as the deployment of DNSSEC: "Proposed laws must not tamper with the technical architecture of the Internet through manipulation of the Domain Name System (DNS), a foundation of Internet security."[18]

Both bills failed, in part because the technical concerns changed the framing from antipiracy to "don't break the Internet." This one legislative episode helps to highlight basic features of Internet Protocol-related governance: the interest in turning to infrastructure for content control; the multistakeholder nature of key debates; tensions between public policy objectives and how technical systems work in practice; and the balance among conflicting values such as—in the case of SOPA/PIPA—intellectual property rights versus speech, innovation, and technical stability.

## The IP Ecosystem and Political Kill Switches

IP has long been at the center of a number of strategies of filtering and censorship, and the examples are numerous: IP addresses can serve as the identity infrastructure (coupled with other information, such as that provided by an Internet Service Provider) to enable blocking of content and people; during DNS hijacking, a fake (spoofed) IP address can be returned instead of the genuine one in order to block access to a website or other online resource; IP filtering is, and has long been, a primary firewall mechanism for shielding a network from unwanted traffic and for filtering (blocking) content, for a variety of reasons; deep packet inspection (DPI) mechanisms in basic Internet switches is used not only to scrutinize the content of a packet for cybersecurity practices and routine network management, but also to co-opt for surveillance purposes.

The IP ecosystem is key to understanding government Internet shutdowns and politically motivated content-control attempts. There are key differences among countries' efforts, due to both countries' network infrastructures and, of course, the spectrum of autocratic to democratic information policy approaches. For example, in 2020, it took the Iranian government more than 24 hours to implement its Internet shutdown, due to the complexity of its infrastructure.[19] Yet, some countries have only several points of infrastructure concentration because of limited international gateways from Internet Service Providers, few or no IXPs within their borders, or even concentrated points of ingress and egress due to undersea cable infrastructure.[20] These concentration points are natural choke points for political ordering.

This architecture of connections, the degree of government control of these architectures, and the degree of a government's power over the private sector all play roles in shaping Internet shutdown approaches and typologies. Governments can implement either total Internet shutdowns (as in the case of India's complete shutdown of the Internet in the Kashmir region for more than 150 days[21]) or more targeted content-control efforts, impacting the human rights, livelihoods, and health of those living in a country or region. Often, the more extensive disruptions are carried out by ordering or asking an Internet Service Provider (ISP) to shut down service entirely, such as withdrawing its BGP-advertised IP routes accessible via its network. In this scenario, the IP addresses normally reachable via that ISP disappear from routing tables. The implementation of these shutdowns can be total or targeted. The Ethiopian government shutdowns in the Tigray region for over two years, and its more recent shutdowns in the Amhara region,[22] are examples of this approach.

Russia's targeted Internet shutdowns in occupied parts of Ukraine, as well as its rerouting of Internet traffic through a Russian state-controlled telecommunications company, combines this shutdown approach with real-world human coercion and threats. Russian soldiers in 2022 reportedly invaded ISP offices in Kherson, Ukraine, at gunpoint force to shutdown or take over these Ukrainian ISPs and route the Internet traffic through Russian networks.[23] Similarly, Russian soldiers in Ukraine physically destroyed equipment such as cell towers, further limiting access to free information and information flow. Journalistic accounts of this phenomenon described how a Russian missile struck down Kyiv's TV tower.[24] During this time, Russian forces damaged or destroyed approximately 15% of Ukraine's Internet infrastructure,[25] illustrating a very physical and material component of cyber warfare.

In addition to these physical disruptions of Ukraine's network infrastructure, Russia concurrently adopted IP-based content-control approaches, including DDoS attacks on Ukrainian banking and government websites.[26]

The so-called Great Firewall of China is perhaps most emblematic of IP-based content-control techniques, such as employing the DNS via DNS poisoning or DNS hijacking. The Chinese government employs DNS filtering of politically forbidden keywords to return invalid IP addresses for certain websites, essentially blocking them.[27] The government uses an array of techniques that identify the source of a transmission or the use of virtual private networks, as well as man-in-the-middle attacks in which the government can issue self-signed SSL certificates to capture transmissions and enact surveillance while remaining undetected.[28] Techniques of active probing investigate any outbound requests, especially to servers outside of China. If this probe identifies the request as being part of a prohibited network such as a specific VPN, it then cancels the request and blocks the transmission via IP.

Taken together, these techniques enable the Chinese government to focus mainly on users inside China accessing content or sites, but also users from outside of the country who seek to investigate critical issues within China, in particular regarding digital rights.[29]

These examples of politically motivated disruptions help to demonstrate the power of the Internet Protocol ecosystem to block content, shutdown access, and otherwise disrupt communication amid complex, social, geographic, economic, and political contexts.

## The IP Ecosystem and Health and Safety of Life

With the Internet integrated into every facet of modern life, it is no surprise that the IP ecosystem has been called upon to aid in government efforts related to citizen safety. As the world grappled with the COVID-19 pandemic, people turned to the Internet for answers and information on how best to treat infections. Unfortunately, malicious actors took advantage of this and created websites purporting to represent biotech companies developing COVID treatments when in fact they were actors using that pretext to collect individuals' personal information.[30] Seeking to illegally profit from the pandemic, these malicious actors would then take that information and use it for fraudulent purposes, including phishing, pharming, and malware, and in one case to sell counterfeit vaccines.

To address these human life and safety concerns, the U.S. Attorney's Office for the District of Maryland took DNS-based action in seizing the domain names in question and redirected them to accurate and reliable COVID-19 information. This is just one of many examples where governments take direct action through elements of the IP ecosystem to address real-world human safety issues.

Another approach is through the encouragement of trusted notifier programs. A trusted notifier program refers to a system whereby a relationship, formal or informal, is established where one party, typically based on an agreed set of criteria, informs the second party of bad behavior, with the expectation that the second party takes appropriate action to address the concern. One of the earliest efforts to elaborate the mechanics of this concept was the Internet and Jurisdiction Policy Network (I&J). Focused on national jurisdictional challenges around the borderless Internet, the group has, among other things, produced a set of norms, criteria, and mechanisms to guide when it might be appropriate to use the DNS layer to address abuse and who should make those decisions.[31]

An early implementation of a DNS trusted notifier program came from NTIA when in 2019 it announced it would work with the U.S. Food and Drug Administration (FDA) and three registry operators (Verisign for.com, Public Interest Registry for.org, and Neustar for.us) in a 120-day pilot program to combat illegal online opioid sales.[32] The effort was discrete in scope, grounded in the FDA's legal authority to enforce U.S. laws, and based on an existing FDA program. When a website met two conditions—offered opioids deemed illegal for sale in the United States and sold them online to U.S. consumers—the FDA had been sending warning letters to the website operators, but getting little or no reaction.

Under the NTIA-facilitated pilot, the FDA began copying the relevant registry operator on their notification letters. The FDA serving as the trusted notifier began alerting the registry that illegal actions were happening in their top-level domain. If the website operator did not address the issue within the timeframes agreed by the registries and the FDA, the relevant registry would review the FDA's notification and assess whether to take further voluntary action. This action could be voluntarily locking the domain, deleting the domain, or placing the domain on hold, as appropriate. The pilot program resulted in close to 30 websites being disabled, and thus reducing the availability of illegal opioids online in the United States, and presumably saving lives.[33] Given the success of the effort, all parties agreed to continue the illegal online opioid sale trusted notifier program.

These examples illustrate how targeted, limited, and proportional use of the Internet Protocol system can be a component of government's strategies related to health and safety.

## Implications of IP as a Content-Control Proxy

The turn to the IP ecosystem for content-control and moderation purposes reveals five broad themes. First is the role of private actors—social media companies, platforms, and the technical actors that provide them with infrastructural support—in setting a number of policies and data collection and retention practices, that de facto define end users' privacy and agency on the Internet. In addition to these rules, which can overlap with national and regional regulations or be in conflict with them, private companies can be key actors in international political controversies by acting on an ad hoc basis. As we have seen with the Wikileaks/EveryDNS case, the decision by the company that was providing Wikileaks with DNS resolution services to stop providing such services eventually led to a temporary "vanishing" of Wikileaks from the Internet from the end user's standpoint.

Infrastructure-based content control also highlights the complexities related to cross-border jurisdiction. Indeed, law enforcement across borders is often made more challenging by different layers of legal instruments, ranging from national laws to international conventions and treaties. The Internet infrastructure, including the core protocols such as IP, are by nature "beyond borders" and can thus be used as tools for action, including in content control, for which legal instruments are unfit. The SOPA/PIPA example, is a case in point, as infringing sites were using domains controlled by actors headquartered outside of the United States, a "problem" the draft legislation proposed to solve by ordering DNS blocking of these sites irrespective of geographic location.

Third, infrastructure-based content control speaks to the broader issue that IP, as a notable "control point" of the Internet, is among the technologies where tensions between principles and practice can be sharp. These range from values such as freedom of expression, openness and participation to data collection, retention, and aggregation. This can eventually lead, at best, to opportunistic business models trading the gratuity of online services for massive data treatment possibilities, leading to profiling and personalization—and at worst, to repression, surveillance, and censorship.

There are also risks that tampering with infrastructure can generate for the broader Internet ecosystem. Using IP filtering, DNS redirection, or other infrastructure-based mechanisms can result in over blocking and other forms of collateral damage. When an Internet Service Provider terminates a home account, for example, this disconnects not only the infringing party (often a teenager) but other siblings accessing information online, parents using broadband access to work from home, and in fact, the entire household. When a website or entire domain name is redirected, filtered, suspended, or seized because it contains pirated media, counterfeit goods, or at the request of law enforcement, access to legitimate content that might be available on that site or in that domain can be impacted.

Finally, another—and linked—question is that of the efficacy of those measures. Disproportional remedies can be ineffective or short lived as the offending content can still be accessed by looking directly for the associated IP address or when the perpetrators shift or hop to a new domain name. More broadly, circumvention measures exist that allow people to work around IP-ecosystem-based filtering, such as using alternative DNS services, employing virtual private networks that mask IP addresses, or using proxy servers.

## Notes

1. Omer Yoachimik and Jorge Pacheco, "Cyber Attacks in the Israel-Hamas War," Cloudflare, The Cloudflare Blog, October 23, 2023. https://blog.cloudflare.com/cyber-attacks-in-the-israel-hamas-war/.
2. Ibid.
3. Meta Hate Speech Policy, https://transparency.fb.com/policies/community-standards/hate-speech/, accessed on September 12, 2023.
4. See, for example, Euronews, "Polish far-right party banned from Facebook over alleged COVID-19 disinformation," January 2022, https://www.euronews.com/2022/01/06/polish-far-right-party-banned-from-facebook-over-alleged-covid-disinformation.
5. See Francesca Musiani, et al., *The Turn to Infrastructure in Internet Governance,* Palgrave Macmillan, 2015 for an in-depth discussion of this phenomenon.
6. See Google's Transparency Report Help on Content Removal issues, https://support.google.com/transparencyreport?hl=en#topic=7295796.
7. PayPal Blog, "Paypal Statement Regarding Wikileaks," December 12, 2010, https://www.thepaypalblog.com/2010/12/paypal-statement-regarding-wikileaks/.
8. See European Union, "Questions and Answers on the Digital Services Act," February 22, 2024, https://ec.europaeu/commission/presscorner/detail/en/QANDA_20_2348.
9. See European Union, "Commission recommends Member States to fast-track DSA governance to enhance response to illegal online content," October 17, 2023, https://ec.europa.eu/commission/presscorner/detail/en/ip_23_5122.
10. ICE Press Release, "HSI Baltimore Seizes 55 Websites that Violated Copyrights by Illegally Live Streaming World Cup Matches," December 12, 2022, https://www.ice.gov/news/releases/hsi-baltimore-seizes-55-websites-violated-copyrights-illegally-live-streaming-world.

11. See, e.g., Sudin Thanawala, "YouTube Video of Baby Dancing to Prince Track Sparks Trial over Copyright," *Associated Press*, October 15, 2015, https://www.cbc.ca/news/entertainment/youtube-video-of-baby-dancing-to-prince-track-sparks-trial-over-copyright-1.3228580.
12. For example, France attempted to set up a three-strikes system via the "HADOPI" law, ultimately withdrawn in 2013 after substantial controversy, very limited practical impact and heavy financial loss. See "France drops controversial 'Hadopi law' after spending millions," *The Guardian*, July 9, 2013, https://www.theguardian.com/technology/2013/jul/09/france-hadopi-law-anti-piracy.
13. See https://www.xfinity.com/support/articles/comcast-dmca-compliance-policy, accessed October 3, 2023.
14. See Francesca Musiani, et al., *The Turn to Infrastructure in Internet Governance,* Palgrave Macmillan, 2015 for an in-depth discussion.
15. Laura DeNardis. *The Global War for Internet Governance.* New Haven: Yale University Press, 2014, pp. 2–3.
16. The Electronic Frontier Foundation "An Open Letter from Internet Engineers to the US Congress," December 15, 2011, https://www.eff.org/deeplinks/2011/12/internet-inventors-warn-against-sopa-and-pipa.
17. Steve Crocker et al., "Security and Other Technical Concerns Raised by the DNS Filtering Requirements in the PROTECT IP Bill," May 2011, Center for Democracy and Technology, https://www.cdt.org/wp-content/uploads/pdfs/Security-Concerns-DNS-Filtering-PIPA.pdf.
18. White House, "Obama Administration Responds to We the People Petitions on SOPA and Online Piracy," January 14, 2022, https://obamawhitehouse.archives.gov/blog/2012/01/14/Obama-administration-responds-we-people-petitions-sopa-and-online-piracy.
19. Eleanor Marchant and Nichole Stremlau, "Internet Shutdowns in Africa: The Changing Landscape of Internet Shutdowns in Africa—Introduction," *International Journal of Communication*, Volume 14, 2020.
20. Justin Sherman, "Cyber Defense Across The Ocean Floor:The Geopolitics of Submarine Cable Security," *Atlantic Council*, September 2021.
21. Sankalp Phartiyal and Fayaz Bukhari, "India's Top Court Says Indefinite Kashmir Internet Shutdown Is Illegal," *Reuters*, 2023.

22. Access Now, "An Overview of Global Internet Shutdowns," May 19, 2023, https://www.accessnow.org/internet-shutdowns-2023/.
23. New York Times, "How Russia Took over Ukraine's Internet in Occupied Territories," August 9, 2022, https://www.nytimes.com/interactive/2022/08/09/technology/ukraine-internet-russia-censorship.html.
24. BBC, "Ukraine conflict: Kyiv TV tower struck by Russian missile," March 1, 2022, https://www.bbc.com/news/av/world-europe-60579847.
25. Al Jazeera, Russia Downed Satellite Network in Ukraine: Western Officials," May 10, 2022, https://www.aljazeera.com/news/2022/5/10/russia-behind-cyberattack-against-internet-network-in-ukraine.
26. NPR, "Ukraine Says Government Websites and Banks Were Hit with Denial of Service Attack," February 15, 2022, https://www.npr.org/2022/02/15/1080876311/ukraine-hack-denial-of-service-attack-defense.
27. Mingshi Wu et al., "How the Great Firewall of China Detects and Blocks Fully Encrypted Traffic," 32nd USENIX Security Symposium, USENIX Security 23, August, 2023, pp. 2653-2670.
28. Josh Chin and Liza Lin, "Surveillance State: Inside China's Quest to Launch a New Era of Social Control," *The British Journal of Criminology*, Volume 63, Issue 2, March 2023, pp. 534–536; see also Dimitrios Vagianos and Glykeria Stavrou, "Surveillance Infrastructure and Artificial Intelligence Challenging Democracy and Human Rights in China," *The Cyprus Journal of Sciences*, Volume 20, May 22, 2023.
29. Stephanie Yang, "As China Shuts out the World, Internet Access from Abroad Gets Harder Too," *Los Angeles Times*, June 23, 2022, https://www.latimes.com/world-nation/story/2022-06-23/china-great-firewall-foreign-domestic-virtual-censorship.
30. HSI investigation results in seizure of three domain names purporting to be biotechnology company websites with COVID-19 treatments, April 7, 2021, https://www.ice.gov/news/releases/hsi-investigation-results-seizure-3-domain-names-purporting-be-biotechnology-company#:~:text=Homeland%20Security%20Investigations%20and%20the,Cyber%20Crimes%20Center%20(C3)%20during

31. See Internet & Jurisdiction Policy Network, Domains & Jurisdiction Program, "Operational Approaches Norms, Criteria and Mechanisms," https://www.internetjurisdiction.net/uploads/pdfs/Papers/Domains-Jurisdiction-Program-Operational-Approaches.pdf.
32. See NTIA, "Supporting the President's Call to Action Against Opioid Abuse," April 2, 2019, https://www.ntia.gov/blog/supporting-president-s-call-action-against-opioid-abuse.
33. See US Food and Drug Administration, "FDA In Brief: FDA Continues Efforts to Curb Illegal Availability of Unapproved Opioids Online," February 1, 2021, https://www.fda.gov/news-events/fda-brief/fda-brief-fda-continues-efforts-curb-illegal-availability-unapproved-opioids-online.

CHAPTER 7

# Internet Protocol Security Entanglements with Geopolitics

The Internet runs on trust. Trust between private networks that conjoin to form the global Internet. Trust in the IP addresses advertised between adjacent networks via Border Gateway Protocol. Trust in the queries returned from the DNS and in the third-party institutions that authenticate websites. And trust in the IP addresses themselves. Is the address authentic or is it being "spoofed" for some malign purpose? Are requests legitimate or part of a DDoS campaign? Are the queries returned authentic or are they designed to redirect someone to an inauthentic site? Much can go wrong when this trust is broken.

Many cybersecurity problems affecting the IP ecosystem are accidents but some are also intentional attacks that exploit the centrality and ubiquity of IP to cause disruption or deception. Some of the most malicious and disruptive attacks on the Internet—sometimes politically motivated—have involved Distributed Denial of Service (DDoS) attacks. DDoS attacks incapacitate a target by flooding it with so many requests that it becomes unavailable for legitimate requests. This approach is "distributed" because it does not originate from a single source but rather from thousands (or more) of unwitting computing devices whose owners are unaware that the devices have been hijacked and implanted with malicious code designed to attack the target with a coordinated flood of requests.



F. M. Alexander et al., *Geopolitics at the Internet's Core*, Information Technology and Global Governance,
https://doi.org/10.1007/978-3-031-89478-7_7

Throughout the years, coordinated DDoS attacks have targeted the DNS itself. On October 21, 2002, a denial of service attack lasting one hour targeted all of the DNS root servers in operation at the time.[1] The assault on the Internet's core infrastructure attracted considerable attention and, since then, the DNS has become more distributed and engineered to achieve site mirroring, load balancing, and replication.

The infamous Mirai botnet and other DDoS attacks exemplify the ongoing entanglements between geopolitics, the Internet's core infrastructure, and cybersecurity. On its surface, the Mirai botnet is a story about disruption of the public-facing websites of Netflix, Twitter, Reddit, and other popular sites. It is also a story about the vulnerability of Internet of Things (IoT) devices to being hijacked and unwittingly used to carry out attacks. The Mirai botnet attack exploited security vulnerabilities in millions of home IoT devices, implanting malicious code that hijacked these devices to flood the attack's targets with so many requests that the targets became inaccessible to those legitimately trying to access them. Any one of these attack characteristics is alarming—the exploitation of vulnerability in the IoT; the ease of carrying out DDoS attacks; or the fact that such major sites were disrupted.

There is a more striking characteristic of the Mirai botnet. This DDoS attack succeeded because it targeted the DNS rather than bombarding the targeted sites directly. More specifically, the attack targeted Dyn, a company that provided DNS resolution services translating domain names into IP addresses, or resolving queries for the affected domain names. This "turn to infrastructure" to exert control or carry out an attack has a long history.[2] As Chapter 6 described, the DNS has been commandeered for political censorship, domain name seizures for intellectual property rights enforcement, and other content-control objectives. It is also used to disrupt communications.

Three young Americans pled guilty to violating the U.S. Computer Fraud and Abuse Act (CFAA) for posting on a criminal forum the Mirai source code used to carry out this disruptive DDoS attack. Some news reports at the time claimed that the young men had created the code to gain an advantage in the video game Minecraft. Almost two decades earlier, a high-profile DDoS attack that affected prominent public-facing websites, including Yahoo!, CNN, Amazon, and the online stock trading site eBay, also involved a young hacker.[3] A Canadian teenager known as "Mafiaboy" pled guilty to the attack and acknowledged that he was able to carry this out using openly and freely available DDoS tools.[4] It is unlikely that the Mirai botnet or the 2000 "Mafiaboy" attack were politically motivated, but often these attacks are.

High-profile, politically motivated DDoS attacks caused significant disruption in Estonia in 2008.[5] Iranian government web sites and other official sites were the target of DDoS attacks after the 2009 election of Mahmoud Ahmadinejad. In the case of Estonia, the attacks disrupted government services, financial services, and some media over a period of three weeks. These DDoS attacks, as well as in-person protests by Russian minorities in Estonia, followed Estonian officials' relocation of a World War II era statue of a Soviet soldier.

Sometimes, DDoS attacks originate from appropriating valid IP addresses (i.e., network prefixes), as in the case of the Mirai botnet, addresses associated with IoT devices. Other types of attack use IP spoofing, the use of forged source addresses. IP spoofing and similar attacks have served to perpetrate fraud, spread misinformation, and disrupt critical communication networks.

The Internet's trust-based routing and interconnection infrastructures have faced similar attacks, whether for economic or political reasons. For example, in April 2018, hackers stole roughly $150,000 in cryptocurrency from users of MyEthernetWallet cryptocurrency wallet by exploiting a BGP routing weakness.[6] Turning to an example with more explicit political import, in December 2017, traffic for a number of prominent American tech companies, including Apple, Facebook, Google, Microsoft, and Twitch, was routed through a Russian ISP under circumstances that, while not entirely explained, were characterized by researchers as "suspicious and intentional."[7]

In the early days of the Internet's development, and certainly during the development of its predecessor network, ARPANET, there was an underlying assumption of familiarity and trust among people and institutions who knew each other. Vint Cerf and Steve Crocker, two Internet pioneers, have pointed out that they were all friends then, working on the early Internet.[8] Trust was assumed. Trust existed then, among people, among ARPANET nodes, among network operators, and in the systems that tracked and resolved names and numbers. As the Internet commercialized and globalized, these inherent trust relationships evolved into technical, rather than human, trust architectures, sometimes successfully and other times problematically. But this evolution from trust among people to trust among systems is a reminder that cybersecurity architectures and trust architectures intersect in complex ways.

The relationship between trust and security as being at the core of today's Internet is already outlined in several works in the existing literature.[9] Many of them point out that, while there is often a conflation between "digital trust" and "digital security," this is misleading, as it supposes a homogeneity between two problems that are not of the same order. Trust can be defined as a relation between actors while security more as a set of processes made concrete by specific tools depending on different contexts.[10] The incorporation of "trust" in "security" is not merely a lexical approximation, but the result of a recurring response to the challenges posed by digital systems.

The complex, interconnected IP ecosystem is at the heart of this relationship between trust, security, and technical architectures, and of how they can be affected by accidents and intentional acts. Global supply chain security concerns around routers have only heightened and further complicated these security concerns at the Internet's core. Given the centrality of the Internet Protocol to the digital economy, this should be one of the highest cybersecurity priorities for society. How secure is the IP ecosystem? What are the main points of trust that require high security? And what is the status of shoring up these trust points?

This chapter examines these questions by focusing on four key areas of IP-related trust architectures: Certificate Authorities, Border Gateway Protocol, the DNS, and IP addresses themselves.

## The "Trust" Institutions Authenticating Everything Online

Sometimes security vulnerabilities and attacks involve and target the "institutions of trust" around the technology. A weak link of Internet security was laid bare in September of 2011 when the Dutch government had to take over the operations of security company DigiNotar. The company provided trust services validating digital certificates, including those vouching for the authenticity of some Dutch government websites online. Hackers infiltrated the company's certificate process to allow false certificates to be issued. These false certificates enabled man-in-the-middle attacks targeting hundreds of thousands of Iranian Gmail users to possibly intercept their email.[11]

The security company hired to investigate the incident dubbed the DigiNotar Certificate Authority breach "Operation Black Tulip." Its preliminary investigation of rogue software found "…the IP addresses of an internal DigiNotar server hardcoded in the software" and that, "Around 300,000 unique requesting IPs to google.com have been identified. Of these IPs > 99% originated from Iran."[12]

The DigiNotar hack is not an obscure footnote in Internet history but rather a notable incident, among others, that helps reveal a trust vulnerability underlying key security functions of the digital economy and society. For end users, trust in underlying systems is the basis of believing a banking website or government site is authentic. Trust is the basic currency of accessing anything in the digital public sphere. Yet here the Internet has an institutional weak spot; and one that is not necessarily about technology but about people.

The security of *everything* is only as strong as the weakest certificate authority listed as a certificate-vouching institution in a browser list. As Internet pioneer David Clark succinctly explained, "If the designers of the certificate authority system to secure access to Web sites had understood that the real tussle would be over which actors would be trusted to vouch for different Websites, they could have designed a different trust framework to limit or prevent these tussles."[13]

This institutional weakness, ironically, underlies one of the most complex technical areas of cybersecurity: authenticating that the website someone accesses is the actual website rather than a deceptive decoy that could be used for financial fraud, identity theft, propaganda, or other malicious purposes.

Anyone trying to access the Amazon website to make a purchase must have trust that the website is authentic and that the exchange of information is kept private. The TLS protocols help establish encrypted communications between the two parties but also use an asymmetric cryptography process called public key cryptography to generate the encryption keys necessary for keeping information private and essentially authenticating the identity of the website. It is straightforward to authenticate an individual based on access controls such as passwords, biometric identification, or two-factor authentication. It is far more difficult to authenticate a web site. A digital certificate authenticating Amazon's public encryption key is necessary to protect the user making a transaction from digital deception.

Who or what vouches for the validity of Amazon's site? These certificates are issued by "trusted third parties" known as certificate authorities, or CAs. Understanding how this works requires understanding public key cryptography. There are two broad approaches to encryption. One is symmetric, or private key, encryption in which each of the parties communicating possesses the encryption key necessary to encode or decode information. The obvious complication is that any transmission of this key in advance makes it vulnerable to interception. The second broad approach that solves this problem is asymmetric, or public key, encryption. The sender and receiver each possess two encryption keys, a private key known only to the one party and a public key accessible to anyone. Here is how it works:

> When a device sends an encrypted message, it looks up the recipient's public key and uses this key to encrypt the message. The recipient then uses the public key and the private key that only this recipient knows to decrypt the message. Originally theorized in the late 1970s by Whitfield Diffie and Martin Hellman, public key systems are the basis for modern encryption standards for email (for example, Secure Multipurpose Internet Mail Extensions, or S/MIME) and web transactions (for example, Transport Layer Security, or TLS).[14]

How can one be sure that the public key is authentically associated with the intended Internet site? The trusted third-party certificate authorities handle this process of vouching for digital certificates. This verification process is one of the most critical trust functions in the Internet governance ecosystem. Web browsers such as Chrome, Edge, Firefox, and Safari "trust" a list of certificate authorities performing this vouching process. There are more than 100 CAs around the world, including prominent private companies such as Comodo (renamed Sectigo) and GoDaddy, but also many other institutions including not-for-profit and governmental.

This institutional system of trust is problematic in that it is only as secure as the least common denominator of institutions trusted by browsers—not trusted by the individuals affected by this digital certificate-vouching process. It is a problem of infinite regress: can one trust the one certifying trust in another one? The website has to be vouched for by a digital certificate which has to be vouched for by a CA which has to be vouched for by another entity? What is the root of this trust?

Problems have followed because of acts by untrustworthy "trusted third parties." As Clark explains, "The problem can be corruption, penetration by malicious parties, or just adverse interests"[15] with the paradigmatic example above of a Dutch CA, DigiNotar, apparently penetrated by Iranians to issue false certificates for Google and Facebook.

Various institutions of Internet governance across the multistakeholder spectrum have worked to raise the security of the CA system, sometimes through establishing voluntary best practices, sometimes through technical standards work, sometimes through not-for-profit services, and sometimes through governmental frameworks. For example, the CA/Browser Forum is an industry consortium of CAs working together to establish standards for the distribution and management of certificates. The Internet Security Research Group (ISRG) operates a non-profit certificate authority called "Let's Encrypt" to provide TLS certificates to hundreds of millions of websites. Standards organizations such as the IETF continuously work on technical standards involved in certificate security. Governments have instituted requirements and regulations for the issuance of certificates. In the United States, for example, NIST has issued guidance related to the security and management of certificates.

Yet problems with certificate authorities have persisted more than a decade after the infamous DigiNotar incident. In November of 2022, security company Symantec assessed that "State-sponsored actors compromised a digital certificate authority in an Asian country during a campaign in which multiple government agencies were also targeted."[16] The attack had been ongoing for six months, and involved a long known advanced persistent threat (APT) known as Billbug. Some reports suggested it was a Chinese government sponsored organization focusing its attention on the Southeast Asia region.[17]

Because the issuance of digital certificates is such a core part of the security scaffolding of the Internet's underlying infrastructure, this point of administration will continue to be a target and an arms race between those who provide trust services and those trying to breach this trust for economic or political gain.

## Trust Between Networks: BGP and Its Flaws

One of our expert interviewees warned, "BGP is a protocol with significant vulnerabilities." That is jarring and so are news headlines such as "China Telecom Routes European Traffic to Its Network for Two

Hours."[18] The U.S.-China Economic Security Review Commission's 2010 annual report to Congress included the following claim:

> For about 18 minutes on April 8, 2010, China Telecom advertised erroneous network traffic routes that instructed U.S. and other foreign Internet traffic to travel through Chinese servers. Other servers around the world quickly adopted these paths, routing all traffic to about 15 percent of the Internet's destinations through servers located in China. This incident affected traffic to and from U.S. government (".gov") and military (".mil") sites, including those for the Senate, the army, the navy, the marine corps, the air force, the office of secretary of Defense, the National Aeronautics and Space Administration, the Department of Commerce, the National Oceanic and Atmospheric Administration, and many others. Certain commercial websites were also affected, such as those for Dell, Yahoo!, Microsoft, and IBM.[19]

This rerouting issue, while geopolitically concerning, was probably not noticed by Internet users. But events that disrupt popular online media sites and social media platforms attract far more attention because users are directly affected. A global outage of YouTube in 2008 resulted from a local action in Pakistan in which the government ordered Pakistan Telecom to block access to a politically controversial video.[20] The blocking of the video should have remained within the country, but leaked beyond the border into the wider Internet, causing YouTube to be inaccessible. RIPE-NCC released a case study of this BGP hijacking event and explained: "On Sunday, 24 February 2008, Pakistan Telecom (AS17557) started an unauthorised announcement of the prefix 208.65.153.0/24. One of Pakistan Telecom's upstream providers, PCCW Global (AS3491) forwarded this announcement to the rest of the Internet, which resulted in the hijacking of YouTube traffic on a global scale."[21]

Whether intentional or accidental, BGP security problems have caused problematic outages. These outages, such as one that disrupted Facebook and Instagram, cause alarm, but also make digital infrastructure more visible to the public. On October 4, 2021, Facebook and its associated Internet applications including Messenger, Instagram, and WhatsApp, experienced a notable worldwide outage. Consistent with the rest of the Internet, Meta's vast private infrastructure relies upon the Internet Protocol, the Domain Name System, and Border Gateway Protocol, a complex system that is easily taken for granted until a problem occurs.

Facebook is not merely a social media company. It is also a private network, just as are Google, all large media companies, Amazon, and other cloud computing and web hosting services. To place the size of these networks in perspective, Facebook operates "tens of thousands of miles of fiber-optic cables crossing the globe and linking all of (its) data centers."[22]

Facebook's outage involved IP addresses, the DNS, and BGP and the interdependencies among these illustrates how errors—whether intentional or not, can have cascading effects throughout complex systems.[23] According to Facebook's internal account, an erroneous command made during routine maintenance caused the outage.[24] The command caused Facebook's own DNS servers to cease resolving queries to translate requested sites into IP addresses. This inability to answer DNS queries, in turn, disrupted the network's ability to advertise the addresses available through its network to other networks, via BGP. Facebook and Instagram "disappeared," at least temporarily.

Like this Facebook example, many of the most significant Internet security attacks of the past half century have directly or indirectly involved the Internet Protocol. As in the case of the Facebook outage, some cybersecurity problems are simply accidents arising from a corporate technical misconfiguration. These can occur when a routine update or a change in an advertised IP route is incorrectly executed. Such misconfigurations lead to routing disruptions that can cause IP packets to be dropped or forwarded to the wrong destination.

These types of incidents can have an immediate, public, and wide scale impact. Nearly a quarter of the network connectivity across Canada ceased to function on July 8, 2022.[25] Mobile and Internet services became unavailable in homes and businesses across the country, impacting the use of online payment systems, access to ATMs, and critical government emergency services such as 911. The restoration of service took several days, prompting calls for the Canadian Radio-Television and Telecommunications Commission (CRTC) to investigate. The CRTC asked Rogers Communications, the company at the center of the breakdown, a series of written questions about the causes of the outage, the impacts felt by emergency services, information on past outages, and how the company planned to compensate customers.[26]

In a forty-page response, portions of which Canadian officials redacted before posting publicly, Rogers Communications admitted a system failure had occurred in their core IP network. The failure was caused by a configuration change during a network update that unexpectedly deleted a routing filter, resulting in the flooding of Rogers distribution routers with IP traffic its network could not handle. Specifically, Rogers stated: "This (network update) caused our IP routing network to malfunction. To mitigate this, we re-established management connectivity with the routing network, disconnected the routers that were the source of the outage, resolved the errors caused by the update and redirected traffic, which allowed our network and services to progressively come back online later that day."[27]

As these examples show, and as Internet service providers working with IP networks clearly state, Border Gateway Protocol (BGP) is a vulnerable protocol even while essential to nearly all global digital communications.

Historically, technical issues and events associated with BGP have been relegated to the Internet's technical community, coordinating institutions, and private network operators. Even when governments have been involved, this usually has been via specialized technical experts. Yet, concerns are rightly rising to the highest level of governmental policymaking. For example, the 2023 United States National Cybersecurity Strategy the Biden White House issued included security concerns about Border Gateway Protocol:

> We must take steps to mitigate the most urgent of these pervasive concerns such as Border Gateway Protocol vulnerabilities, unencrypted Domain Name System requests, and the slow adoption of IPv6. Such a "clean-up" effort to reduce systemic risk requires identification of the most pressing of these security challenges, further development of effective security measures, and close collaboration between public and private sectors to reduce our risk exposure without disrupting the platforms and services built atop this infrastructure.[28]

Efforts to shore up security at the Internet's core is more than a "clean-up effort" but rather a crucial set of design and coordination efforts involving a wide variety of actors and institutions across the entirety of the multistakeholder Internet Protocol community and across layers upon layers of Internet architecture.

Strengthening the security of the public core of the Internet was also the first norm-setting recommendation of the Global Commission on the Stability of Cyberspace in 2019, and in particular a call for agreements by state and non-state actors to agree to not attack this public core.[29]

How exactly does BGP work? Networks are only able to communicate with each other because of BGP. It is the core inter-domain routing protocol that enables networks to exchange information at their interconnection points. The institutions that operate networks (i.e., autonomous systems) make business agreements to interconnect their networks and exchange BGP routing information between these interfaces. BGP operates at the boundaries between autonomous systems, essentially routing domains. Each autonomous system (assigned its own unique autonomous system number, or ASN) advertises a set of IP addresses reachable through its domain.

As David Clark defines Border Gateway Protocol very clearly in *Inventing an Internet*, the protocol is "the global routing protocol used among autonomous systems on the Internet. An AS can use one of a number of routing protocols internally but must communicate with other ASs using BGP."[30]

The core governance issue of BGP is that it assumes authenticity and by default trusts the routing paths provided by AS numbers. This trust by default design allows for the most effective and efficient routing of IP traffic, but the lack of validation or verification allow for the potential of misdirection and/or interception, introducing network vulnerabilities. As Ashwin Matthews explains, the topological structure of BGP is built upon "multiple centres of power, at different geographical scales [where] smaller networks rely on larger networks to carry traffic to destinations across the internet, while larger networks employ the staff and tools required to manage their more highly connected topological positions, in a complex web of technical–economic-political dependencies."[31] BGP developers designed the protocol so that it could flexibly support the addition of new networks to the Internet's structure. What was not originally designed in, however, was a security overlay that would mitigate against accidental misconfigurations or false advertised routes. Networks sometimes "made claims through BGP about routes to which they could carry traffic, which in actuality they could not reach."[32] BGP has been subject to ongoing failures, technical, administrative, and intentional attacks aimed at interception or diversion of internet traffic; these failures have engendered responses that are "both social and technological."[33]

One fundamental BGP vulnerability is that it is relatively easy for network operators to unintentionally generate route leaks. A significant episode occurred on June 12, 2015 when Telekom Malaysia began announcing approximately 176,000 of prefixes to an AS operated by

Level3, which then announced these prefixes to its network peers and customers. This resulted in a BGP leak, given that Telekom Malaysia's action was interpreted by the network as an indication that all of these prefixes were reachable through its network. As a result, the network was bombarded with more traffic than it usual. Level3 was routing all this traffic, having erroneously accepted the prefixes, but Telekom Malaysia was unable to handle these requests—either in terms of reachability or capacity with the result of having to drop packets.[34]

Discussions have continued about what the solutions to these problems could be, and how to practically implement them. There has long been consensus that BGP needs to be improved, but less agreement about exactly what proposals put forward by academic and industry communities to follow. In short, "there is a remarkable lack of consensus on what needs to be secured or validated, and the approach to be taken, preventing solutions to get critical support to move their deployment forward."[35]

Technical standardization efforts to address this security need have included the IETF's BGPsec (see RFC 8205) which specifies how to sign and validate announcements and AS paths between networks. This design is dependent upon RPKI, or Resource Public Key Infrastructure, to cryptographically validate the origins of paths, making it dependent upon a global cryptographic key management process. To state in the simplest terms, this system validates and authenticates that the entity announcing routes is authorized to do so. Like all cryptographic key management processes, RPKI requires certificate authorities that distribute and validate the assigned keys. The RIR system currently performs this validation for those opting in to the system. As RIPE-NCC explains about RPKI and their role as a certificate authority: "RPKI proves the association between specific IP address blocks or ASNs and the holders of those Internet number resources. The certificates are proof of the resource holder's right of use of their resources and can be validated cryptographically… We act as a trusted Certificate Authority (CA) and issue certificates to resource holders. Certificate Authorities verify that the public key in the generated certificate is the public key of the identified party."[36]

This cryptographic signing approach seems like a desirable security solution, but is not universally deployed. RPKI raises governance concerns about centralized control of such an important system, political concerns about whether governments could revoke certificates for political reasons, and technical concerns about the complexity and computational resources of the system.[37]

Security actors implementing "best practices" for routing security seem so far to be following the most appropriate way to proceed. A notable example of widely agreed-upon (and voluntary) best practices is the Mutually Agreed Norms for Routing Security (MANRS), a global initiative supported by the Internet Society. MANRS promotes specific "tailored, relevant" actions and programs for different types of actors in the routing security field, including network operators, IXPs, Content Delivery Networks (CDNs) and equipment vendors.[38] Some of these suggested best practices include: definition by network operators of clear routing policies and implementation of a system that ensures correctness of their announcement; implementation of anti-spoofing filtering; maintenance of a globally accessible and up-to-date contact information, to facilitate coordination between network operators; and preservation of a public, documented routing policy.[39]

Researchers in Internet measurement have recently conducted a first analysis of the MANRS ecosystem in order to assess to what degree operators' actually meet MANRS recommendations, finding uneven levels of rigor among them.[40] In November 2023, the Internet Society partnered with the Global Cyber Alliance (GCA) in an effort to try and scale deployment of MANRS, promising that "ISOC will focus on funding and support through training and global advocacy activities, while GCA will provide the secretariat function and operate the MANRS Observatory."[41] The 2023 MANRS Annual Report marked its tenth anniversary and predicted growth in its voluntary membership and in its partners.[42]

## Securing the DNS

In 2014 the world was captivated by the unexplained disappearance of Malaysia Air flight 3870. Triggering one of the most extensive multi-year searches in aviation history, the plane and the remains of the 239 people on board were never found. Imagine the following year going to the Malaysia Air website to check on your ticket, or the flight status of a loved one and seeing instead the image of a lizard in a top hat and the message: "404—plane not found." This is what happened in 2016 when the Malaysia Air website was hacked by the group Lizard squad.[43] Taking advantage of gaps in the airline's security, the hackers were able to redirect Internet users to a false website.

As has been mentioned, the early development of the IP ecosystem, including the Domain Name System, was done largely by individuals who knew the institution, if not the exact person, on the other end of the network with which they were communicating. These first hand direct personal connections meant that a trust relationship between the parties was inherent and security was not specifically included in the original IETF-developed DNS standards.

The DNS, often referred to as the phone book of the Internet, is the system of converting long, hard to remember IP numbers to easy to remember names. As an example, instead of typing the IP address 142.250.190.78 (or the longer binary number represented by this dotted decimal shorthand notation: 10001110111110101011111001001110) to reach the Google search, a user simply types google.com. The DNS is largely invisible to most users, but without it or without app intermediaries, users might be forced to memorize long numbers to access Internet content, or to reconfigure names every time a number reconfiguration occurred. A less friendly user interface would have severely limited the utility and pace of the Internet's commercialization and development.

A traditional DNS query can be broken down into steps. First, a user types a domain name into a web browser or clicks a link or takes some other action to initiate the query. Then, the user's device will seek out the IP number associated with the domain name requested. If the website has been visited before by the user the information could be stored or saved in the DNS cache or memory of the user device. If it is a common domain name, the information could be stored in the recursive DNS servers used by the network from which the user is accessing the Internet. Recursive DNS servers are deployed throughout networks to increase speed and limit the number of requests being made directly to authoritative servers. Authoritative servers store the DNS record, the mapping of the domain name to the IP number, directly configured by the DNS administrator for a particular top-level domain name. If the request is for new information, it will be transferred over to an authoritative DNS server. In step three, the DNS record is accessed. And in the final step, the DNS record is transmitted to the user's computer, transferring the user to the website requested. The process, from initiation to completion, takes milliseconds and relies on a distributed hierarchy of trust. Specifically, trust that the information requested in the four-step process described above is accurate, including that the DNS cache, the temporary storage of the results of earlier DNS lookups.

To prevent DNS data from being corrupted with bad information, the IETF in the 1990s began to develop Domain Name System Security Extensions (DNSSEC) standards. And while security protocols were agreed upon, their deployment across the Internet was slow with the weakest link in any network being the default security level.

Deployment of DNSSEC received a boost when in 2008, researcher Dan Kaminsky identified a DNS cache poisoning vulnerability that "allowed attackers to send users to malicious sites and hijack email."[44] DNS cache poisoning or spoofing involves an IP address in the DNS resolver's cache or memory being replaced by an IP address that redirects users to a compromised site controlled by attackers. Kaminsky's discovery of an attack vector that allowed DNS cache poisoning of almost all DNS nameservers in the world proved to be an incentive for action given the global scale of the threat. Stakeholders pushed to have DNSSEC deployed at the top of the DNS hierarchy, the authoritative root zone file, with the theory that trust would be maintained and flow through the networks. Applying DNSSEC to the zone file would be applying a tamper proof seal, similar to a wax seal on a letter as was the custom in the Middle Ages, to the address book of the Internet.

Until 2016, the authoritative root zone file was produced through a process administered by NTIA, given the U.S. government's historical role and stewardship of the DNS, involving ICANN and Verisign. In this three-legged stool, ICANN in performance of the IANA functions processed change requests from TLD operators, NTIA verified and authorized the request, and Verisign as the root zone maintainer implemented the changes and published the authoritative root zone file (Fig. 7.1).

In response to the Kaminsky-identified vulnerability, NTIA consulted with stakeholders through a Notice of Inquiry seeking input on six different possible models for deploying DNSSEC at the root.[45] Based on the feedback received, NTIA picked a model and instructed ICANN and Verisign to submit a testing and evaluation plan, before ultimately authorizing final deployment on July 16, 2010.[46]

The role of NTIA in root zone administration was the source of much geopolitical debate for twenty years at the ITU and in the five-year WSIS process, as described in Chapter 5. Not only were root zone file updates for global top-level domains (gTLDs) subject to NTIA authorization, country-code top-level domain names (ccTLDs), something that many countries saw as their national flag in cyberspace, were also subject to a process administered by another country. In addition, this placed NTIA as

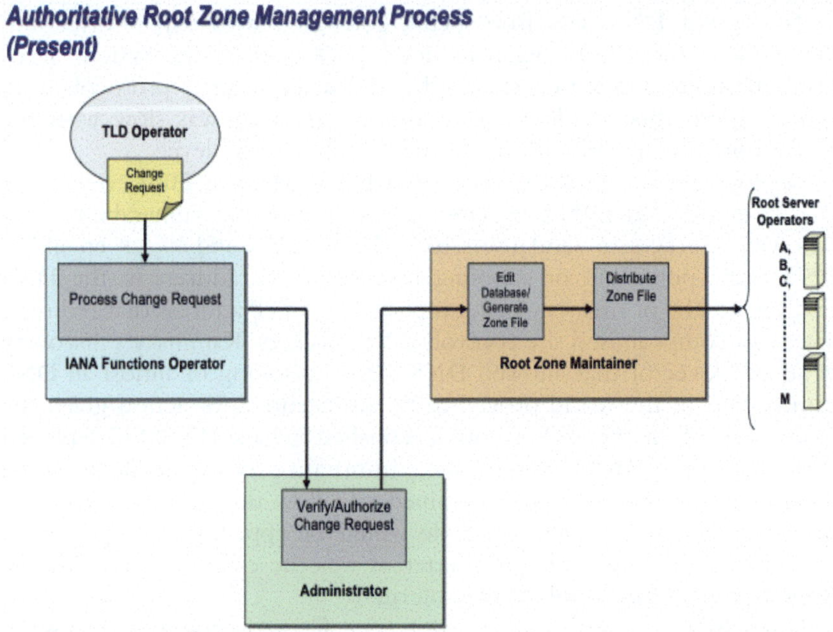


**Fig. 7.1** Original NTIA image of pre-2016 authoritative root zone management process

the sole decision-maker on the trust model chosen for DNSSEC deployment. Further complicating matters from a geopolitical perspective was that the management and administration of ccTLDs was distributed by John Postel in the early days of the Internet to academic institutions or friends, sometimes with no connection to the country with which the ccTLD represented.

After the 2016 IANA stewardship transition, the role of NTIA was changed and a direct agreement between ICANN and Verisign was established for production and maintenance of the DNS authoritative root zone file.[47] While this removed the unique role of the U.S. government in the process, the production of the rootzone and the DNS cryptographic key rollover still occurs in the United States, leaving lingering jurisdictional concerns for some nations. And periodically ccTLD re-delegation requests will surface as countries look to assert local or national laws and control over their ccTLD.

While DNSSEC cannot prevent all attacks against the DNS, and while deploying DNSSEC is complicated, unauthorized changes to DNS data can be identified and users are prevented from being redirected, if DNSSEC is deployed. Consequently, ICANN and other cybersecurity stakeholders have continued to push for broader DNSSEC deployment as one of the tools to combat malicious activity targeting DNS infrastructure. Post the 2010 deployment at the authoritative root, ICANN began including DNSSEC obligations in its system of contracts. Registries that operate generic top-level domains (gTLDs) are now required to deploy DNSSEC and ICANN-accredited registrars are now required to support DNSSEC. In 2020, ICANN announced that all 1195 gTLDs had deployed DNSSEC.[48]

The deployment process among country-code top-level domain name operators (ccTLDs) is more complex as ccTLDs operate in a variety of local policy and regulatory constructs and are not subject to a single system of agreements. Some operate under direct contracts with their respective government (i.e., U.S.) while others operate in a more privatized management system (i.e., UK). As of June 14, 2021, ISOC reported that out of 250 ccTLDs, 81 were fully DNSSEC operational.[49] ICANN offers support and training to ccTLDs in an effort to achieve universal DNSSEC deployment, including working with other partners like the International Telecommunication Union (ITU). And in 2021, a DNSSEC Deployment Guidebook for ccTLDs was issued and translated in the six official U.N. languages to facilitate broader adoption.[50]

Highlighting that security solutions are never foolproof, in 2023 German researchers exploited a DNSSEC design flaw to develop the first DNSSEC-based algorithmic complexity attack.[51] Named “KeyTrap” by the research team, the vulnerability exposed that “with just a single DNS packet” a DNS resolver could be misdirected to a malicious nameserver whose query response causes the DNS resolver to “consume most or all of its own CPU resources.”[52] By exhausting the CPU resources, a successful KeyTrap attack would disrupt connectivity rendering Internet-based applications like web browsing, email, and social media unavailable. While the research team worked with vendors to develop patches to contain this vulnerability, “completely preventing the attacks requires fundamentally to reconsider the underlying design philosophy of DNSSEC, i.e., to revise the DNSSEC standards.”[53]

## Trusting the IP Address Itself

Trust in IP addresses themselves is clearly at the core of the entanglements between protocols, security, and geopolitics. At the heart of the ability of placing one's trust in IP addresses are crucial questions such as whether an address is authentic, or is being "spoofed" for an illegitimate purpose; whether requests are legitimate, or part of a DDoS campaign; whether the returned queries are authentic, or designed to redirect someone to a fraudulent site. In addition to topics already addressed in this chapter, this section examines the issue of trust in IP by examining examples of the malicious activities that can break trust in IP addresses (primarily DDoS attacks and IP spoofing), and by briefly introducing some cases in which, because of the global nature of IP, geopolitics often intertwines with trust and security challenges.

Having previously introduced the DDoS phenomenon in this book, but to emphasize its connection to IP addresses, it is useful to recall the objective of DDoS attacks. They are meant to incapacitate a target by flooding it with requests so that it becomes unavailable for legitimate requests. This flood of malicious requests is "distributed" because it originates from a high number of devices that have been hijacked for this purpose.

Many types of DDoS attacks are able to co-opt the Internet Protocol ecosystem. Two types of attack, in particular, one a protocol process attack (TCP/SYN) and one a volume-based attack (ICMP) helps to explain this connection.[54]

One of the important tasks of the Transport Control Protocol, or TCP, is to establish a connection between two points, such as a computer (a "client") and a web or email server (a "server"). These two devices exchange a sequence of messages that essentially serve as a three-way handshake acknowledgment. The client sends a specific type of TCP packet with a predetermined sequence of bits known as a SYN (synchronization) flag to the server. The server sends back an acknowledgment sequence of bits known as a SYN-ACK message (synchronization acknowledgment) to the client. In the final part of opening up the connection between the client and server, the client sends a final ACK message (acknowledgment) to the server. This final part of the handshake is what is exploited in a TCP/SYN DDoS attack, along with "IP spoofing." A forged IP address from a client computer sends the first synchronization message, and receives the acknowledgment from the server, but then does not send the final acknowledgment message. While the server awaits this final message, the communication channel is held open, consuming server resources. Numerous devices carrying out this method simultaneously result in disruption of the server.

ICMP flood attacks are volume-based attacks, but historically also co-opt IP to carry out disruptions. It starts with "pinging," meaning simply to test the reachability of an IP address, such as via the Internet Control Message Protocol, or ICMP. Pinging involves sending a request to the IP address of the targeted device and then waiting for a reply from the device. This process can be exploited by bombarding a targeted device with a high volume of ping requests, which prompts the target to reply, consuming processing capacity and taking up network bandwidth.

Often linked to these (and other) DDoS attacks are practices of IP spoofing, where a malicious actor changes the source or originating IP address to hide from where an IP packet with its contents originates. That malicious actor creates packets and changes the source IP address. IP spoofing is most often used in DDoS or man-in-the-middle attacks[55] against specific devices or infrastructures. This IP spoofing, in essence, disguises the originating IP address in order to conduct malicious activity. Indeed, malicious actors can use botnets to send geographically dispersed packets,[56] in line with the DDoS attack's goal to overwhelm a system or infrastructure with voluminous traffic, causing it to malfunction or crash. Prevention in these cases is difficult, because of the originating IP address' hidden identity. Simply put, the IP spoofing generates unfounded trust within the IP ecosystem, enabling attackers to bypass security measures and get their packets accepted.

In order to accomplish this, malicious actors need to obtain a trusted IP address so that their packet can enter the recipient network or intercept an IP packet so they can switch their own IP address for the intercepted trusted address. Unfortunately, there are tools available to facilitate such malicious activity. It is difficult for an end user to identify IP spoofing, as the IP address looks like a legitimate one. However, there are other tools such as packet filtering systems available for identifying IP spoofing.

Mistrust in a particular IP address can also happen by mistake, when specific actors think that they are in the presence of DDoS attacks or IP spoofing phenomena, which in turn triggers collateral damage. An interesting example of this occurred in 2020. CenturyLink, an Internet backbone provider, disrupted Internet traffic by thinking it was blocking one mistrusted IP address. Some popular websites experienced hours-long outages. Cloudflare reported: "Globally, we saw a 3.5% drop in global traffic during the outage, nearly all of which was due to a nearly complete outage of CenturyLink's ISP service across the United States."[57]

Originally, CenturyLink thought a disruption was due to a DDoS attack from a specific IP address. Thus, Century Link's Operations Engineering Team set out to block what they thought was the malicious actor's IP address. Unfortunately, when they implemented the system to block bad IP addresses (in this case, a single IP address), a technical flaw translated this single IP address into several IP addresses, triggering multiple blockages, causing Internet outages. This is an example of trust gone awry: mistrust of one IP address through an accidental flaw multiplied into myriad blockages and subsequent outages.[58]

Maintaining trust in IP addresses is a core feature of the IP/security/geopolitics entanglement, and the potential attacks to this trust are multiple and malicious. Thus, it is hardly surprising that a number of guidelines aimed at developing best practices for preventing or mitigating DDoS attacks and IP spoofing have been proposed, starting with the IETF's May 2000 Request for Comments 2827.[59] Such best practices suggestions are primarily targeted at organizations, and include encouragements to create a DDoS response plan, to know one's typical Internet traffic pattern, and to monitor traffic in real time. Interestingly, a recurring suggestion is also to "move to the cloud," given that the "cloud has more bandwidth than on-premise resources [...] and the nature of the cloud means many servers are not located in the same place."[60]

As geopolitical strategies are increasingly embedded in technology, IP addresses will certainly continue to be a bone of contention in terms of security, just as they will continue, as Chapter 6 suggested, to be used for blocking.

## Normal Accidents and Normal Attacks

The IP ecosystem is both appropriated for attacks and itself a target of attacks. This has historically been the case and, because of IP's centrality to the entire digital economy and society, will likely continue. A system initially developed when individuals knew everyone at the other ends of the network has evolved into a ubiquitous global network with countless interconnection points. This shift from inherent trust in colleagues and friends to the need to develop and deploy security standards and tools to erect trust like a scaffolding has made security in the IP ecosystem as much about the institutions and governance structures as it is about the technology. And advancements in technology and computing power only serve to reinforce that security is never perfect and never done.

"Most high-risk systems have some special characteristics that make accidents in them inevitable, even normal," wrote Charles Perrow in his 1999 book *Normal Accidents: Living with High-Risk Technologies*.[61] Although Perrow was writing prior to the explosion of the Web and focusing on nuclear, chemical, military, genetic engineering, and other complex technologies, he could have been writing about Internet architecture. IP-based security problems can stem simply from misconfigurations and cascading interactions among complex, interconnected, large-scale systems. In other words, they are sometimes accidents. The systems complexity Perrow addressed was relegated to each unique technological system. In the contemporary era, digital systems interconnect with each of these systems, making the cascading effects of an outage or misconfiguration in one area potentially affecting all areas.

Yet some seeming accidents are intentional attacks, sometimes with the goal of making such attacks appear to be accidental. Increasingly, there is evidence of non-state actor attacks acting at the behest of a nation-state government. As the number of actors with the requisite skills to implement attacks increases, governments and private companies alike are concerned both with the requisite capacity for countering such attacks and for ways in which to handle attribution, only increasing geopolitical tensions.

With the deployment and operation of the Internet largely in the hands of the private sector, IP security-related decisions have historically been highly privatized, decentralized, and the province of the variety of multistakeholder institutions and actors, of which the average user is unaware, discussed in Chapter 2. This is changing as governments at both national and international levels delve deeper into the infrastructure layer of the Internet and IP-based systems become further entrenched in daily life. Whether it be efforts by the European Union to impose secure DNS resolution infrastructures, interference in multistakeholder processes related to BGP by the U.S. domestic telecom regulator, or proposals from a high-level commission of global experts for governments to refrain from conducting cyber-operations that disrupt the public core of the Internet, the geopolitical dimensions of IP security, like security itself, will never be fully resolved.[62]

## Notes


1. Paul Vixie et al., "Events of 21-Oct-2002," ISC/UMD/Cogent Event Report, November 24, 2002.
2. Francesca Musiani et al., eds., *The Turn to Infrastructure in Internet Governance*, Palgrave MacMillan, 2016.
3. Lee Garber, "Denial-of-Service Attacks Rip the Internet," *IEEE Computer Magazine*, April, 2000, pp. 12–17.
4. Federal Bureau of Investigation Press Release, "Mafiaboy Pleads Guilty," Washington, DC, January 19, 2001, http://www.fbi.gov/news/pressrel/press-releases/mafiaboy-pleads-guilty.
5. Marc Donner, "Cyberassault on Estonia," *IEEE Security & Privacy Magazine*, Volume 5, Number 4, August 2007, pp. 4–5; Phillip M. Lutscher, et al., "At Home and Abroad: The Use of Denial-of-service Attacks during Elections in Nondemocratic Regimes," *Journal of Conflict Resolution*, Volume 64, Issue 2–3, 2020, pp. 373–401; Stefan Kirchner, "Distributed Denial-of-Service Attacks Under Public International Law: State Responsibility in Cyberwar," *IUP Journal of Cyber Law*, Volume 8, Issue 3, 2009, p. 10.
6. Peter Loshin, "BGP routing security flaw caused Amazon Route 53 Incident," *TechTarget*, April 25, 2018, https://www.techtarget.com/searchsecurity/news/252439945/BGP-routing-security-flaw-caused-Amazon-Route-53-incident.
7. Dan Goodin, "'Suspicious' Event routes traffic for big-name sites through Russia," *Ars Technica*, December 13, 2017, https://arstechnica.com/information-technology/2017/12/suspicious-event-routes-traffic-for-big-name-sites-through-russia/.
8. Computer History Museum, Interview of Steve Crocker (interview by James L. Pelkey), Recorded April 26, 1988, in Washington, DC., https://archive.computerhistory.org/resources/access/text/2017/12/102738690-05-01-acc.pdf.
9. Helen Nissenbaum, "Securing trust online: Wisdom or Oxymoron," *Boston University Law Review*, Volume 81, Number 3, June 2001, pp. 635–664.
10. Coye Cheshire, "Online Trust, Trustworthiness, or Assurance?" *Daedalus*, Volume 140, Number 4, 2011, pp. 49–58.

11. Fox-IT, Interim Report, "DigiNotar Certificate Authority Breach, Operation Black Tulip," September 5, 2011, https://www.sec.gov/Archives/edgar/data/1044777/000119312511241796/dex992.htm, accessed March 31, 2024,
12. Fox-IT, Interim Report, "DigiNotar Certificate Authority Breach, Operation Black Tulip," September 5, 2011, https://www.sec.gov/Archives/edgar/data/1044777/000119312511241796/dex992.htm, accessed March 31, 2024.
13. David D. Clark, *Designing an Internet*, The MIT Press, 2018, p. 175.
14. For a more detailed description of public-key cryptography and Certificate Authorities, see Laura DeNardis, *The Global War for Internet Governance*, Yale University Press, 2014, pp. 93–95.
15. David Clark, *Designing an Internet*, The MIT Press, 2018, 204.
16. Symantec Threat Intelligence Team Blog, "Billbug: State-sponsored Actor Targets Cert Authority, Government Agencies in Multiple Asian Countries," November 15, 2022, https://symantec-enterprise-blogs.security.com/blogs/threat-intelligence/espionage-asia-governments-cert-authority.
17. The Hacker News, Researchers Say China State-backed Hackers Breached a Digital Certificate Authority, November 15, 2022, https://thehackernews.com/2022/11/researchers-say-china-state-backed.html.
18. Ionut Arghire, "China Telecom Routes European Traffic to Its Network for Two Hours," *Security Week*, June 10, 2019, https://www.securityweek.com/china-telecom-routes-european-traffic-its-network-two-hours/.
19. U.S.-China Economic and Security Review Commission, "2010 Report to Congress," November, 2010, p. 244, https://www.uscc.gov/sites/default/files/annual_reports/2010-Report-to-Congress.pdf.
20. RIPE-NCC News Release, "YouTube Hijacking: A RIPE NCC RIS Case Study," March 17, 2008, https://www.ripe.net/publications/news/youtube-hijacking-a-ripe-ncc-ris-case-study/.
21. Ibid.
22. https://engineering.fb.com/2021/10/05/networking-traffic/outage-details/.

23. See Laura DeNardis, "Facebook's Global Outage Wasn't the Result of a Hack, but Big Political Questions Lurk Behind It," *Washington Post Monkey Cage*, October 8, 2021.
24. https://engineering.fb.com/2021/10/05/networking-traffic/outage-details/.
25. Ellen Francis. "Outage in Canada leaves millions without internet; ATMs, 911 lines hit", *Washington Post,* July 9, 2022, https://www.washingtonpost.com/world/2022/07/09/canada-network-outage-rogers-communications-internet/ (accessed March 31, 2024).
26. See Canadian Radio-Television and Telecommunications (CRTC), "Telecom—Commission Letter addressed to Ted Woodhead (Rogers Communications Canada Inc.), July 12, 2022.
    https://crtc.gc.ca/eng/archive/2022/lt220712.htm (accessed March 31, 2024).
27. See Ted Woodhead, Chief Regulatory & Government Affairs, Rogers Communications Canada Inc. letter to Claude Doucet, Secretary General, CRTC, July 22, 2022, p. 1, https://crtc.gc.ca/otf/eng/2022/8000/c12-202203868.htm.
28. White House, National Cybersecurity Strategy, March 2023, p. 24.
29. Final Report of the Global Commission on the Stability of Cyberspace, 2019, p. 8. https://hcss.nl/wp-content/uploads/2019/11/GCSC-Final-Report-November-2019.pdf.
30. David Clark, *Designing an Internet*, The MIT Press, 2018, p.357. A non-academic reference to consult is TechTarget, "BGP Tutorial: How the routing protocol works," https://www.techtarget.com/searchnetworking/feature/BGP-tutorial-The-routing-protocol-that-makes-the-Internet-work.
31. Ashwin Mathews, "The Myth of the Decentralised Internet," *Internet Policy Review,* Volume 5, Number 3, 2016. https://doi.org/10.14763/2016.3.425.
32. Mathews, ibid.
33. Mathews, ibid.
34. A more detailed explanation of the case can be found at https://www.bgpmon.net/massive-route-leak-cause-internet-slowdown/.
35. Cecilia Testart, "Reviewing a Historical Internet Vulnerability: Why Isn't BGP More Secure and What Can We Do About it?" in Proceedings of TPRC 46: The 46th Research Conference on Communication, Information and Internet Policy 2018,

August 15, 2018, Available at SSRN: https://ssrn.com/abstract=3141666.
36. RIPE-NCC, "What is RPKI?" accessed at https://www.ripe.net/manage-ips-and-asns/resource-management/rpki/what-is-rpki/.
37. For an analysis, please see Brenden Kuerbis and Milton Mueller, "Internet Routing Registries, Data Governance, and Security," *Journal of Cyber Policy*, Volume 2, Number 1, pp. 64–81, https://doi.org/10.1080/23738871.2017.129092; and also Brenden Kuerbis and Milton Mueller, "Negotiating a New Governance Hierarchy: An Analysis of the Conflicting Incentives to Secure Internet Routing," *Communications and Strategies*, Number 81, March 21, 2011, pp. 125–142, https://ssrn.com/abstract=2021835.
38. https://www.manrs.org/programs/.
39. MANRS Implementation Guide on Github, https://github.com/manrs-tools/manrs-docs/blob/main/pdf/MANRS-Network-Implementation-Guide.pdf, accessed March 31, 2024.
40. Cecilia Testart, et al., "Mind your MANRS: Measuring the MANRS Ecosystem," In *Proceedings of the 22nd ACM Internet Measurement Conference*, October, 2022, pp. 716–729, https://dl.acm.org/doi/pdf/10.1145/3517745.3561419.
41. Leslie Diagle and Andrei Robachevsky, "Achieving Greater Heights for MANRS," November 2, 2023, https://www.manrs.org/2023/11/achieving-greater-heights-for-manrs/.
42. MANRS, "MANRS Community Report 2023: 10 Years On, Still Growing Strong—MANRS," January 2024.
43. ABC News, "Malaysia Airlines Hit by Lizard Squad Hack Attack," January 16, 2015, https://abcnews.go.com/Technology/malaysia-airlines-hit-lizard-squad-hack-attack/story?id=28489244.
44. Thu T. Phan, "The Great DNS Vulnerability of 2008 by Dan Kaminsky," Duo Labs, April 26, 2015, https://duo.com/blog/the-great-dns-vulnerability-of-2008-by-dan-kaminsky.
45. See NTIA, "Enhancing the Security and Stability of the Internet's Domain Name and Addressing System" October 9, 2008, https://www.ntia.doc.gov/legacy/frnotices/2008/FR_DNSSEC_081009.pdf.

46. See NTIA, "Commerce Department, ICANN and VeriSign Deploy New Technology to Enhance the Security and Stability of the Internet," July 16, 2010, https://ntia.gov/press-release/2010/commerce-department-icann-and-verisign-deploy-new-technology-enhance-security.
47. See ICANN, "Rootzone Maintainer Agreement," September 28, 2016, https://www.icann.org/en/stewardship-implementation/root-zone-maintainer-agreement-rzma.
48. See ICANN "Domain Name System Security Extensions Now Deployed in all Generic Top-Level Domains," December 23, 2020, https://www.icann.org/en/announcements/details/domain-name-system-security-extensions-now-deployed-in-all-generic-top-level-domains-23-12-2020-en.
49. See ISOC, "ccTLD DNSSEC Status 2020-06-14," https://www.internetsociety.org/wp-content/uploads/2021/06/2021-06-14-2021-06-14.png.
50. See ICANN, "DNSSEC Deployment Guidebook for ccTLDs," November 12, 2021, https://www.icann.org/en/system/files/files/octo-029-12nov21-en.pdf.
51. Elias Heftrig, Haya Schulmann, Niklas Vogel, and Michael Waidner, "The KeyTrap Denial-of-Service Algorithmic Complexity Attacks on DNS." ATHENE & Goethe-Universitat Frankfurt & TU Darmstadt & Fraunhofer SIT, January 2024, https://www.athene-center.de/fileadmin/content/PDF/Technical_Report_KeyTrap.pdf.
52. Thomas Claburn, "Just One Bad Packet Can Bring Down a Vulnerable DNS Server Thanks to DNSSEC," *The Register*, February 13, 2024, https://www.theregister.com/2024/02/13/dnssec_vulnerability_internet/.
53. Cornelia Reitz, "Serious Vulnerability in the Internet Infrastructure: Fundamental design flaw in DNSSEC discovered," *Presseportal*, February 13, 2024, https://www.presseportal.de/pm/173495/5713546.
54. Laura DeNardis, *The Global War for Internet Governance*, Yale University Press, 2014, pp. 100–101.
55. Man-in-the-middle attacks refer to instances when malicious actors use IP spoofing to mimic a targeted system, thus receiving that system's packets and then responding by using the received packets and responding with malware infused in the packet.

56. See the earlier mentioned GitHub example.
57. Matthew Prince, Cloudflare Blog, "August 30th 2020: Analysis of CenturyLink/Level(3) outage," https://blog.cloudflare.com/analysis-of-todays-centurylink-level-3-outage.
58. "CenturyLink Took Down 3.5% of the Internet Trying to Block a Single IP Address," September 2, 2020, https://techmonitor.ai/technology/data-centre/centurylink-flowspec-outage.
59. Paul Ferguson, RFC 2827, "Network Ingress Filtering: Defeating Denial of Service Attacks Which Employ IP," May, 2020, https://www.rfc-editor.org/info/bcp38.
60. See, for example, Security Scorecard, "10 Best Practices to Prevent DDoS Attacks," August 16, 2021, https://securityscorecard.com/blog/best-practices-to-prevent-ddos-attacks/.
61. Charles Perrow, *Normal Accidents: Living with High-Risk Technologies*, Princeton University Press, 1999, p. 4.
62. EU https://ec.europa.eu/info/funding-tenders/opportunities/portal/screen/opportunities/topic-details/cef-dig-2021-cloud-dns-works, FCC https://www.fcc.gov/document/fcc-launches-inquiry-internet-routing-vulnerabilities, GCSC https://hcss.nl/gcsc-norms/.

CHAPTER 8

# The Role of the Internet Protocol Ecosystem in Inclusion

While the Internet Protocol ecosystem has played a crucial role in enabling growing connectivity and access to digital resources, the economic and social benefits of this growth are unevenly distributed. There are multiple digital divides. IP addresses are not evenly distributed around the world. Participation in standards-setting organizations has its own barriers. The global distribution of Internet Exchange Points has become more distributed but still concentrated in the West. Language gaps also exist in digital spaces, with dominant languages supported and local languages sometimes missing from technologies, code, and user interfaces.[1]

Yet policy and scholarly attention to digital divides have historically focused on last mile access (broadband connectivity) and sometimes local networks, often missing geopolitical contexts and the broader underlying infrastructure beyond end user access. Access itself encompasses far more than connectivity, such as whether an individual or an organization or a country has the skills to use the connection.[2] These areas entangle with the IP ecosystem in various ways, such as the advent of internationalized domain names and the push for "universal acceptance" of languages, cultural divides in the IP ecosystem institutions, and inequities in the skill sets necessary to participate.[3] Work on internationalized domain names has enabled access in a variety of languages. As of 2022, one could access



F. M. Alexander et al., *Geopolitics at the Internet's Core*, Information Technology and Global Governance,
https://doi.org/10.1007/978-3-031-89478-7_8

the Internet in non-ASCII characters via 91 top-level domain names and 61 country-code top-level domains.[4]

The 2001 *Human Development Report*—the first United Nations Development Program report to focus on what it then called "new technologies" and human development—provided a baseline for understanding approaches toward a more inclusive Internet and how these approaches have changed (or not) over time.[5] The 2001 report uses the nation-state as the key analytical category. While the 2019 Report, by comparison, still uses the nation-state as a key category, it argues that "groups with lower human development have systematically less access to a wide range of technologies" and, further, that "gaps in advanced technologies are widening." Such gaps "can also become barriers not only in accessing services or enabling economic transactions but also in being part of a 'learning society'."[6] By 2019, this Report, housed in a multilateral organization, recognizes a broader range of access, outcomes, and exclusions.

What are the outcomes of such access? And which individuals, depending on nationality or any individual characteristics, benefit or, conversely, are deprived of the benefit of connecting to the IP ecosystem? Outcomes of Internet connection vary by social status, in that those with higher social status achieve more valuable outcomes, exacerbating existing social class divides.[7] Such divides and outcomes include additional barriers such as those the differently abled face in many different countries.[8] How do questions concerning participation in governance and inclusion related to accessibility, gender, human rights, etc. emerge? Answers to bridging possible divides and to achieving meaningful inclusion call for an understanding both of the complex IP ecosystem and related capacity development approaches as well as to underlying geopolitical forces.[9]

Noting an overemphasis on last mile access in digital divide concerns is not to diminish the ongoing digital divide challenges around Internet connectivity. For good reasons, multistakeholder models in the Internet governance space have increased attention to strengthening access-related capacities. Civil society organizations, along with alliances and partnerships with other non-state actors, have joined nation-state governments in the capacity-building spaces to improve access. Numerous organizations, as well as scholars, collect data related to physical access. UNESCO reports that "Despite progress in recent years, only 36% of Africa's population had broadband Internet access in 2022… (Even the presence of broadband access does not imply that all citizens have that access or have the skills to utilize that access and furthermore, the)...substantial digital gender gap (35% versus 24% in 2020) and a significant divide in digital skills continues to hamper the continent's progress towards achieving Internet Universality."[10]

Like other elements of the Internet ecosystem, access also has geopolitical dimensions. A dispute between the Islamic Republic of Iran and Starlink, a private satellite service and division of SpaceX, helps demonstrate the key link between access and geopolitics. The dispute centered on Iranian citizen access to the Internet via Starlink. On February 23, 2023, the Islamic Republic of Iran submitted a document to the ITU Radio Regulations Board concerning the operation of Starlink connections in Iran.[11] The complaint, which followed Iran's Internet shutdowns in response to the 2022–23 widespread protests, requested that all Starlink connections originating in Iran be disabled. Iran argued that such connections went against its government's regulations and the Board ultimately ruled in its favor. At its 94th meeting, the Radio Regulations Board called on Norway (the notifying administration) and the United States (the associated administration) to disable Starlink terminals operating within Iran. The Board concluded that while the terminals were probably brought into Iran from localities where Starlink was authorized to provide service and was using IP addresses outside Iran, Starlink should be able to geolocate those terminals within Iran—where that government did not authorize Starlink to operate—and disable them.

The Radio Regulations Board's discussion of this matter at its 94th meeting also elicited comments from the Ghanaian member who noted that some of its citizens had also deployed Starlink connections without government authorization for Starlink to operate in Ghana. Responding to these discussions, the member from Morocco reported that immediately after the earthquake in his country, volunteers set up satellite connections (through unauthorized services). The Moroccan government issued temporary authorization for those satellite connections to enable citizens to connect to the Internet following the disaster.

Iran's actions in this case underline geopolitical forces at play in the broad Internet access and governance ecosystem. Iran chose the exact venue/institution to bring its complaint, a venue that is multilateral in nature and that does not have a history of non-governmental participation.[12]

Beyond these access issues, this chapter examines specific dimensions of inclusion and exclusion, sometimes even invisible, in relation to the

IP ecosystem, and how these dimensions are embedded in geopolitical tensions and sociocultural contexts. The potential for inclusion or exclusion spans the many elements of the IP ecosystem. From the critical Internet resources of domain names and IP addresses to the surrounding governance institutions, ranging from regional Internet registries to standards organizations, the IP ecosystem holds the potential for inclusion or exclusion. The history of Internet governance is replete with objectives of bringing about a more universal or inclusive Internet. Yet the global, complex, and interoperable nature of IP intersecting with varying nation-state territorial sovereignty perspectives has shaped and continues to shape discussions and debates around inclusion and what actors should be involved.[13]

The following sections address three different layers of "meaningful inclusion" (or exclusion) embedded within the Internet Protocol ecosystem: access to critical Internet resources; participation in and use of standards; and inclusion in IP-supporting systems. The chapter concludes with a discussion about how to reorient inclusion toward greater absorptive capacity throughout all layers of the IP ecosystem beyond access.

## Access to Critical Internet Resources

While the subject of geopolitical flashpoints around critical Internet resources has been covered in earlier chapters, IP addresses and domain names are also key tools for digital inclusion. Without these critical Internet resources and the phonebook function the DNS provides, the interconnection of networks and the global access to information resources would be much more complex and limited. This makes the availability, distribution, and access to IP addresses and domain names indispensable to achieving meaningful inclusion. Domain names, because they are based on alphanumeric human language, have had the added historical dimension of the original language characters used only being derived from the American Standard Code for Information Interchange, or ASCII.

The institutions and actors involved in the management of critical Internet resources and the establishment of associated technical standards have undertaken a variety of activities to expand access to and the use of IP addresses and domain names. The IETF, as far back as the 1990s, agreed on the protocols to expand the number of available IP addresses to meet the world's growing needs. The regional Internet registry system has expanded over the years to five, one per region, to facilitate a more globally distributed IP address resource allocation. The IETF also took up the issue of expanding domain names into non-ASCII characters so that languages other than English could be used. The first Internationalized Domain Name for Applications (IDNA) protocol was adopted by the IETF in 2003 and was updated in 2008.[14] This standard has facilitated the deployment of IDNs in both the country-code and generic top-level domain space by ICANN and registry operators. And while the original name space had seven top-level domains, after multiple rounds of expansion efforts by ICANN, this expanded by 2025 to more than one thousand gTLDs.[15]

Even though the actors and institutions involved in critical Internet resource standards and allocation have taken steps to expand availability and access, historic disparities continue. In the case of domain names, the concentration of companies involved in the domain industry primarily continues to be in the West. The uptake and adoption of IPv6 has been much slower than anticipated given the limited incentives to shift and the lack of direct interoperability with IPv4. One challenge is that "transitioning to IPv6 did not offer network operators, enterprises, or vendors any clear advantages in the short term, required some expenditure, and was another protocol to manage when few IPv6 services were available."[16] To encourage IPv6 uptake and adoption some governments have mandated shifts in government networks and have included IPv6 requirements in procurement contracts. The OECD undertook work to examine the economic benefits of the transition and, in 2012, ISOC initiated World IPv6 days, since which "global IPv6 traffic has grown more than 5000%."[17]

In the context of domain names, while the IETF finalized the IDNA standard to accommodate non-ASCII characters and ICANN expanded the number of diverse gTLDs, the meaningful use of IDNs requires that all actors involved in the Internet user experience take some action. ICANN has launched a work program on "universal acceptance" geared toward ensuring "that all domain names, including new top-level domains, Internationalized Domain Names (IDNs), and email addresses are treated equally and can be used by all Internet-enabled applications, devices, and system."[18] This effort has included training, readiness assessments, and the creation of an annual Universal Acceptance Day to build awareness. ICANN has also taken steps to build global diversity and representation in the operation of gTLD registry operators by establishing an applicant support program to provide both financial and non-financial resources, including a USD $2 million fund, as it takes steps to further expand the number of gTLDs.[19]

## Capacity-Building and Inclusion in Technical Standards

Internet standards have society-wide implications in that they shape not only the global technical architecture but also have significant economic and political implications. The intersections between standards and inclusion are numerous, as addressed in *Opening Standards: The Global Politics of Interoperability* (MIT Press 2011). The development and adoption of open standards contributes to the extent to which information and communication technologies are distributed globally and whether these products are affordable in emerging markets. Whether standards are openly published determines the capacity for implementing these standards in products and enabling economic competition among interoperable products. Open publication of standards also enables access to the specifications for the purpose of understanding and holding to account design components with public interest implications. Whether or not standards have underlying intellectual property restrictions on their use, such as standards-embedded patents, has capacity-building and inclusion connections. If companies throughout the world had to pay royalties on the use of Internet standards in order to embed them in their products, this could have a direct limiting effect on innovation and on economic competition beyond first-mover advantage. Said another way, a lack of standardization can be a technical barrier to trade. The question of who participates, or is permitted to participate, in standards-setting organizations is salient because involvement carries with it the capacity to shape not only technical architectures but societal interests from privacy to security.

As early as 2003, because of all of the aforementioned intersections of capacity-building, inclusion, and standards, the United Nations WSIS Geneva Declaration of Principles specifically called out the critical role of standardization in developing countries:

> Standardization is one of the essential building blocks of the Information Society. There should be particular emphasis on the development and adoption of international standards. The development and use of open, interoperable, non-discriminatory and demand-driven standards that take into account needs of users and consumers is a basic element for the development and greater diffusion of ICTs and more affordable access to them, particularly in developing countries. International standards aim to create an environment where consumers can access services worldwide regardless of underlying technology.[20]

As part of the WSIS process, this emphasis on standardization and development continued in the Geneva Plan of Action and in the 2005 Tunis Agenda for the Information Society, both underlining the critical role of open and interoperable standards in the international system.[21]

The Telecommunication Standardization Sector of the ITU (ITU-T), in their "Bridging the Standardization Gap" project on improving standards capacity in the developing world, published a research project on "Measuring and Reducing the Standards Gap" in 2009.[22] While focused on nation-state capacity, the quantitative metrics used in this project try to assess standards capacity in key categories such as development capacity, government standards policies, national standards use and adoption, and human factors such as number of standards experts, standards courses in higher education, conferences or standards-development meetings held within the country, and government funding of standards training, among other measurements.

The ITU's Development Sector (ITU-D) has also focused on capacity development. Given its international intergovernmental organization status, it focuses on nation-states and donor-recipient model approaches to absorptive capacity. Its work especially deals with telecommunication specifications and various supporting systems aspects of the IP ecosystem but also builds on partnerships with private sector organizations. Other international standards-setting institutions have also done specific, sustained work on building greater absorptive capacity and participation in standardization. For example, the International Organization for Standardization (ISO) has a capacity-building program, both for the objectives of facilitating trade and building capacity in developing countries, through training courses and technical assistance, among other investments.[23]

More specific to the Internet Protocol, IETF procedural norms have contributed to the capacity for inclusion in standardization: participatory openness, free availability of standards, and minimal restrictions, if any, around intellectual property rights use in standards. Participation can be measured in many ways, but inclusion would not be possible at all without the underlying procedural openness in the IETF of anyone being able to contribute to standards, attend events, or participate in core working groups. Because of the cost to attend in-person meetings around the world, the remote participation capacity also contributes to inclusivity. Other factors necessary to assess IETF inclusivity include the global distribution of meetings and representational diversity, both in contributors and those in leadership positions.

The IETF's intellectual property rights (IPR) approach arguably has contributed the most to innovation and economic capacity-building around Internet hardware and software, as well as to the rapid global growth of the network. The policy generally requires disclosure of any IPR related to standards development and giving normative preference to these rights to be licensed on either a royalty-free basis or under reasonable and non-discriminatory, or RAND, terms.

Efforts to build human capacity in standardization have spanned nearly all standards organizations. The Internet Society has consistently worked toward this goal, through fellowship programs to build expertise from developing countries, Internet governance courses, and also capacity-building partnerships. Inclusion goals are baked into ISOC's mission: "supports education in developing countries specifically, and wherever the need exists; promotes professional development and builds community to foster participation and leadership in areas; fosters an environment for international cooperation, community, and a culture that enables self-governance to work; serves as a focal point for cooperative efforts to promote the Internet as a positive tool to benefit all people throughout the world; and provides management and coordination for on-strategy initiatives and outreach efforts in humanitarian, educational, societal, and other contexts."[24]

All of these dimensions of inclusion—all works in progress—speak to the multidimensional aspects of capacity-building related to strengthening absorptive capacity, not merely developing the technical standards but the ability for these standards to be adopted and absorbed across geographies and societies.[25]

## Inclusion Through IP-Supporting Systems

The supporting systems that form the infrastructural scaffolding of the Internet Protocol IP have various points of connection with inclusion. These include the Domain Name System, the global routing system, the worldwide network of authoritative root servers, and Internet Exchange Points and other interconnection infrastructure. The DNS, for example, has expanded in overall number of top-level domain names and the accommodation of different scripts and languages in domain names, as well as their character length. Yet, the systems used by many software applications to validate domain names and email addresses are still derived from the early days of the DNS. This can lead to glitches and/or inability for some end users to conduct online transactions without receiving error messages. There are initiatives to raise awareness of such issues and develop technical solutions. One of these is the Universal Acceptance Steering Group (UASG), a 2015-founded consortium of more than 120 "companies, governments and community groups." [26] The UASG Communications Working Group is working toward a technical standard to ensure that all domain names and email addresses can be used by all Internet-enabled applications, devices, and systems.

Historically, a critical mass of authoritative name servers—the root servers—were located in the United States. ICANN and the organizations managing DNS infrastructure have worked toward implementing and maintaining a greater decentralization of root servers. Having local instances of root servers is important to improve national and regional Internet resiliency in those regions, but also to improve the security and resilience of the Internet globally. In December 2022, ICANN and regional partners deployed the first ICANN Managed Root Server (IMRS) cluster in Africa.[27] Prior to the IMRS cluster installation, ICANN reported that 35 to 40 percent of the DNS query traffic was traveling outside of Africa for resolution. The IMRS cluster enabled many more DNS root queries to be handled within the continent. This localization contributes to inclusion by "stimulating Internet access and strengthening Internet stability for its users," and for security as the IMRS is meant to provide higher bandwidth and data processing capacity to possibly alleviate some of the heavy and sudden traffic deriving from DDoS attacks.[28]

Internet Exchange Points may be an even more crucial dimension of inclusion within the IP ecosystem. IXPs are the physical and logical infrastructure points at which network operators connect and exchange traffic based on private contractual agreements to do so. These network operators are actually a heterogenous collection of institutions including local ISPs, content delivery networks, large media companies, cloud computing services, large backbone networks, mobile phone providers, and many more. The number of IXPs has grown over time but are still unevenly distributed. The presence or absence—or the scarcity versus abundance—of IXPs in a country or a region has immediate implications for inclusion. The presence of an IXP means that Internet traffic flows do not have to rely on IXPs outside of the country, thus ensuring enhanced connectivity and more efficient routing. A 2020 Internet Society report studying Kenya and Nigeria's IXP growth points out the important effects linked to the presence of an IXP within a country: IXPs increase the speed of local exchange, catalyze locally hosted content and services, and contribute to Internet usage, thereby increasing Internet penetration.[29] Yet, several countries in the world do not have an IXP or only have one.[30] The presence of an IXP additionally contributes to ease (and lower cost) of access to the IP ecosystem, thus improving physical access opportunities. For all these reasons, ISOC, sometimes partnering with governments and the private sector, seeks to be an active force in catalyzing the growth of IXPs, and sees its role as identifying and helping to supply what an IXP needs in order for it to work and especially the requisite technical expertise.[31]

The establishment and the development of an IXP is likely to always depend on a multiplicity of factors, including the existing regulatory framework, the identified business opportunities for private actors, and the envisaged benefits for a country or a region's population. The entanglement of these factors is especially sensitive and potentially controversial in "Global South" regions, due on one hand to the scarcity of these facilities, and on the other hand, the arguably greater need for inclusion-fostering infrastructures, as a detailed academic assessment of the establishment of Mexico's first IXP in May 2014 illustrated.[32] This case study, still one of few examining IXPs as a fully fledged Internet governance actor, sheds light on "realities in which the power of telecommunications incumbents and the lack of market competition prevent IXPs from becoming stable infrastructures,"[33] precisely in those countries and regions that would need them most to foster access and inclusion via the increased technical and economic stability of their regional Internet infrastructures.

## Achieving Meaningful Inclusion: Addressing Limits of Inclusivity

Examining entanglements between the IP ecosystem and inclusion helps to emphasize the importance of "absorptive capacity"—a sponge-like ability to integrate new knowledge or new skills at the individual, organizational, nation-state or regional level.[34] This concept is somewhat analogous to capacity-building or development, but focusing more on the recipient culture, politics, and power as well as on technical architecture. Integral to building absorptive capacity are elements of trust and interoperability. For example, the design of the IPv6 standard providing an expansion of the IP address space was an integral part of capacity-building and inclusion, but not a sufficient one. The cost of upgrading and the conservative momentum of existing installed technology served as a counterweight that has historically slowed adoption. Lack of expertise within governments, and many other contextual and human factors, can also serve as barriers to absorption. The broader forces of absorptive capacity need to embody other spurs to adoption including economic incentives, government procurement policies adopting the technology, industry commitment to implementing dual stack protocols, and institutional distribution of addresses around the world.

A similar adoption impediment has evolved around IDNs over time. Approving new language scripts is necessary but not sufficient. Universal acceptance requires embedding this into systems. An analogous friction arises around the supporting systems of the IP ecosystem, such as IXPs and the DNS. As new features are introduced, there is a gap between embodiment in infrastructure and the uptake and universal acceptance of these new tools in practice.

Inclusion in standardization also has to extend far beyond the procedural openness of allowing (or even inviting) people to participate in the design to increase multistakeholder participation geographically and across stakeholder communities from policymakers to citizens. For least developed communities, having resources to financially sustain the time of experts, and supporting logistics, is similarly critical. The grant programs advanced by some of the core institutions of Internet governance have begun to grapple with these issues, as well as government investment.

Beginning in the late 2010s and early 2020s, civil society began focusing on what it called a "human-centric" Internet. Specifically, a network that accounts for human rights, diversity, and bottom-up and participatory approaches to Internet governance. Yet geopolitical tensions shape even responses to calls for a more human-centric internet.[35] What is sometimes missing in approaches to capacity-building or development is a perspective from the bottom-up, including from a range of different divides.

Inclusion and capacity-building is no more exempt from the geopolitical tensions between cyber sovereignty and multistakeholder governance than other dimensions of Internet governance. Whether or not one adopts a multistakeholder or a nation-centric stance, the intersectionality and complexity of the IP ecosystem, especially as it relates to inclusion, calls for strengthening of absorptive capacities including technical absorptive capacities as much as human capacities.

Many international institutions—including the ITU, the OECD, UNESCO, the United Nations Development Program, the World Bank, all in addition to regional and global Internet governance institutions and numerous NGOs—have advanced programs and resources toward cultivating capacity in the digital sphere. The very mission of the ITU-D is strengthening capacity globally. Since 2019, the ITU has expanded its focus beyond governments to include citizens with the creation of its Digital Transformation Centres (DTC) Initiative partnering with Cisco in order to "support(ing) countries to strengthen digital capacities of citizens, particularly in the underserved communities. The selected DTCs become part of a global network of institutions to accelerate the uptake of digital technologies among citizens and boost the capacity of young entrepreneurs and SMEs to succeed in the digital economy."[36]

The OECD offers another nation-state-centered lens into capacity-building. A 2021 OECD Report recognizes the complexity of digital divides and the need for global digital cooperation. It includes calls for ensuring human rights and for limiting digital authoritarianism. Highlighting continuing inequalities, it also calls on nation-state governments for greater inclusion of women and for handling the challenges of digital inequalities. Even here with the inclusion of mentions about human rights and global cooperation, one can sense the tensions between nation-state governments as actors and a more global IP-ecosystem-matched vision.

One among many examples of a non-governmental, multistakeholder organization addressing inclusion is the Global Forum on Cyber Expertise

(GFCE). The GFCE considers itself a global not-for-profit multistakeholder organization with 130 members from around the world and all sectors, including the ITU, nation-states, regional organizations, the World Bank, private sector companies, and civil society organizations. A mixed capacity-building/development model, "Building cyber capacity provides the necessary foundation for countries to strengthen their cyber resilience through developing skills and capacity that address threats and vulnerabilities arising from cyberspace. It is therefore our mission to strengthen cyber capacity and expertise globally through international collaboration and cooperation."[37]

Describing only these few examples helps surface key questions about what type of absorptive capacity is needed, who defines and frames what capacities are lacking, and what entities are "lacking?" The answers lie in recognition of both the nature of the IP ecosystem itself and evolving technologies as they interact with cultures, societies, geopolitics, and economics as will be discussed in the final chapter. Further, recalling decades-long attempts at successful and unsuccessful capacity-building and the United Nations Sustainable Development Goals with their targets of 2030 reminds one of the needs for amplifying absorptive capacity regarding individual, organizational, and interorganizational leadership in state and non-state actors alike:

- Including a focus on technical along with policy absorptive capacities;
- Crafting strategies that are human-centric and adopt bottom-up elements (as those in design thinking approaches), matching sociocultural and historical contexts;
- Remembering that some successful collaborations or partnerships include both cooperative and competitive elements; and
- Recognizing that the IP ecosystem is a critical part of meaningful inclusion.

Finally, as Risse-Kappen[38] pointed out in 1994, "ideas do not float freely." Learning or knowledge diffusion along with technology diffusion interacts with systemic and domestic political variables. The transformative change surrounding the end of the Soviet system highlights the then-understudied interactions between ideas and their contexts, especially, the international flow of ideas and domestic institutions and structures. Often missing in such historical explorations are intersections with technical infrastructures.

The work of this book serves as a reminder that the transnational flow of ideas/framing of Internet Protocol-related capacity-building or inclusion, interacts dynamically both with technical infrastructures and with domestic and international institutions. Understanding inclusion in the information society requires consideration of the distributed nature of the IP ecosystem with its myriad Internet governance institutions and actors as well as the interactions with technical standards and emerging technologies. These intersections are neither hierarchical nor linear. Thus, approaches to inclusion should involve models that complement the kaleidoscopic design of IP and reflect its very nature. The final chapter highlights ongoing opportunities arising from emerging technologies in the context of geopolitical tensions.

## Notes

1. Meital Kupfer, "A More Inclusive Internet for Who? Non-English Speakers in Digital Spaces," Internet Society Foundation, February 20, 2023, https://www.isocfoundation.org/2023/02/a-more-inclusive-internet-for-who-non-english-speakers-in-digital-spaces/.
2. Eszter Hargittai, ed., *Handbook of Digital Inequality*, Elgar, 2021 and Van Deursen and van Dijk, JAGM, "The First-level Digital Divide Shifts From Inequalities in Physical Access to Inequalities in Material Access," *New Media and Society*, Volume 21, Issue 2, 2019, pp. 354–375.
3. According to ICANN, universal acceptance refers to ensuring access "including new top-level domain names, internationalized domain names, and (that) email addresses are treated equally and can be used by all Internet-enabled applications, devices and systems. (It) provides the gateway to the next billion Internet users."
4. Pitinan Kooarmornpatana and Sarmad Hussain, "Internationalized Domain Name Annual Report 2022," ICANN, 2023.
5. United Nations Development Programme, *Human Development Report 2001*, "Making New Technologies Work for Human Development," United Nations, 2001, https://www.undp.org/publications/human-development-report-2001.

6. United Nations Development Programme, *Human Development Report 2019*, “Beyond Income, Beyond Averages, Beyond Today: Inequalities in Human Development in the 21st Century”, United Nations, 2019, p. 201.
7. Alexander Van Deursen and Ellen Helsper, “The Third-Level Digital Divide: Who Benefits Most from Being Online?” *Communication and Information Technologies Annual*, Emerald Group Publishing Limited, 2015, pp. 29–52.
8. See Gerard Goggin et al., “Disability, Technology Innovation and Social Development in China and Australia.” *Journal of Asian Public Policy* Volume 12, Number 1, 2019, pp. 34–50 or Filippo Trevisan and Derrick L. Cogburn, “Technology and Accessibility in Global Governance and Human Rights: The Experience of Disability Rights Advocates” *Journal of Information, Communication and Ethics in Society*, Volume 18, Number 3, 2020, pp. 377–391.
9. For an overview of technology adoption and capacity-building in developing countries, see: Nanette Levinson “Technology and Development in International Communication,” *Oxford Research Encyclopedia of International Studies,* Oxford University Press, June 2020, pp. 1–31.
10. UNESCO, “Bridging the Digital Divides,” October 17, 2023, https://www.unesco.org/en/articles/bridging-digital-divides?hub=66940.
11. See minutes of the ITU Radio Regulation board 94th Meeting at R23-RRB23.3-C-0015!!PDF-E.pdf (itu.int); See also Freedom House, *Iran: Freedom on the Net 2023 Country Report* | and Farzaneh Badiei, “Islamic Republic v. Starlink: Will The ITU Fragment Satellite Internet?” January 29, 2024, https://digitalmedusa.org/islamic-republic-v-starlink-will-the-itu-fragment-satellite-internet/.
12. The Radio Regulations Board consists of 12 members, each nominated by a nation-state government, and elected through a government only voting process. https://www.itu.int/en/ITU-R/conferences/RRB/Pages/default.aspx.
13. See Mark Raymond and Justin Sherman, “Authoritarian Multilateralism in the Global Cyber Regime Complex: The Double Transformation of an International Diplomatic Practice,” *Contemporary Security Policy,* Volume 45, Number 1, 2023, pp. 110–140 for a

nuanced analysis of digital sovereignty and emergent "authoritarian multilateralism."

14. See, John Klensin, "Internationalized Domain Names for Applications (IDNA): Background, Explanation, and Rationale," IETF, August 2010, https://datatracker.ietf.org/doc/html/rfc5894.
15. See ICANN, "List of Top-Level Domains," https://www.icann.org/resources/pages/tlds-2012-02-25-en.
16. Internet Society, "Frequently Asked Questions (FAQ) on IPv6 Adoption and IPv4 Exhaustion," https://www.internetsociety.org/deploy360/ipv6/faq/.
17. See OECD, "The Economics of the Transition to Internet Protocol version 6 (IPv6)," Working Party on Communication Infrastructures and Services Policy, , November 28, 2014, https://one.oecd.org/document/DSTI/ICCP/CISP%282014%293/FINAL/En/pdf and ISOC, World IPv6 Launch, last accessed April 13, 2014, https://www.worldipv6launch.org.
18. ICANN, "Universal Acceptance," https://www.icann.org/ua.
19. ICANN, "Applicant Support Program," https://newgtlds.icann.org/en/applicants/candidate-support.
20. World Summit on the Information Society, *Declaration of Principles, Building the Information Society: a Global Challenge in the New Millennium, Principle 44. Document* WSIS-03/GENEVA/DOC/4-E, December 12, 2003, http://www.itu.int/wsis/docs/geneva/official/dop.html.
21. World Summit on the Information Society, Tunis Agenda, Document WSIS-05/TUNIS/DOC/6(Rev. 1)-E, November 18, 2005.
22. ITU-T Bridging the Standardization Gap, "Measuring and Reducing the Standards Gap," December 4, 2009, https://www.itu.int/dms_pub/itu-t/oth/32/02/T32020000010001PDFE.pdf.
23. See, for example, International Organization for Standardization, "ISO Action Plan for Developing Countries, 2021-2025, 2021, https://www.iso.org/publication/PUB100374.html.
24. https://www.internetsociety.org/mission/.
25. Absorptive capacity refers to the abilities of an organization or a group of organizations to soak up new knowledge and/or new technologies. This concept builds on the early work of Wesley M. Cohen and Daniel A. Levinthal, "Absorptive Capacity: A New

Perspective on Learning and Innovation," *Administrative Science Quarterly*, Volume 35, 1990, pp. 128–152.

26. UASG Communications Working Group, "Why UA? Understanding the Social and Economic Benefits of Universal Acceptance," April 20, 2022, https://uasg.tech/2022/04/why-ua-understanding-the-social-and-economic-benefits-of-universal-acceptance/.
27. Rangan, Ashwin, "ICANN IMRS Cluster Brings a More Resilient and Stable Internet to Africa," ICANN Blogs, December 6, 2022, https://www.icann.org/en/blogs/details/icann-imrs-cluster-brings-a-more-resilient-and-stable-internet-to-africa-06-12-2022-en.
28. Ibid.
29. Michael Kende, "Anchoring the African Internet Ecosystem: Lessons from Kenya and Nigeria," Internet Society, 2020, https://www.internetsociety.org/wp-content/uploads/2020/06/Anchoring-the-African-Internet-Ecosystem-Lessons-from-Kenya-and-Nigeria.pdf.
30. Packet Clearing House, *Internet Exchange Point Directory Reports*, http://www.pch.net/ixpdir/summary.
31. Internet Society, "The Internet Exchange Point Toolkit & Best Practices Guide: How to Maximize the Effectiveness of Independent Network Interconnection in Developing Regions and Emerging Markets, Collaborative Draft," February 2014, https://www.internetsociety.org/wp-content/uploads/2021/04/Global-IXPToolkit_Collaborative-Draft_Feb-24.pdf.
32. Fernanda R. Rosa, "Internet interconnection infrastructure: Lessons from the Global South," *Internet Policy Review*, Volume *10, Number* 4, 2021.
33. Ibid.
34. Wesley Cohen, and Daniel Levinthal, "Absorptive Capacity: A New Perspective on Learning and Innovation," *Administrative Science Quarterly*, 1990, pp. 128–152 or H. Emre Yildiz et al., "Reconceptualizing Absorptive Capacity: The Importance of Teams as a Meso-level Context," *Technological Forecasting and Social Change*, Volume 199, 2024.
35. Nanette Levinson, "Idea Entrepreneurs: The United Nations Open-Ended Working Group & Cybersecurity," *Telecommunications Policy,* 45, 2021.

36. See ITU, "Digital Transformation Centres Background," https://academy.itu.int/itu-d/projects-activities/digital-transformation-centres-initiative.
37. See https://thegfce.org/about-gfce/.
38. Thomas Risse-Kappen, "Ideas Do Not Float Freely," *International Organization*, Volume 48, Number 2, 1994, pp. 185–214.

CHAPTER 9

# Geopolitical and Technical Futures of the Internet Protocol

The Internet, despite many of the challenges addressed in this book, is one of the most transformative technologies to have ever been invented, leading the world into the era of digital transactions, telemedicine, global access to knowledge, social media, and the Internet of Things. The COVID-19 pandemic only accentuated the vital importance of the Internet for healthcare, distance learning, entertainment, and connecting families unable to see each other in person. It also perhaps marked a turning point for the ways in which humans work now and into the future, moving many parts of the world and many occupations to increasingly hybrid settings, or even completely online. At the same time, it accentuated existing inequalities, online harassment, and privacy concerns, and made more visible the presence of internet infrastructure in a range of critical domains from energy to transportation.

Underneath these concerns, the Internet Protocol and its surrounding technical and institutional ecosystem have been at the center of this transformation—both the opportunities and the challenges. This is not as much to define the Internet as IP—although that definition had some consensus but not unanimity among the experts surveyed for this book—but to acknowledge the enduring centrality of the Internet Protocol and surrounding ecosystem even throughout changes in its technical design and institutional governance structures. To be sure, as



F. M. Alexander et al., *Geopolitics at the Internet's Core*, Information Technology and Global Governance,
https://doi.org/10.1007/978-3-031-89478-7_9

one surveyed expert summarized, "Outside of the technical or research community, I'd doubt many people would equate IP as a technical definition of the Internet. Most people equate the Internet with the currently most successful applications and their use, not the enabling underlying protocols."[1]

It is true that the evolution of applications—from the Web to social media to the Internet of Things—is what has been so transformative over decades. But this book hopefully contributes to pulling back the curtain to make visible the protocological infrastructure underpinning the digital world and the geopolitical battles over IP unfolding over decades and helping to emphasize why IP—and control over IP—matter greatly to the world.

The rise of artificial intelligence applications in the twenty-first century would also not be possible without the Internet. There arguably would be no usable AI without the Internet. Using generative AI as an example, the massive stores of data that provide training inputs to large language models or image generation programs originate from or are accessed primarily over the Internet. Immediate feedback from users accessing these programs over the public Internet further refines these generative AI systems. The Internet's infrastructure—from cloud computing and content hosting services to broadband access—serves as the very scaffolding of AI systems. Generative AI applications themselves are part of the Internet application ecosystem just like the Web or video streaming. And many of the longstanding lessons and structures of Internet governance are shaping AI governance discussions, especially problems around content moderation, privacy, user consent, intellectual property, antitrust, and security. As an example, the earliest agreement was an OECD values-based set of principles targeting governments and all stakeholders in their respective roles on how best to achieve trustworthy stewardship of AI.[2]

Reciprocally, AI has diffused into the Internet's architecture at all layers. Machine learning techniques are at the heart of many cybersecurity mechanisms detecting DDoS attacks and other irregular patterns that indicate the presence of malware or unauthorized network intrusions. Internet search engines are fully dependent upon AI to efficiently sort through massive quantities of information and try to return the most relevant, accurate, or personalized search returns, sometimes simultaneously and instantaneously performing language translation of returned content. AI-shaped data analysis and personalization fuels the advertising revenue business models underlying much of the information society and prioritizes or recommends everything from YouTube videos and social media feeds to recommended products on Amazon.

That AI and the Internet are entangled in every way further solidifies the Internet's place as a historic innovation while further complicating public policy problems, for example, around security, mass surveillance, labor transformations, deception, inequality, and polarization. Many warnings about AI follow the same historical trajectory of warnings about the collapse or destruction of the Internet (or even society) as the technology has evolved. Some of these concerns came from those who themselves helped design the digital world. In 1995, Ethernet inventor Robert Metcalfe, a respected technologist and founder of a prominent early switch manufacturer 3Com, predicted that the Internet would collapse, in part because of its rapid growth.[3] Web inventor Tim Berners-Lee has more recently and harshly criticized how the Web has shifted from a decentralized and open model to a small number of concentrated platforms based on proprietary architectures, monopolization, and revenue model in which society has voluntarily handed over personal data. As Berners-Lee told Vanity Fair, the Web has "ended up producing–with no deliberate action of the people who designed the platform–a large-scale emergent phenomenon which is anti-human."[4]

How is it that the Internet Protocol ecosystem—the core of the Internet creating a common address space and consistent global routing, interoperability, and interconnection system—has *endured massive political, social, and technological changes*? Massive technical changes include the rise of new applications such as the Web, social media, the Internet of Things, and generative AI. Perhaps the greatest transformation is the rise of societal dependence on the Internet for everything from financial to health care systems.

While more out of view from Internet users, there have also been massive changes in the institutional system of Internet governance. Internet governance is not static any more than technology is static. The institutional system has shifted significantly over time, distributed over countless multistakeholder actors. Just one of these transformations was the shift from U.S. stewardship of names and numbers to a once-new institution, ICANN. There are new Regional Internet Registries, new battles over cyber sovereignty versus multistakeholder governance, new data localization laws, new privacy laws, new cybersecurity organizations, and new technologies of Internet governance. Throughout all of this, the Internet Protocol has endured.

Even the language around the Internet is mercurial. Nomenclature is inherently inconsistent. Information superhighway. Video on demand. Online world. Small i internet or capital I Internet? Cyberspace or Internet or Digital? Will the word digital endure as quantum technologies advance? Anyone involved in technology policy has experienced the constant code switching such as using "cyber" when talking about national security or "Internet" when discussing access to information, economic growth, or speech rights, even when the technologies and the policy issues being discussed are the same. The Internet Protocol has underpinned all of this.

What has accompanied the constancy of the Internet Protocol, even as it evolved, is the constant geopolitical pressure and conflict over the IP ecosystem. As the Internet has become more enmeshed in society and has continued to grow in users and innovative new applications, it has become ever more entangled in geopolitical conflict. To what extent has this geopolitical pressure ruined or fragmented the Internet? Kieron O'Hara's and Wendy Hall's book *Four Internets: Data, Geopolitics, and the Governance of Cyberspace* (2021) explores the emergence of and tensions around different approaches to governing the Internet from a relatively open Internet to what the author's describe as the Beijing paternal Internet.

An independent task force of the Council on Foreign Relations declared, somewhat controversially, in 2022 that "the era of the global Internet is over" in part because the Internet is "less free, more fragmented, and less secure."[5]

It is true that the experience of the Internet in one part of the world—whether as a user, government official, or developer—is quite different than in other parts of the world. There is uneven distribution, uneven filtering and censorship, and uneven economic opportunity. As one of our survey experts warned: "the 'splinternet' is a reality already, with Governments of countries like China and Russia using the network to control its citizens' access to information and ability to communicate. User experience of fragmentation is likely to continue, much along "East vs West" political lines, but perhaps the next major technical advance on the Internet might reunite the end-to-end nature of the Internet."[6]

Even while exploring critical issues of fragmentation, security, and repression, the underlying Internet Protocol ecosystem provides the structural building block for enabling the distribution of information—including reports about fragmentation—to almost everywhere in the world. Countless attempts to redesign the Internet Protocol core of the Internet—even as IP has evolved to address security and access issues—have indeed been a feature of modern society, from a "new IP" to blockchain Web 3.0 efforts.

One of the global experts surveyed for this book summed up this pressure on the Internet Protocol: "The state of IP makes me feel a little bit sad, because it's such a brilliant, lightweight concept and has enabled so much innovation to sit on top of it. It's truly a wonder, and I don't think enough people really reflect on how extraordinary the TCP/IP set of protocols have been in simply providing interconnection without compelling adherence to a particular ideology, set of applications or geographical location."[7]

Amid all of these constant changes and pressures, why has the Internet Protocol ecosystem—including a consistent global address space—remained at the center of the Internet and of society? This concluding chapter examines why the Internet Protocol system has endured over time amid geopolitical, technical, and societal transformations and explores its prospects for its future given this ongoing pressure.

## The Normal Cycle of Technology as a Proxy for Geopolitics

History has established—and this book has tried to elaborate—that the core technologies of the Internet have constantly been brought to the center of controversies, geopolitical debates, and power struggles over the digital economy and society. The proliferation of the Internet into almost every aspect of daily life mirrors the increase in governmental interest in Internet governance. This is not merely about governments focusing on basic connectivity issues and how to ensure that their citizens can take advantage of the benefits the Internet offers. It is also not only about basic public interest concerns such as protecting privacy and addressing the security risks of the networks. Control over the design and governance of core digital technologies now help determine economic power and political power from the nature of the relationship among governments, the private sector, and citizens to the nature of global warfare.

While it can be justifiable to default to the notion that democratic leaning states behave one way and more authoritarian regimes behave another, the key point is that all of the 193 governments that make up the United Nations—as well as non-state actors—enter into the many Internet governance control struggles over the core and hidden infrastructures enabling the global Internet. This infrastructure is and will continue to be a space of control and power.

The contested spaces examined in this book support five key geopolitical themes that will likely endure and will likely perpetuate the normal cycle of technology as a proxy for geopolitics. The first is the tension between *bordered nations and a borderless Internet*. State and non-state actors alike reach across borders over decentralized and distributed technical architecture, leading to tensions between cybersovereignty approaches such as data localization laws versus how the Internet works in practice. In turn, sometimes regulatory approaches established in one region—because so many companies do business in many nations—have harmonizing legal effects on other regions. The EU's GDPR privacy regulation is a possible example.

The second theme likely to endure is how governments and other actors seek to achieve economic or political objectives by *co-opting Internet infrastructure*. Chapter Six took up one example of this phenomenon, how the Domain Name System and other technical points of control in the IP ecosystem have routinely been co-opted to filter or block content. With IP-based networks so diffuse and their impacts so broad, governments looking to achieve an outcome have begun to delve deeper and deeper into the underlying Internet infrastructure. Whether it is modifying standards, using the domain name system to filter or block content, or hijacking routes as a vector in nation-state conflict, governments' activity is increasing. This has resulted in techniques such as governments using IP addresses for identifying citizens, hackers using DDoS attacks for dissident objectives, or law enforcement use of infrastructure for intellectual property rights enforcement.

One of the surveyed experts for this book captured this phenomenon of co-opting infrastructure well: "We can see considerable evidence that some (governments in particular, but not solely them) are uncomfortable with the power that the Internet gives individuals, and that they have started to reach for the handy levers of putting controls back into the network."[8]

Another thematic force shaping the geopolitics of infrastructure is, of course, the *politics of technical design* itself. In the case of IP, this is evident in both attempts to redesign IP entirely and replace it with a new standard and the actual practices of incrementally redesigning IP, such as extending the size of the address space to enable greater connectivity or overlaying security features on core protocols. The social shaping of technical design is far older than the Internet and will continue to be a feature of society. As one of the book's surveyed experts expressed, "I hope we will still have IP as the core of the internet architecture, and I hope we will see the policies that boundaries between cultures and jurisdictions (that will not have gone away) can be implemented as policies. And not by breaking the internet architecture."[9]

*Internet infrastructure is privatized*, and will continue to be highly privatized, as the majority of networks and systems are owned, funded, and operated by for profit corporations. While no single actor, corporation or government, controls or owns the entirety of the Internet, the decisions of private companies, either unilaterally or in response to law or societal pressure have had the most direct impact. The most attention to this issue resides around content, such as the so-called techlash against the concentrated power of large technology and media companies. But the privatization of all layers of the information and communication sphere has been both a destabilizing force for governments and a site of delegated censorship and surveillance over citizens. ICANN's decision to turn down the Ukrainian request to disrupt Russian Internet connectivity by, in part, withdrawing IP addresses is an example of the power even not-for-profit but also arguably multistakeholder private entities have in the digitally mediated public sphere.

Closely related to the above themes in Internet governance and addressed throughout this book and especially in Chapter 2, *multistakeholder arrangements largely make up the Internet governance ecosystem*. IP addresses, protocols, and systems are mediated by a multistakeholder ecosystem of design entities, governance entities, and usage contexts. Larry Lessig influenced a generation of legal scholars with his 1999 book *Code and Other Laws of Cyberspace* explaining how behavior online, like offline, is regulated by four overlapping and concurrently acting modalities. Only one of these modalities involves law. The other three are: markets, such as economic forces of supply and demand or privatized governance via business models based on data collection; norms, such as cultural or institutional approaches to content moderation in platforms;

and, of course, technical architecture, such as standards design as a force shaping public policy. Many of these modalities comport with the points of control and power dynamics between the design, implementation, usage, and governance of IP addresses.

Who possesses critical resources? Who distributes them and on what procedural or distributional basis? Who is behind the standards design and what procedural and participatory norms shape this design? How are IP addresses used to block content or identify people? And many more questions of power and influence.

The technological artifact that is an IP address–in its design, use, supporting systems, and governance—elucidates eight points of control and power that help explain why IP resides at the center of so many controversies. These points of infrastructure power are summarized in Table 9.1.

**Table 9.1** Eight points of power within the IP ecosystem

- **Architectural Design**—Authority over design of the Internet protocols and supporting systems and the procedural and participatory norms shaping this design and essentially enacting technically mediated public policy, such as around privacy, security, and access
- **Distributional Forces**—Control over the distribution of Internet addresses and how and whether these resources are re-distributed over time sectorally, geographically, either administratively or via markets
- **Possessorship**—Influence via who historically "possesses" or "acquires" the ability to use an IP address over time and what influence, for example, holders of large IP address blocks have over the overall system
- **Intermediation Power**—Power via co-opting or otherwise using IP-related infrastructure for blocking content, disrupting communication, surveilling, or profiting politically or economically
- **Extraterritoriality**—Control by bringing IP addresses, protocols, systems, and governance into cross-border, global policy conflicts
- **Securitization**—The security decision points around the IP ecosystem and decisions mediating values tensions between the need for strong security to protect the economy, privacy, and critical infrastructure and the need for weaker security for law enforcement, intelligence, and cyber offense
- **Forces of Identification**—Decisions about anonymity, personal identity, authentication, and traceability that determine everything from individual privacy to protection from identity theft and harassment online
- **The Politics of Structuralization**—The power dynamics behind attempts to procedurally or institutionally shape or reconfigure the governance system administering IP addresses

As long as these terrains of influence exist within the Internet Protocol ecosystem, the cycle of politicization around the technology will likely continue.

## Normal Geopolitical Pressure to Redesign the Internet Protocol

The Internet Protocol has hardly been a static technology. This book, especially Chapters 3 and 4, has addressed many significant evolutions. Perhaps most notably, a major redesign effort was the selection of the next-generation protocol—IPv6—that would expand the size of the IP address space to accommodate the rapid internationalization and commercialization of the Internet. In the same 1990s time period, the introduction of Classless Inter-Domain Routing (CIDR) replaced the system essentially requiring large blocks of IP addresses handed out to institutions for a more flexible allocation size. IPsec and other security protocols, including DNSSEC, were introduced to provide greater security via cryptography. Engineers have augmented the Internet Protocol to apply in new settings, such as the Internet of Things, and responded to demand for greater security and greater quality of service.

While the Internet Protocol and surrounding standards and systems have not been static, they have consistently retained the basic technical characteristics that make them arguably the common denominator of the Internet: a common, global address system, common technical standards that enable interoperability, and shared supporting systems such as the Domain Name System translating names into numbers.

But attempts to redesign the Internet, sometimes from scratch, have proliferated. These efforts have sometimes focused on replacing the IP ecosystem entirely and sometimes involved radical redesign adjacent to IP. For example, some of these redesign efforts have centrally involved overlaying new technologies, such as work on a "Quantum Internet" or replacing some functions with a decentralized blockchain-based architecture.

Some of these initiatives are arguably "thought experiments," such as RINA (Recursive Internet Architecture),[10] proposed by French engineer and computer scientist Louis Pouzin, former inventor of Cyclades, one of the first packet-switching networks. Several of these projects' technical soundness and feasibility have, however, already been heavily criticized.[11] Other initiatives are able to gain broader and stronger traction, such as the Chinese "NewIP" effort. This project could be described as a "clean slate" initiative attempting to not only redesign the protocol system but also dislodge the institutional system responsible for designing and administering the technologies. One of the experts surveyed for this book explained that "The reasons for 'NewIP' and all the variants of that idea are often posed as improvements of all the things IP got wrong, but there is precious little evidence that these are features generally needed or, in some cases, actually wanted except by those who want to control traffic more."[12]

The ITU has been at the center of many of the control struggles over the Internet Protocol, from the historic controversy over who would control Internet addresses to the appearance of NewIP proposals. In the case of NewIP, as one of the experts surveyed summarized, "I haven't seen any 'redesigns' whose purpose was to facilitate fragmentation, but I haven't seen any real technical specifications for any of the so-called "redesigns" (in particular, the Huawei so-called "new IP" never contained any technical details)."

After many criticisms of the redesign proposals in the ITU, more incremental proposals began surfacing, but with the same impact: "a loss of interoperability and therefore a loss of the single global Internet and enhanced risks of surveillance, tracking and human rights violations."[13] One surveyed expert called this incremental approach adopting "guerilla tactics to start blowing apart the current IP edifice."[14]

It is nearly impossible to disconnect state redesign efforts from the overarching philosophy of cybersovereignty intensively challenging the so-called multistakeholder system. Perhaps the most consistent actor in this space is the Russian Federation. Domestically, Russia put in place a variety of rules to ensure state control of the Internet within its borders.[15] Internationally, they focused on pushing for a cybersecurity treaty through the UN General Assembly processes, while criticizing but participating in the multistakeholder Internet governance system. In 2020, the Russian Federation began to directly call for changes in the Internet governance system. Harking back to policy positions from the 2003–2005 WSIS discussions and ignoring the results of the IANA stewardship transition as detailed in Chapter 5, in August 2020, former President and Prime Minister and then Deputy Chair of the Russian Security Council, Dmitry Medvedev asserted that the United States fully controlled the domain name system and that the system needed to change.[16]

Similar statements from other Russian officials followed and to kick off 2022, the Russian Federation attached a statement to the January meeting report of the ITU Council Working on Internet-related public policy specifically calling for "the transformation of the existing Internet governance system in order to exclude the influence of any unilateral political restrictions or commercial interests on it and ensure the safety, integrity, continuity, stability, sustainability and security of the global critical infrastructure."[17]

This was all coupled with the Russian Federation's nomination of a candidate for the ITU's powerful Secretary General position, Rashid Ismailov, and the implication that the ITU would be the place to execute this change to the multistakeholder system. The competing candidate for the ITU Secretary General, which was decided in a secret paper ballot election process, was from the United States. This led some to suggest the outcome of this election would determine the future of the Internet.[18] In the end, on September 29, 2022, Doreen Bogdan-Martin, the U.S. candidate, won by an overwhelming majority, 139 votes to 25. Bogdan-Martin ran on a vision of inclusivity, partnerships, and connectivity, and is the first woman to lead the ITU since it was founded in 1865.

Another example was the discussion in the European Union around their second Network and Information Security directive (NIS2). As part of an effort to increase cyber resiliency, the European Commission (EC) staff proposal included a series of provisions related to the domain name system that would among other things result in Brussels having regulatory oversight of root server operations. This proposal was in stark contrast to the existing system where the 13 root server operators are included as part of the ICANN administered multistakeholder technical Internet governance system. Not only was the proposal inconsistent with longstanding European support for multistakeholder Internet governance as a general matter given it proposed the DNS be subject to government oversight, the EC proposal was extraterritorial in nature as it asserted jurisdiction over the entire global system.[19] A variety of European and non-European stakeholders weighed in objecting, including RIPE-NCC who operates one of the root servers in Europe.[20]

Technical redesign-based challenges to the multistakeholder Internet governance system also occur in the United States. Under the guise of being strong in the face of the Russian invasion of Ukraine, the U.S. Federal Communications Commission (FCC), began looking into how to secure Internet routing by issuing a Notice of Inquiry (NOI).[21] Citing

Russia's hijacking of Internet routes in Ukraine as part of its incursion, the FCC asked for information about vulnerabilities threatening the security and integrity of Border Gateway Protocol (BGP). Tying the effort directly to the FCC's role in the security of communications networks broadly and the previous work of an FCC industry advisory committee, the NOI represented the first ever direct engagement of the FCC in Internet governance issues in a regulatory manner. Prior to this, U.S. efforts related to the DNS had largely been led by NTIA given its role with respect to ICANN and the U.S.' long standing support for multistakeholder Internet infrastructure governance. While the NOI recognized the role of existing Internet Protocol institutions such as the IETF, ICANN, and the RIRs, it specifically put forward the idea of U.S. domestic regulation, via the FCC, as way to resolve a global IP challenge and as a means to ensure U.S. leadership and counter Russian aggression:

> *Commission's Role.* Ensuring continued U.S. leadership requires that we explore opportunities to spur trustworthy innovation for more secure communications and critical infrastructure... We seek comment on our authority to promote the security of Internet routing through regulation, including as it may apply to wireless and wireline Internet Service Providers, Internet Exchange Providers, interconnected VoIP providers, operators of content delivery networks, cloud service providers, and other enterprise and organizational stakeholders.[22]

Close to fifty parties responded to the NOI within the 60-day window for both the comments and reply comments, with various points of view on the questions posed by the FCC.[23] The majority of commenters however opposed a direct regulatory role for the FCC in Internet routing. Arguing that FCC regulation would be ineffective and unwarranted given the global nature of the Internet, they instead recommended the FCC work with other U.S. government agencies to convene stakeholders to develop voluntary best practices, fund research into improving routing security, and consider secure routing requirements for U.S. government contractors. This included the IAB which filed comments pointing out that "the IETF will continue to evolve the BGP protocol to meet the needs of new network structures and applications, with a strong focus on security."[24]

NTIA, which coordinates interagency views and represents the U.S. Executive Branch before the independent FCC in addition to being the lead agency on DNS issues, filed reply comments suggesting interagency cooperation, provided examples of existing U.S. government work in this area, and called on the FCC to engage in multistakeholder efforts. More pointedly, NTIA stated that "regulation by the Commission over Internet routing could set a damaging precedent in support of international Internet regulation, in contrast to standing USG policy."[25]

The clear message in support of multistakeholder solutions as opposed to domestic regulation was however undercut nearly three months past the comment deadline when NTIA with a simple transmission cover note attached, forwarded to the FCC the comments of the Department of Homeland Security's Cybersecurity and Infrastructure Security Agency (CISA). CISA in its individual agency comments articulated its concerns with respect to the lack of secure routing as it relates to U.S. national security and called for more forceful steps. Specifically, "CISA recommends that the FCC investigate and consider methods to drive down this risk by utilizing all of its statutory authorities."[26] The CISA comments were then publicly welcomed by FCC Chair Jessica Rosenworcel, something that did not occur when, in May, NTIA filed the presumably interagency coordinated comments.[27]

The examples detailed above, which as of this writing, have yet to come to resolution, demonstrate that technology-driven challenges to the multistakeholder model are emerging from a wide range of state actors, in both liberal democracies as well as more authoritarian regimes. Even in the United States, which arguably, has championed the multistakeholder model most overtly, the FCC's taking up the issue of whether or not to regulate domestically secure Internet routing illustrates that the default to seek regulatory or government mandated solutions to Internet governance issues occurs if stakeholders do not remain vigilant or if the existing IP governance institutions fail to address a problem.

The overall multistakeholder approach and its underlying, though always contested, principles of openness and participation have generally contributed to economic growth and expressive liberty and clearly emerged victorious in the early battles detailed in Chapter 5. Yet, there are many unknowns. Will one technical governance approach ultimately dominate into the future of geopolitical unknowns? It is possible that different governance approaches will evolve around various Internet governance issue sets or that Internet fragmentation is intensified by non-uniform choices made around geopolitical pressures.

One Internet expert consulted for this book raised an entirely different concern. While there will continue to be efforts to fundamentally change

IP, "there is no reason to believe that people will not try other solutions, including outside of IP, to gain more control over their networks and communication."[28]

Attention needs to be paid to these battles as there are costs to losing what have been the successes of both the prevailing architecture and governance model. Whether driven by technological need or political expediency, these control battles continued over decades and will likely continue into the future.

## Challenges to IP from Quantum to Outer Space

Speculating about emerging information technologies is precarious, even a fool's errand, because innovation in this space proceeds so rapidly. The inception of ARPANET is in living memory. The Web, social media, smartphones, and artificial intelligence certainly are. Two things can be certain. The Internet's next chapter will also see significant and rapid technological transformations, many not yet fully envisioned. And this rapid innovation co-produces, and is reciprocally constructed by social change. As STS scholar Sheila Jasanoff summarizes in *The Ethics of Invention*, "Our inventions change the world, and the reinvented world changes us."[29]

Yet, anticipating change is, and has always been, a central enterprise in technology governance. Anticipatory governance especially embeds the recognition that technical and standards design is part of public policy rather than simply *ex post facto* regulation or technical administration after a new technology is developed. When focusing on the institutional components of the IP ecosystem—whether governments, international organizations, regional organizations, standards-setting bodies, private sector, technical sector, or civil society—the question of governance, as opposed to governments, arises around emerging technologies as it does in current architectures.[30] Traditional anticipatory governance discussions limit themselves to the inclusion of technical experts with government policymakers, as they discuss possible policy options regarding emerging technologies. Yet the IP ecosystem, with the presence of polycentric governance,[31] means going beyond the traditional definition of anticipatory governance. It is particularly useful to update the anticipatory governance concept with a more inclusive definition of those who should be actually involved in anticipatory governance. Such usage complements the multistakeholder model highlighted in parts of the IP ecosystem.

The contemporary Internet already differs from the traditional "screen-based" Internet in profound ways. In *The Internet in Everything: Freedom and Security in a World with No Off Switch* (2020), DeNardis explained how digital technologies have already leapt from human-facing display screens into the physical world of objects all around us. This cyber-physical, or Internet of Things, transformation co-transforms technology policy from concerns in two dimensional screens to three-dimensional space in which national security, privacy, and human safety issues are dramatically heightened. The Internet is in the body, medical devices, energy sensors, home appliances, agricultural systems, food production systems, and in clothing.

This transformation of the Internet from a communication system to being embedded directly in the physical world speaks to a starting point for investigating emerging and intersectional governance terrains. It is no longer possible to separate online and offline spaces. Internet policy is now directly entangled with other policy issues such as energy policy, environmental policy, consumer safety, medicine, outer space exploration and discovery, as well as continuing to be fully integrated within international relations, national security, human rights, and economic policies.

The current trajectory of design, investment, and interest suggests that the Internet will further move into infinitesimally small and astronomically large spaces. These small cyber-physical spaces for IP addresses include objects in and around the body, including neuroscientific, medical, and diagnostic devices.

Elon Musk's Neuralink project implanting chips into the human brain[32] attracts arguably the most public attention, understandably so because of the safety, security, and privacy questions and the existential blurring of boundaries between human and machine. But human-implantable computer chips are already well developed, at least those dependent upon RFID communication, for security applications and for storing health information. The simple versions of RFID medical-implant technology are not unlike the microchips injected into pets and livestock to provide unique identification numbers. Far more consequentially, cardiac implants, insulin pumps, and other body-implanted cyber-networked objects have wireless connections which in turn can connect to or be controlled by devices on the public Internet. And emerging capabilities in neurotechnology are becoming a terrain of warfare.[33]

Emerging, network-connected biotech devices and systems accessed over the Internet, even with proprietary components, raise many questions about the prevailing architectures and governance norms around the Internet. Will these devices be addressable with unique IPv6 addresses or use a different, possibly more closed system of identification? What authentication and trust architectures are necessary to provide maximal human safety and national security? To what extent are the prevailing standards bodies, such as the IETF, and coordinating institutions, such as ICANN, relevant in this domain? Are open standards for interoperability still important or will proprietary architectures have a resurgence to design fragmentation into the system? Just as major application and device advancements (IoT, the Web, industrial control systems) created new exigencies and demands upon the core technologies of the Internet, so too will biotechnology advancements, all with attending geopolitical tensions and impacts.

Quantum technologies will also likely have direct entanglements with the Internet Protocol and surrounding systems. Internet standards communities are already undertaking quantum standards work such as with the formalization in the IETF of the Quantum Internet Research Group (QIRG)[34] and work taking place within NIST, the ITU, ISO, and many other standards bodies and industry consortia. Vinton Cerf, known as the father of the Internet for his work on TCP/IP and other foundational Internet Protocols and technologies, has predicted that, in the very near future, "we will see some serious applications of quantum computing to solve one or more optimization problems in mechanical design, logistical scheduling, or resource allocation that would be impractical with conventional supercomputing."[35]

Quantum technologies—including quantum computing and quantum sensing, among other applications—would be a fundamental shift from digital technologies. The Internet's longstanding design is digital, based on discrete units and predictable information science that enable any type of information to be represented by a combination of 0s and 1s and then formatted, compressed, encrypted, and transmitted. The systems and protocols addressed in this book are based on this basic premise of discrete units of 0s and 1s. Quantum approaches, in contrast with this digital approach, exist at a more atomic level of photons and electrons, using atomic objects to represent quantum bits. Quantum bits are theoretically able to take on either a 0 or 1 at any given moment because of a quantum mechanics property of superposition. Without attempting to explain the underlying physics, the takeaway is far greater processing capability.

To what extent will a quantum Internet emerge that provides a fundamentally new architecture that connects quantum end nodes, or a quantum overlay on the existing architecture? Even before these possibilities, there will continue to be new design proposals trying to shore up the existing architecture of the Internet—especially the public key cryptography providing so much of society's digital trust architecture—from the prospect of quantum computers overpowering these encryption approaches. The European Union Agency for Cybersecurity (ENISA) summarizes in this way the threat to cybersecurity by quantum computing: "We have known for more than two decades that the development of a sufficiently large and practical quantum computing machine will render most cryptographic systems insecure, radically transforming the existing threat model and endangering our infrastructure."[36]

Whether or not the Internet Protocol ecosystem transforms because of quantum innovations at this atomic level, it is more certain that it will move into astronomically large spaces. One of these areas is likely to be the development of a solar-system Internet.[37] Digital communications on Earth already rely deeply upon satellites: financial systems, national security command and control networks; anything requiring GPS position tracking such as Google or Apple maps; and entertainment and television programming. These systems connect ultimately to or through the public Internet. As communication systems extend further off Earth, to what extent will the underlying technologies have to be redesigned to meet unique atmospheric and positional conditions? NASA is already working on LunaNet, a communication system around the moon; and the European Space Agency is working on its own Moonlight project.

Engineers in multiple institutions are working on a solar-system Internet that would bring the Internet much further off planet. The Interplanetary Chapter of the Internet Society produced a groundbreaking (or maybe spacebreaking) report on "Solar-System Internet Architecture and Governance."[38] Deep-space communication historically involves Earth to device communication. The idea of a solar system or interplanetary Internet is to create a distributed mesh network in space that interconnects many nodes and networks to each other rather than only a point-to-point network back to Earth. Similar to the early Internet, it may not be possible to envision the types of applications—commercial or public—that could use such a network. Perhaps the solar-system Internet will support space settlements and space stations and other human exploration. It could connect deep-space telescopes, planet-based rovers, and other modes of discovery.

The idea of a deep-space Internet sounds futuristic but the idea dates back to 1998, even before the widespread commercialization and globalization of the Web, when Vinton Cerf began discussing the concept while in residence as a distinguished visiting scientist at the Jet Propulsion Laboratory (JPL) in California.

A solar-system network would require many of the technical coordinating functions of the terrestrial Internet. For example, it will need unique identifiers for addressing of nodes, possibly regions, and network domains in space. Who will maintain this identification space and allocate and assign unique numbers, if they indeed are required to be unique? Will ICANN's mandate rise into space, or will another organization enter this domain? Already, ISO has a Consultative Committee for Space Data Systems (CCSDS) formed by the major space agencies (including NASA, JAXA, ESA, CNSA, CSA and others) to establish standards and solve shared space network problems. This Consultative Committee has established the Space Assigned Numbers Authority (SANA) for the purpose of registering standards-related identities.[39]

Given the history of control struggles and politicization of addressing over Internet history, especially the controversy over transitioning IANA stewardship authority from the U.S. government, it is possible that similar conflicts will arise over space network addressing functions. There is also the open question of whether adversarial states funding space networks will want a common addressing scheme.

A technical and administrative complication of extending the Internet into deep space, in short, is that the Internet Protocol and other core technical systems will have to adapt to the unique conditions of space. The combination of harsh atmospheric conditions, latency caused by astronomical distances, constantly moving nodes due to planetary rotation, disruptions from space debris and natural causes, and even lack of time consistency among different planetary gravitational fields, necessitates significant modifications to Internet architecture in space. Even the architecture and back and forth queries of the DNS would not be ideal in space because of latency and will have to be replaced or augmented.

What is "sovereignty" in space? Geopolitical concerns are similarly upended because there is no traditional sovereignty in space. Roughly contemporaneous to the inception of ARPANET, the United Nations

General Assembly adopted the so-called "Outer Space Treaty" addressing a range of subjects (e.g., nuclear non-proliferation) and declaring space not subject to sovereign appropriation.[40] This does not mean that there will not be territorial disputes over outer space or tensions in space networks that follow discussions of cybersovereignty on earth.[41] Sovereignty is already complicated by cross-border digital technologies[42] and is likely to be further complicated as the Internet moves off Earth.

The work underway to create a new space-Internet architecture has generally been referred to as "delay-tolerant networking" (DTN) or sometimes delay and disruption tolerant networking.[43] For example, the IETF has a delay-tolerant networking research group within the Internet Research Task Force and has been working on protocols that respond to the unique requirements of space. Some of the approaches include building storage capability on network nodes and creating technical responses to large and variable transmission delays, intermittently connectivity and normalized disruptions. Initial work has been on "Bundle Protocol" (BP) addressing these difficult constraints.[44] Similar standardization work is also underway, among other efforts, in ISO's Consultative Committee for Space Data Systems, including the CCSDS "Space Packet Protocol" Recommended Standard.[45]

As a solar-system Internet develops, it will likely follow the Internet governance tensions of the past, such as the question of what institution becomes the authoritative source of the core protocols that possibly replace or work in a hybrid manner with the IP ecosystem. Similar to how the Internet of Things developed, there could be multiple competing organizations until working solutions materialize. But as the Interplanetary Networking Special Interest Group (IPNSIG) report expressed in the context of dual efforts in the IETF and the CCSDS, "There is an open question regarding the management and authority of the standards: which standards organization is the proper authority for developing and publishing standards and ensuring that implementations conform to them."[46]

If the Internet moves further off planet and a true solar-system Internet develops over the next half century, it seems certain that new protocols will be introduced, even if in hybrid adjacency to IP, raising questions of standards control and also the appropriateness and feasibility of interconnecting with the terrestrial Internet, especially given the national security and international relations dimensions of space programs.

In the context of emerging technologies, one surveyed expert argued that "The Internet stays the same,"[47] as new requirements such as new services (e.g., blockchain) and new physical interfaces (e.g., new cellular standards) are introduced. Looking at a more remote future, another argued:

> It is highly unlikely as well as very disappointing from a technology perspective if, a hundred years from now, the world is still using DNS and IP protocols as the basis for routing. Hopefully, sometime before 2123 smart people will have developed something better (more efficient and more elegant).

Regardless of whether adaptations or full modifications to architecture emerge, responding in the short term to emerging terrains from quantum to the solar-system Internet, is necessary to maintain the overall core security and stability of the Internet.

## The Enduring Internet Protocol and Its Geopolitics

Considering how rapidly communication technology changes—telegraph, telecom, analog, digital—it is remarkable that the Internet Protocol and surrounding systems have endured for so long and continue to be at the center of the digital world. The Internet Protocol can carry a sense of historical inevitability because it is so entrenched in the global digital sphere. There was, however, nothing preordained about the design and selection and even redesign of IP. There were alternatives that were discarded and contentious global battles fought. And while these conflicts occurred among technologists, private industry, and technical bureaucrats, out of sight of everyday Internet users, the outcome of each skirmish has shaped both the availability and use of the Internet around the world.

The progression of the Internet Protocol has endured crises all along the way, born in crisis, redesigned to address a crucial crisis of address scarcity, and responding and adapting to massive technological changes:

- ***Foundational struggle***: the design, selection, and choice of TCP/IP over OSI protocols;

- ***Expansion struggle***: the selection of a new version of IP—IPv6—to address the need for exponentially more Internet addresses during the Internet's rapid growth;
- ***Oversight struggle***: the transition of the stewardship of the Internet Assigned Numbers Authority (IANA) functions from the U.S. government to the global Internet community.

Having emerged the winner versus the Open Systems Interconnection protocol suite in what is commonly referred to as the Internet-OSI standards war of the late twentieth century, it is not an exaggeration to say, the Internet Protocol arose within conflict. Disagreements flared over which institution was the appropriate venue for developing common global standards, intergovernmental bodies such as the ITU or more open and multistakeholder institutions such as the IETF. Tensions also emerged during the process of revising IP to expand the number of available IP addresses, as well as questions of control and responsibility for the distribution of IP addresses during the Internet's rapid commercialization and globalization.

At the heart of all of these struggles was the question of control, both economic and political. These fights manifested in disagreements over how and where decisions were made, who could be involved in the decisions, and the role of each stakeholder group in decision-making processes. As each crisis has risen and been resolved, the Internet Protocol has remained, even as it has adapted and evolved.

Why is there still "the Internet Protocol" when almost everything else has continually changed over time? What is it about IP that makes it so resilient? Historian of technology, Thomas Hughes, describes a conservative "technological momentum" in the standards for large-scale systems that create an inertia difficult to displace.[48] The Internet Protocol ecosystem touches everything in society from smartphones to industrial systems, a massive sociotechnical transformation unfolding over more than a half century. He is not at all suggesting technological determinism but acknowledging the investment, pervasiveness, and massive installed user base in which prevailing standards embed. A technical expert surveyed for this book summarized this well: "Scale breeds stasis. IP exists as a software (and occasionally hardware) module on billions of devices supported by tens of thousands of support agencies (or even not supported at all). If the protracted transition to IPv6 has taught us anything then the sheer scale of the task of changing every IP software stack is incredibly forbidding. These days it's far cheaper and easier to leave IP alone and change application behaviors."[49]

Society and technology reciprocally co-produce this prevailing architecture, while also shaped by powerful interests and always confronted by exciting new innovations. One of this book's surveyed experts explains the tension between entrenched and emerging technologies:

> "Communication networks mandate a level of uniformity in behavior. Without such a base level of uniformity then we simply cannot communicate at all. The role of the innovator is to disrupt this uniformity and attempt to carve out a niche of opportunity. If this succeeds and there is a distinct early adopter advantage to be had, then it is possible (though not assured) that the innovation gathers market momentum. If this continues the innovation becomes part of the incumbent set of technologies of the Internet environment. Failure within this process implies that the adopters of this technology remain a niche subset of users, and the technology remains a niche technology that can be characterized as fragmentary or divisive."[50]

A common global address space and common and global open standards without restrictions on their use are a core reason why the Internet has grown and new applications flourished. The design of the Internet itself—interoperability standards and a common address space—are such a fundamental part—and technical necessity—of the architecture; and the Internet Protocol, IP addresses, and surrounding protocols and systems are deeply entrenched in this architecture.

An important part of this entrenchment is because of the logical rather than physical nature of the architecture: "Despite the way number resources are distributed geographically, the plain fact is that IP addresses aren't really 'in a place' on the Internet, because there's nothing about IP to tie datagrams to geopolitical boundaries."[51]

The legitimacy of this entrenched system is not based on state power. It derives in part from technical expertise and what Chapter 2 described as the radical governance innovation. With the majority of today's Internet infrastructure owned and operated by private companies, unlike previous communications networks, questions of legitimacy, authority, and accountability persist as it relates to public policy objectives. In the multistakeholder model legitimacy comes from technical expertise and accountability derives from transparency, openness, and active stakeholder engagement.

Perhaps openness and interoperability have, up to the present moment, won. Development and design have been open in participation; implementation and adoption has been voluntary and not mandated from on high; and the institutional process of technical coordination around these systems evolved, while not perfectly, into a multistakeholder structure. Bottom-up, voluntary standardization does not automatically translate into usage. The push for OSI did not result in OSI as the common protocol stack; the design and availability of IPv6 did not mean it was adopted in a widespread manner. Inversely, practice and widespread adoption, if a particular protocol is "recognized as valid" can prove more effective than big and institution-based and -fostered standardization.[52]

As this book has described, the technical architecture has endured ongoing geopolitical conflicts and challenges: surveillance controversies, fragmentation challenges, attempts to overlay cybersovereignty authority on cross-border technology, co-optation for content blocking, and governmental pressure on the institutions of coordination supporting core systems.

The outcomes of these design struggles and geopolitical tensions, although technically complex and somewhat out of view from Internet users, have shaped every aspect of the modern Internet. The ensuing interoperability afforded by a universal set of protocols has catalyzed competition among different tech companies and enabled global connectivity and its accompanying social and political opportunities and challenges. Some of these historical struggles also foreshadowed later Internet governance debates such as concerns about movements toward proprietary enclosure, Internet fragmentation, digital inclusion, and government attempts to impose sovereign borders on the global network.

This pressure will only continue. As one Internet expert added, "data is a source of geopolitical power and competition and is seen as central to any country's economic and national security. Artificial intelligence will increase this strategic instability."[53]

For all these reasons, the Internet Protocol has proven to be enduring and resilient as a standard, fending off competitors and redesign efforts over the years and becoming deeply entrenched—both architecturally and institutionally - in everything. The Internet Protocol may arguably be in a "long cycle."[54] Economists and international relations scholars focusing on innovation, as well as historians analyzing digital technology highlight the presence of "long cycles."[55] As Hilbert (2020) argues, long waves or long cycles match different overarching paradigms. He highlights three examples: the transformation of materials (stone, bronze, and iron); the industrial revolution, (the transformation of energy); and the transformation of information. Further, Hilbert argues that innovation theory names long cycles after technologies and that long waves or cycles have tended to become shorter over the years. Indeed, there is a rhythm to these cycles, with long periods of small improvements punctuated by turbulent times (characterized by mismatches between the techno-economic and the social-institutional arenas).

These theories seem to mirror Thomas Kuhn's earlier work on scientific change. The history of science and technology is, again, a history of massive change. Thomas Kuhn's influential 1962 book *The Structure of Scientific Revolutions* portrayed the scientific process as relatively calm periods of advancement punctuated by crisis-induced revolutions.[56] The clearest example of this process, and the inherent politics of change, is the Copernican revolution that brought about a shift from a geocentric view to a heliocentric view of the universe. The period before the shift involves different epistemic communities (with often incommensurable world views) adhering to their existing paradigms even in the face of incontrovertible anomalies until something shifts and they see, essentially, a different world.

It would be an exaggeration to suggest that this type of epistemic incommensurability and subsequent revolution could possibly explain conflicts in Internet governance, such as cybersovereignty world views versus the multistakeholder governance model, or even technological conflicts, such as the early contention between TCP/IP and OSI adherents Chapter 3 described. But each approach and each community of adherents have their own interests, epistemological commitments, ideologies, and nomenclature. Is the Internet Protocol itself a revolution? If the category "revolution" is meaningful, the Internet certainly is a technological and societal revolution. But the Internet would not be possible without a specific protocol ecosystem, along with hardware and software advances that collectively created a new paradigm for information exchange, economic activity, and communication. One major question remains and that question relates to the future of the Internet Protocol. What punctuates change in long cycles—there is a long cycle then a period of turbulence—what catalyzes change between such periods? Has not the Internet Protocol ecosystem experienced layers of turbulence throughout its development, implementation, and politicization? The theories or paradigms highlight disruptive new technologies, but there can be uncertainties such as the emergence of a global pandemic or world war. These events can escalate turbulence and punctuate long cycles. Cultures and values continue to shape institutional responses and thus, the dialogue or debates continue.

As one of the book's surveyed experts warned, "Avoiding fragmentation will take both vigilance across multiple standards bodies, and positive, proactive advocacy to global south about why the OG (Original) Internet Protocols matter and are better than the alternatives. It will also take substantial financial investment in a 'deal' for global south...Without this, I do think some form of deep-seated fragmentation is inevitable."

If the general "state of IP ten years ago is basically the same" as of this writing, it is also possible, that "Not much will change within ten years" with the existing infrastructure even while Internet policy struggles continue around "the power and profits of dominant companies" and tensions over ongoing and even "increased restrictions on speech."[57] There are social and economic benefits of this constancy of a generic IP, analogous to water and electricity supply.[58]

The societal stakes of the Internet Protocol ecosystem will only increase as digital (and possibly quantum) networks embed further into humans, objects, financial systems, medicine, the Earth, and into the solar system. Massive technological change will continue from artificial intelligence to neuroscience and biotech interfaces not yet envisioned. If history is any indication, the rising stakes of these new applications will be accompanied by ongoing geopolitical struggles and crises. Indeed, they have already begun.

And yet the Internet continues, with IP at its core.

## Notes

1. Expert survey conducted by authors.
2. Organization for Economic Cooperation and Development (OECD), "Recommendation of the Council on Artificial Intelligence," May 22, 2019, https://legalinstruments.oecd.org/en/instruments/OECD-LEGAL-0449.
3. Robert M. Metcalfe, "From the Ether," *InfoWorld*, December 4, 1995.

4. Katrina Brooker, "I Was Devastated," *Vanity Fair*, July 1, 2018, https://www.vanityfair.com/news/2018/07/the-man-who-created-the-world-wide-web-has-some-regrets.
5. Independent Task Force No. 80, "Confronting Reality in Cyberspace: Foreign Policy for a Fragmented Internet," *Council on Foreign Relations*, July 2022, https://www.cfr.org/task-force-report/confronting-reality-in-cyberspace.
6. Expert survey conducted by authors.
7. Expert survey conducted by authors.
8. Expert survey conducted by authors.
9. Expert survey conducted by authors.
10. Jacques-André Fines Schlumberger, "RINA, un Projet Pour l'internet de Nouvelle Generation," 2019, https://la-rem.eu/2019/09/rina-un-projet-pour-linternet-de-nouvelle-generation/.
11. Stéphane Bortzmeyer, "Un Nouveau Raseur de Table Veut Faire Un Meilleur Internet," Blog de Stéphane Bortzmeyer, May 2009, https://www.bortzmeyer.org/table-rase-et-john-day.html.
12. Expert survey conducted by authors.
13. Expert survey conducted by authors.
14. Expert survey conducted by authors.
15. See, Russian State Duma News, "Sovereign Internet Law Adopted," April 16, 2019, http://duma.gov.ru/news/44551/.
16. See ICANN, "Country Focus Report: Russian Federation Internet-Related Laws and United Nations Deliberations," Annex 4, January 19, 2021, https://www.icann.org/en/system/files/files/ge-006-19jan21-en.pdf.
17. See ITU, "Report of the 17th Meeting of the Council Working Group on Internet-related Public Policy Issues," Annex 2 Statement of the Russian Federation, January 24, 2022, https://www.itu.int/md/S22-RCLINTPOL17-C-0006/en.
18. See Mercedes Page, "The Elections for the Future of the Internet," *The Interpreter*, February 24, 2022, https://www.lowyinstitute.org/the-interpreter/election-future-internet.
19. See European Commission, "Proposal for a Directive of the European Parliament and of the Council on Measures for a High Common Level of Cybersecurity across the Union," December 16, 2020, https://ec.europa.eu/info/law/better-regulation/have-your-say/initiatives/12475-Cybersecurity-review-of-EU-rules-on-the-security-of-network-and-information-systems_en.

20. See, RIPE-NCC, "Response to the European Commission's Proposed NIS2 Directive," March 2021, https://www.ripe.net/participate/internet-governance/multi-stakeholder-engagement/ripe-ncc-response-to-nis-2-directive_march-2021.pdf.
21. See, Federal Communications Commission, "In the Matter of Secure Internet Routing," PS Docket 22-90, February 28, 2022, https://www.fcc.gov/ecfs/file/download/DOC-5fd06b819e800000-A.pdf?file_name=FCC-22-18A1.pdf.
22. IBID, page 7, paragraph 14.
23. See, Federal Communications Commission, PS Docket 22-90, https://www.fcc.gov/ecfs/search/search-filings/results?q=(proceedings.name:(%2222-90*%22))&page=0&limit=50.
24. See, IAB comments on FCC PS Docket 22-90, April 8, 2022, p. 2, https://www.fcc.gov/ecfs/search/search-filings/filing/1041122696562.
25. See NTIA reply comments on FCC PS Docket 22-90, May 10, 2022, p. 9, https://www.fcc.gov/ecfs/search/search-filings/filing/1051046709420.
26. See CISA comments on FCC PS Docket 22-90, June 28, 2022, p. 4, https://www.fcc.gov/ecfs/search/search-filings/filing/10707962804139.
27. Publicly available Tweet by FCC Chair Jessica Rosenworcel, July 8, 2022, https://twitter.com/jrosenworcel/status/1545485688082161670?s=10&t=Wj1SDi9d-vq4GL3ZjKZ9Rw.
28. Expert survey conducted by authors.
29. Sheila Jasanoff, *The Ethics of Invention: Technology and the Human Future*, Norton, 2016, p. 1. See also, Sheila Jasanoff, ed., *States of Knowledge: The Co-Production of Science and the Social Order*, Routledge, 2006.
30. See Carolina Aguerre, Malcolm Campbell-Verduyn and Jan Aart Scholte, eds,. *Global Digital Data Governance: Polycentric Perspectives,* Routledge 2024 or Mark Raymond and Justin Sherman, "Authoritarian Multilateralism in the Global Cyber Regime Complex: The Double Transformation of an International Diplomatic Practice," *Contemporary Security Policy*, Volume 45: Number 1, 2024, pp. 110-140.
31. Carolina Aguerre, Malcolm Campbell-Verduyn, Jan Aart Scholte, eds. *Global Digital Data Governance: Polycentric Perspective,* Routledge, 2024.

32. Rolfe Winkler, "Elon Musk Says Neuralink Has Implanted Brain Chip in Human," *Wall Street Journal*, January 30, 2024.
33. See, for example, Joseph DeFranco, Diane DiEuliis, and Jim Giordano, "Redefining Neuroweapons: Emerging Capabilities in Neuroscience and Neurotechnology", *PRISM*, Volume 8, Number 3, 2019.
34. Rodney Van Meter and Stephanie Wehner, "Vision for a QIRG: Quantum Internet Research Group," 2018, https://datatracker.ietf.org/meeting/101/materials/slides-101-irtfopen-van-meter-and-wehner-vision-for-a-quantum-internet-research-group-01.
35. NextGov, "The Year Ahead: 3 Predictions from the 'Father of the Internet' Vint Cerf," January 5, 2021, https://www.nextgov.com/ideas/2021/01/year-ahead-3-predictions-father-internet-vint-cerf/171171/.
36. European Union Agency for Cybersecurity (ENISA), "Post-Quantum Cryptography: Current State and Quantum Mitigation," 2021, p. 28, https://www.enisa.europa.eu/publications/post-quantum-cryptography-current-state-and-quantum-mitigation.
37. Laura DeNardis, "Interplanetary Internet Governance," CIGI Paper No. 277, Centre for International Governance Innovation, June, 2023. https://www.cigionline.org/publications/interplanetary-internet-governance/.
38. Interplanetary Networking Special Interest Group (IPNSIG), "Solar-System Internet Architecture and Governance," September, 2023. Available at, https://www.ipnsig.org/.
39. The Consultative Committee for Space Data Systems, "Space Assigned Numbers Authority (SANA)—Role, Responsibilities, Policies, and Procedures," CCSDS 313.0-Y-3, Yellow Book, October 2020, https://public.ccsds.org/Pubs/313x0y3.pdf.
40. United Nations Resolution Adopted by the General Assembly, 2222 (XXI), "Treaty on Principles Governing the Activities of States in the Exploration and Use of Outer Space, including the Moon and Other Celestial Bodies," 1967, https://www.unoosa.org/oosa/en/ourwork/spacelaw/treaties/outerspacetreaty.html.
41. See, for example, Scott Pace, "U.S. Space Policy and Theories of International Relations: The Case for Analytical Eclecticism," *Space Policy*, January 2023.
42. See, for example, Milton Mueller, "Against Sovereignty in Cyberspace," *International Studies Review*, 2020, Volume 22,

pp. 779-801; Timothy Wu, "Cyberspace Sovereignty?—The Internet and the International System," *Harvard Journal of Law and Technology* Volume 10, Issue 3, 1997, pp. 647–66; and David R. Johnson and David Post, "Law and Borders: The Rise of Law in Cyberspace," *Stanford Law Review*, Volume 48, Number 5, 1996, pp. 1367-1402.

43. Vint Cerf, et al., Informational RFC 4838, "Delay-Tolerant Networking Architecture," April 2007.
44. Scott Burleigh, et al., RFC 9171, "Bundle Protocol Version 7," January 2022, https://datatracker.ietf.org/doc/rfc9171/.
45. The Consultative Committee for Space Data Systems, Recommendation for Space Data Standards, "Space Packet Protocol," Recommended Standard CCSDS 133.0-B-2, June 2020, https://public.ccsds.org/Pubs/133x0b2e1.pdf.
46. Yosuke Kaneko, Vinton Cerf, Scott Burleigh, Maria Luque, and Kiyohisa Suzuki, IPNSIG Strategy Working Group Report, "Strategy Toward a Solar System Internet for Humanity," June 2021, p. 28, https://ipnsig.org/wp-content/uploads/2021/10/IPNSIG-SWG-REPORT-2021-3.pdf.
47. Expert survey conducted by authors.
48. Thomas Hughes, *American Genesis: A History of the American Genius for Invention*, Penguin Books, 1989, pp. 462–63.
49. Expert survey conducted by authors.
50. Expert survey conducted by authors.
51. Expert survey conducted by authors.
52. On this point, see, concerning the example of the Signal Protocol, Ksenia Ermoshina, Francesca Musiani, 2019, "Standardising by Running Code: the Signal Protocol and De Facto Standardisation in End-to-End Encrypted Messaging," *Internet Histories*, Volume 3, Numbers 3-4, pp. 343-363.
53. Expert survey conducted by authors.
54. Nanette Levinson, "Ideas, Institutions, and E-volution: The Internet Governance Ecosystem," paper presented at the Annual Meeting of the IAMCR Law Section, July 2007.
55. See, for example, work by Giovanni Dosi, "Technological Paradigms and Technological Trajectories: A Suggested Interpretation of the Determinants and Directions of Technical Change." *Research Policy,* Volume 11, Number 3, 1982, pp. 147–162 or Martin Hilbert, "Digital Technology and Social Change: The

Digital Transformation of Society from a Historical Perspective," *Dialogues in Clinical Neuroscience,* Volume 22, Number 2, 2020, pp.189–194. Even work in international relations discusses long cycles and international politics; see Joshua Goldstein, "The Possibility of Cycles in International Relations." *International Studies Quarterly,* Volume 35, Number 4, 1991, pp. 477–480.

56. Thomas S. Kuhn, *The Structure of Scientific Revolutions*, The University of Chicago Press, 1962. See, also, his early book, *The Copernican Revolution*, 1957.
57. Expert survey conducted by authors.
58. Expert survey conducted by authors.

# Technical Appendix

IPv4 addresses are represented in decimal using "dotted decimal notation." Translating that 32-binary number into dotted decimal simply involves: dividing the binary number into four groups of eight bits; translating each binary octet into its decimal equivalent; and separating each decimal number with a dot. The first eight bits of the Internet address above are 00010011, which translate (recalling that each placeholder is a multiple of two) from binary into decimal as:

$0(128) + 0(64) + 0(32) + 1\,(16) + 0(8) + 0(4) + 1(2) + 1(1) = 19$

In summary, the following translates each of the binary octets into decimal.

$00010011 = 0 + 0 + 0 + 16 + 0 + 0 + 2 + 1 = 19$

$00101000 = 0 + 0 + 32 + 0 + 8 + 0 + 0 + 0 = 40$

$10000001 = 128 + 0 + 0 + 0 + 0 + 0 + 0 + 1 = 129$

$00100001 = 0 + 0 + 32 + 0 + 0 + 0 + 0 + 1 = 33$

Putting this all together, the shorthand notation of this one IPv4 address is 19.40.129.33. It may not be necessary to understand this nomenclature to understand conflicts over IP address space governance, but it helps to demystify and pull back the curtain on more abstract parts of the technical architecture.



F. M. Alexander et al., *Geopolitics at the Internet's Core*, Information Technology and Global Governance,
https://doi.org/10.1007/978-3-031-89478-7

Discussing or managing an IPv6 address, because each is so much longer, involves a shorthand notation that uses the longer hexadecimal numbering system.[1] Also called "Hex" or base-16, the hexadecimal numbering system has sixteen unique characters. Given that there are only ten unique numbers in the everyday decimal system (0 through 9), hexadecimal adds letters of the alphabet to count higher (0, 1, 2, 3, 4, 5, 6, 7, 8, 9, A, B, C, D, E, and F). To continue counting in hexadecimal is identical to counting in decimal. Once the sixteen symbols are expended, a second placeholder is added and the counting begins in the new place: 0, 1, 2, 3, 4, 5, 6, 7, 8, 9, A, B, C, D, E, F, 10, 11, 12, 13, 14, 15, 16, 17, 18, 19, 1A, 1B, 1C, etc.

The shorthand format for representing a 128-bit long IPv6 address can be understand using the following example of a single address, (taken from an example in Protocol Politics: The Globalization of Internet Governance, MIT Press, 2009, p. 238–240).

11111011101110010101100000100001000000100110010101110
100011001001001111000100100001000000111000011011101000100
110110100100100001

Converting the address to hexadecimal makes it less unwieldy for humans to use, such as while configuring a server. The convention is to break the 128-bit number into eight groupings of sixteen bits and convert each of the sixteen bits into hexadecimal numerals, separated by a colon. One hexadecimal numeral equals four binary digits as follows:

| *Hexadecimal* | *Binary equivalent* |
|---|---|
| 0 | 0000 |
| 1 | 0001 |
| 2 | 0010 |
| 3 | 0011 |
| 4 | 0100 |
| 5 | 0101 |
| 6 | 0110 |
| 7 | 0111 |
| 8 | 1000 |
| 9 | 1001 |
| A | 1010 |

[1] Please see "Internet Protocol Version 6 (IPv6) Addressing Architecture," RFC 3513, April 2003.

| *Hexadecimal* | *Binary equivalent* |
|---|---|
| B | 1011 |
| C | 1100 |
| D | 1101 |
| E | 1110 |
| F | 1111 |

Referring to the table, the long IPv6 number above translates into shorthand hex notation by converting each grouping of sixteen bits into its associated four numeral hex equivalent:

1111 1101 1101 1100 = FDDC
1010 1100 0001 0000 = AC10
1000 0001 0011 0010 = 8132
1011 1010 0011 0010 = BA32
0100 1111 0001 0010 = 4F12
0001 0000 0111 0000 = 1070
1101 1101 0001 0011 = DD13
0110 1001 0010 0001 = 6921

Putting this all together, the long IPv6 address above is represented in hexadecimal as:

FDDC:AC10:8132:BA32:4F12:1070:DD13:6921

Many IPv6 addresses (not the example above) have numerous zeros, which can be compressed in the notation by eliminating the zeros. Thus, a hypothetical address such as FDDC:0000:0000:0000:0000:1070:0001:0001 can be further compressed as FDDC::1070:1:1.

Hexadecimal is used throughout digital systems and computer science as a way to manageably represent binary code. As shown in the IPv6 example above, one hexadecimal symbol represents four bits. This hex shorthand is used for everything from representing color codes (to digitize colors to show in an image, for example) and for encryption keys and digital certificates. Using a completely hypothetical example, a 128-bit encryption key (a unique pattern of 128 zeros and ones used to encrypt and/or decrypt information) would reduce down to a 32-long hex number such as 7FF4 12D0 EE23 4C89 1321 CF99 E6FF 2011.

# Books Referenced


Abbate, Janet, *Inventing the Internet*, MIT Press, 1999.

Aguerre, Carolina, Malcolm Campbell-Verduyn, Jan Aart Scholte, eds. *Global Digital Data Governance: Polycentric Perspective,* Routledge, 2024.

Bijker, Wiebe E., Thomas P. Hughes, and Trevor Pinch, *The Social Construction of Technological Systems*, MIT Press, 1987.

Bowker, Geoff and Susan Leigh Star, *Sorting Things Out: Classification and its Consequences*, The MIT Press, 1999.

Carr, Madeline, *U.S.Power and the Internet in International Relations: The Irony of the Information Age,* Palgrave MacMillan, 2016.

Clark, David D., *Designing an Internet*, MIT Press, 2018.

De Lombaerde, Philippe, *Handbook of Regional Cooperation and Integration*, Edward Elgar Publishing, 2024.

DeNardis, Laura, *Opening Standards: The Global Politics of Interoperability,* MIT Press, 2011.

DeNardis, Laura, *Protocol Politics: The Globalization of Internet Governance*, MIT Press, 2009.

DeNardis, Laura et al., eds., *Researching Internet Governance: Methods, Frameworks, Futures*, MIT Press, 2020.

DeNardis, Laura, *The Global War for Internet Governance*, Yale University Press, 2014.

Galloway, Alexander, *Protocol: How Control Exists after Decentralization*, The MIT Press, 2004.

Ermoshina, Ksenia and Francesca Musiani, *Concealing for Freedom: The Making of Encryption, Secure Messaging, and Digital Liberties*. Mattering Press, 2022.





F. M. Alexander et al., *Geopolitics at the Internet's Core*, Information Technology and Global Governance,
https://doi.org/10.1007/978-3-031-89478-7

Haggart, Blayne, Natasha Tusikov, and Jan Aart Scholte, eds., *Power and Authority in Internet Governance: Return of the State?* Routledge, 2021.

Hargittai, Eszter, ed., *Handbook of Digital Inequality*, Elgar, 2021.

Hughes, Thomas, *American Genesis: A History of the American Genius for Invention*, Penguin Books, 1989.

Jasanoff, Sheila, *States of Knowledge: The Co-Production of Science and the Social Order*, Routledge, 2006.

Jasanoff, Shiela, *The Ethics of Invention: Technology and the Human Future*, Norton, 2016.

Kuhn, Thomas S., *The Structure of Scientific Revolutions*, The University of Chicago Press, 1962.

Musiani, Francesca et al., eds., *The Turn to Infrastructure in Internet Governance*, Palgrave MacMillan, 2016.

Perrow, Charles, *Normal Accidents: Living with High-Risk Technologies*, Princeton University Press, 1999.

Radu, Roxana. *Negotiating Internet Governance*, Oxford University Press, 2019.

Russell, Andrew, *Open Standards and the Digital Age*, Cambridge University Press, 2014.

Santaniello, Mauro and Nicola Palladino, *Legitimacy, Power, and Inequalities in the Multistakeholder Internet Governance*, Palgrave Macmillan, 2021.

# Index





F. M. Alexander et al., *Geopolitics at the Internet's Core*, Information Technology and Global Governance,
https://doi.org/10.1007/978-3-031-89478-7

The manufacturer's authorised representative in the EU is Springer Nature Customer Service Centre GmbH, Europaplatz 3, 69115 Heidelberg, Germany. If you have any concerns regarding our products, please contact ProductSafety@springernature.com

Printed and bound by CPI Group (UK) Ltd, Croydon, CR0 4YY
30/09/2026
02225567-0001